practical
digital
preservation

A how-to guide for
organizations of any size

practical
digital
preservation

A how-to guide for
organizations of any size

ADRIAN BROWN

An imprint of the American Library Association

Chicago • 2013

First published in the United Kingdom by Facet Publishing, 2013.
This simultaneous U.S. Edition published by Neal-Schuman,
an imprint of the American Library Association, 2013.

16 15 14 13 12   5 4 3 2 1

ISBN: 978-1-55570-942-6 (paper)

Composition by by Facet Publishing Production in Palatino Linotype
and URW Linear typefaces.

Contents

Acknowledgements

This book would never have been possible without the knowledge, insights, comments, support and assistance of a great many people, in the course of building digital preservation services in three different organizations over a period of 16 years. While I cannot begin to list all of those who have inspired, encouraged or otherwise prompted so many of the ideas herein, I would like to acknowledge and thank a number of people who have, directly or indirectly, been pivotal in its creation:

- Kathy Perrin at English Heritage, for allowing me the freedom to experiment, and develop my early ideas about digital preservation
- David Ryan, now of the Royal Household, for giving me the opportunity to apply those ideas on a large scale at The National Archives (TNA), and all my former colleagues in the Digital Preservation Department at TNA
- Dr Caroline Shenton, Director of the Parliamentary Archives, for supporting and encouraging me throughout the writing of this book, and providing so much constructive comment
- the staff of the Parliamentary Archives, the Digital Preservation Project team at the Houses of Parliament, and in particular Alison Heatherington, for her sterling work, steadfast support and critical feedback on the draft manuscript
- Dave Thompson at the Wellcome Library, Ed Fay at the LSE Library, and Kevin Bolton of Manchester Archives+, for so generously sharing their time and practical experiences
- the team at Facet, and in particular Louise Le Bas, Sarah Busby, Lin Franklin and Jenni Hall, who have guided the book from inception to publication.

While I would love to attribute any errors, inaccuracies or omissions to an unfortunate format migration error, they must remain the responsibility of the author.

I would also like to thank all the individuals and organizations who have given permission to reproduce illustrations: Figures 2.3 (University of Nottingham), 4.1 (Tessella Ltd), 4.5, 8.3 (English Heritage), 6.5, 8.8, 9.1 (Crown copyright), 6.7 (Viv Cothey and Gloucestershire County Council), 9.2 (Cheshire Archives and Local Studies), 9.5 (London School of Economics and Political Science), and 9.6 (Wellcome Library, London). Figures 7.1 and 7.2 have been redrawn by the author from originals created by the International Federation of Library Associations (IFLA) Study Group on the Functional Requirements for Bibliographic Records, and the PREMIS Editorial Committee respectively. Crown copyright material is reproduced under the terms and conditions of the Open Government Licence, version 1.0.

This book is dedicated to the two people who made it, and everything that led to it, possible in the most fundamental way, through their boundless support, belief and patience: my Mum and, most of all, Sally.

This glossary is necessarily restricted to terms that are either specific to, or have a distinct meaning within, the field of digital preservation. Specialist terms within the libraries, archives, museums and IT communities are not generally included.

Accessioning: The process of bringing *digital objects* under the physical and intellectual control of a *digital repository*.

AIP: See *Archival Information Package*.

API: See *Application Programming Interface*.

Application Programming Interface (API): A specification for an interface that allows software components to communicate, and typically used by software developers to enable different software tools to interoperate.

Archival Information Package (AIP): An *information package* that is preserved within an *Open Archival Information System (OAIS) digital repository*.

Authenticity: The quality of trustworthiness of a record – in this context a *digital object*. Authenticity provides the assurance that a record is what it purports to be and has demonstrably not been tampered with or otherwise corrupted. Authenticity arises from the *reliability*, *integrity* and *usability* of the record.

Bit: The fundamental unit of digital information storage, which can have a binary value of either 1 or 0.

Bitstream: A sequence of *bytes*, which has meaningful common properties for the purposes of preservation. A bitstream may be a *file* or a component of a file.

Bitstream preservation: The aspect of preservation management that is concerned with maintaining the *integrity* of every *bitstream* ingested into the *digital repository*, by ensuring that a demonstrably *bit*-perfect copy can be retrieved on demand, for as long as required.

Byte: A unit of digital information and measure of data volume, normally equivalent to eight *bits*.

Call for bids: See *invitation to tender*.

Characterization: The aspect of *logical preservation* that is concerned with understanding the nature of *digital objects*, including their technical and *significant properties*.

Checksum: A value calculated by an algorithm based on the *bit*-level content of a *file*, such that any change to that content will result in a different checksum value. Checksums can therefore be used to detect changes to data, and hence perform *integrity checks*.

Cloud computing: The provision of IT resources as services across a network. Such services can be provided at a number of levels, including Infrastructure-as-a-Service, Platform-as-a-Service and Software-as-a-Service.

Content information: See *information object*.

Data object: A technological instantiation of an *information object*, composed of one or more *bitstreams* and dependent on a specific technical environment to provide access.

Digital asset register: A record of an organization's digital information assets, which quantifies the value and risk of loss in each case.

Digital linear tape: A common format of magnetic tape data storage technology.

Digital object: An entity which is the target for preservation. Depending on context, it may refer to an *information object* or a *data object*.

Digital preservation: The process of maintaining a *digital object* for as long as required, in a form which is *authentic*, and accessible to users.

Digital repository: A combination of people, processes and technologies, which together provide the means to capture, preserve and provide access to *digital objects*.

DIP: See *Dissemination Information Package*.

Disk image: A bit-level copy of a digital storage device, such as a hard disk, usually encoded in a single *file*.

Dissemination Information Package (DIP): An *information package*, derived from one or more *AIPs*, and supplied to an end-user by an *OAIS digital repository* as a result of a request for access.

Document Type Definition (DTD): A formal syntax for defining a document type in XML or HTML.

DTD: See *Document Type Definition*.

Emulation: The class of *preservation actions* that entail transforming a technology environment to allow a *digital object* to be accessed in its original form.

Exabyte: A unit of measurement of data volume, equivalent to 1000 *petabytes*.

Extensible Markup Language (XML): A markup language for encoding information in human-readable and machine-readable form.

File: A *bitstream* which is managed by a file system as a single, named entity.

File Transfer Protocol (FTP): A protocol for transferring digital *files* across a network.

Fixity: See *integrity*.

Format: A predefined structure for organizing a *file* or *bitstream*.

FTP: See *File Transfer Protocol*.

Information object: The conceptual object of preservation. An information object is realized as meaningful information by interpreting a *data object* through its associated *representation information*.

Information package: A logical container defined by *OAIS*, and composed of an *information object (content information)* and associated *preservation description information*.

Ingest: The final stage of *accession*, in which one or more *AIPs* are generated from a *Submission Information Package (SIP)* and stored in a *digital repository*. Physically, this requires the *files* to be moved into a permanent storage location within repository control, and the *metadata* to be incorporated into the relevant metadata management regime.

Integrity: The aspect of an *information object's authenticity* that depends on it being protected against unauthorized or accidental alteration.

Integrity checking: The process of testing the *integrity* of a *data object*, typically using a *checksum*. This is a key aspect of *bitstream preservation*.

Invitation to tender: A formal procurement procedure whereby potential suppliers are invited to submit bids to provide a product or service. The term can also refer to the document issued as part of this process, detailing the customer's requirements for the product or service.

Linked open data: A method of publishing structured data using standard web technologies, so that it can be linked together for machine processing.

Logical preservation: The aspect of preservation management that is concerned with ensuring the continued *usability* of meaningful information content, by ensuring the existence of a usable *manifestation* of an *information object*.

Manifestation: A specific *data object* that instantiates an *information object*. Multiple manifestations can exist for any given information object.

Metadata: The set of information required to enable content to be discovered, managed and used by both human agents and automated systems. Literally 'data about data'.

Metadata Encoding and Transmission Standard (METS): A widely adopted *metadata* standard for encoding descriptive, administrative and structural metadata.

METS: See *Metadata Encoding and Transmission Standard*.

Migration: The class of *preservation actions* that entail transforming a *digital object* into a form which can be accessed in a new technology environment.

Migration pathway: A specific *migration* process for transforming between a source and target *format* of *data object*.

Normalization: The process of *migrating digital objects* to new *formats* at the point of *ingest*, in order to minimize the number of formats to be managed within a *repository*.

Open Archival Information System (OAIS): A *digital repository* that conforms to the *OAIS Standard*.

Open Archives Information System (OAIS) reference model: An international standard (ISO 14721: 2003) defining a high-level functional model for a *digital repository*.

OWL: See *Web Ontology Language*.

Persistent identifier: A reference to a *digital object* which uniquely refers to it, and can be relied on to remain meaningful (capable of being interpreted as referring to that object) for at least as long as the object itself exists.

Petabyte: A unit of measurement of data volume, equivalent to 1,000 *terabytes*.

PREMIS: A preservation *metadata* scheme, now an international *de facto* standard.

Preservation action: The process of enacting and validating a *preservation plan*. This forms the final stage of *logical preservation*, and results in the generation of a new *AIP*. Two major classes of preservation action are *migration* and *emulation*.

Preservation description information: The information that is required to preserve an *information object* in an *OAIS digital repository*, and which comprises provenance, reference, fixity, context and access rights information.

Preservation planning: The aspect of *logical preservation* that is concerned with identifying threats to the continued availability and *usability* of *authentic digital objects* and, if such threats are identified, determining appropriate countermeasures. It incorporates the process of *technology watch*.

Quarantine: A process that occurs during *accession*, whereby a *SIP* is isolated from other systems until it has been confirmed to be free from any malicious software.

RDF: See *Resource Description Framework*.

Refreshment: The process of copying data from one storage device to another, of the same or different type, for the purposes of *bitstream preservation*.

Reliability: The aspect of an *information object's authenticity* that depends on it being a full and accurate representation of the cultural or business activity to which it attests. This requires the establishment of trust in the curatorial processes used to manage the object throughout its lifecycle, and the continued ability to place the object within its original context.

Representation: See *manifestation*.

Representation information: The set of information required to interpret a *data object* as a meaningful *information object*, or a component of a technical environment that supports interpretation of that object (such as a software tool or hardware platform).

Representation information registry: A systematic collection of *representation information* or locatable references to information held elsewhere, which exposes that information for discovery and processing by human or automated systems. The most common forms of registry are format registries, which specialize in representation information about formats, and tools registries, which provide information about preservation tools and services.

Resource Description Framework: A family of specifications for describing and modelling information in the Semantic Web.

SAN: See *Storage Area Network*.

SDK: See *Software Development Kit*.

Significant property: Any intrinsic property of an *information object* that contributes to the assertion of its *authenticity*.

SIP: See *Submission Information Package*.

Snapshot: An archived, time-delimited instance of a website.

Software Development Kit (SDK): A set of tools for creating applications for a particular software package, operating system or hardware platform.

Storage Area Network (SAN): A network by which storage devices are made available to multiple computers.

Submission Information Package (SIP): An *information package* that is supplied for *ingest* into an *OAIS digital repository*. The ingest process results in the creation of one or more *AIPs* from the SIP.

Technology watch: The process of monitoring technological changes, in order to detect those that may affect the continued *usability* of a *digital object*. It forms one element of *preservation planning*.

Terabyte: A unit of measurement of data volume, equivalent to 1000 gigabytes

Uniform Resource Identifier (URI): A protocol for identifying networked resources, such as web content.

Uniform Resource Locator (URL): A type of *URI* that identifies the resource and its location. It therefore acts as an address for networked resources such as web content.

URI: See *Uniform Resource Identifier*.

URL: See *Uniform Resource Locator*.

Usability: The aspect of an *information object's authenticity* that depends on it being accessible by authorized users, across time and changing technical environments. This requires that it is locatable and retrievable by users, capable of representation in a current technical environment, and that it supports interpretation by users.

Validation: The process of confirming that a *bitstream, SIP* or *metadata* object is complete, accurate and correctly formed, or that a *preservation action* has been performed in accordance with a specified *preservation plan*, to a defined quality level.

Web archiving: The set of processes used to capture copies or *snapshots* of web resources for permanent preservation.

Web Ontology Language (OWL): A family of formal languages for creating ontologies, primarily for use in the Semantic Web.

XML: See *Extensible Markup Language*.

1

Introduction

1.1 Introduction

Picture a scene: in a county record office somewhere in England, a young archivist is looking through the morning post. Among the usual enquiry letters and payments for copies of documents is a mysterious padded envelope. Opening it reveals five floppy disks of various sizes, accompanied by a brief covering letter from the office manager of a long-established local business, explaining that the contents had been discovered during a recent office refurbishment; since the record office has previously acquired the historic paper records of the company, perhaps these would also be of interest? The disks themselves bear only terse labels, such as 'Minutes, 1988-90' or 'customers.dbf'. Some, the archivist recognizes as being 3.5" disks, while the larger ones seem vaguely familiar from a digital preservation seminar she attended during her training. On one point she is certain: the office PCs are not capable of reading any of them. How can she discover what is actually on the disks, and whether they contain important business records or junk? And even if they do prove of archival interest, what should the record office actually do with them?

Meanwhile, a university librarian in the mid-west USA attends a faculty meeting to discuss the burgeoning institutional repository. Introduced a few years ago to store PDF copies of academic preprints and postprints, there is increasing demand from staff to store other kinds of content in a much wider range of formats, from original research data, to student dissertations and theses, teaching materials and course notes, and to make that content available for reuse by others in novel ways. How, the librarian ponders, does the repository need to be adapted to meet these new requirements, and what must the library do to ensure the long-term preservation of such a diverse digital collection?

Finally, in East Africa, a national archivist has just finished reading a report from a consultant commissioned to advise on requirements for preserving electronic records. The latest in a series of projects to develop records management within government, he knows that this work is crucial to promoting transparency, empowering citizens by providing them with access to reliable information, reducing corruption and improving governance through the use of new technologies. The national archives has achieved much in recent years, putting in place strong records management processes and guidance. But how to develop the digital preservation systems necessary to achieve the report's ambitious recommendations, with limited budgets and staff skills, and an unreliable IT infrastructure?

This book is intended to help these people, and the countless other information managers and curators around the world who are wrestling with the challenges of preserving digital data, to answer these questions. If I had been writing it only a few years ago, my first task would have been to explain the need for digital preservation at length, illustrated no doubt with celebrated examples of data loss such as the BBC *Domesday* disks, or NASA's Viking probe.[1] Today, most information management professionals are all too aware of the fact that, without active intervention, digital information is subject to rapid and catastrophic loss – the warnings of an impending 'Digital Dark Ages' have served their purpose. Hopefully, they are equally alive to the enormous benefits of digital preservation, in unlocking the current and long-term value of that information. Instead, their principal concern now is how to respond in a practical way to these challenges. There is a sense that awareness of the solutions has not kept pace with appreciation of the potential and the problems.

Such solutions as are widely known are generally seen as being the preserve of major institutions – the national libraries and archives – with multi-million pound budgets and large numbers of staff at their disposal. Even if reality often doesn't match this perception – many national memory institutions are tackling digital preservation on a comparative shoestring – there is no doubt that such organizations have been at the vanguard of developments in the field.

The challenges can sometimes appear overpowering. The extraordinary growth in the creation of digital information is often described using rather frightening or negative analogies, such as the 'digital deluge' or 'data tsunami'. These certainly reflect the common anxieties that information curators and consumers have about their abilities to manage these gargantuan volumes of data, and to find and understand the information they need within. These concerns are compounded by a similarly overwhelming wave of information generated by the digital preservation community: no one with any exposure to the field can have escaped a certain sense of despair at ever keeping up to date with the constant stream of reports, conferences, blogs, wikis, projects and tweets.

In writing this book, my goal has been to demonstrate that, in reality, it is not only possible but eminently realistic for organizations of all sizes to put digital preservation into practice, even with very limited resources and existing knowledge. I have sought to do so through a combination of practical guidance, and case studies which reinforce that guidance, illustrating how it has already been successfully applied in the real world.

1.2 Who is this book for?

This book is intended to be of value to anyone with an interest in the practice of digital preservation, but is primarily aimed at existing and prospective practitioners in:

- **smaller memory institutions**, such as libraries, archives, museums and galleries, which have a core mission to collect, preserve and provide access to information or artefacts
- **institutional archives and libraries**, which collect, preserve and provide access to the information resources created or used by their organizations in support of their core mission; examples include business archives and institutional repositories.

In other words, it is written for the vast range of organizations outside the national cultural memory institutions that want and need to develop the ability to collect, preserve and provide access to digital information. Although it should be of interest to policy makers within these organizations, it is intended primarily for those who are, or are hoping to be, responsible for digital preservation at a practical level.

The underlying aim of digital preservation can be stated very simply:

> To maintain the object of preservation for as long as required, in a form which is authentic, and accessible to users.

This book shows how you can build practical solutions to achieve that aim. It begins by looking at how to approach developing a digital preservation capability, from raising initial awareness, and gaining the necessary mandate and resources, to beginning an organized programme of work to put in place the appropriate people, systems and processes. It then examines in detail what the practice of digital preservation actually involves, from initially acquiring content to making it available to users. It should not be assumed that this requires monolithic IT systems; one of the central arguments of this book is that digital preservation is an *outcome*, which can be achieved by many different means, and at varying levels of complexity, to suit the needs and resources of the organization in question.

1.3 Minimum requirements

The entry level for digital preservation is actually very low – indeed, the premise of this book is that it is entirely realistic for small organizations to implement credible services. However, it must be recognized that there are minimum requirements for an organization to build a digital preservation service. These are:

- **Motivation**: First and foremost, an organization must have the desire to address the digital preservation challenge. Doing so is likely to be a lengthy process, by turns as frustrating as it is rewarding, and a substantial level of motivation is essential to persevere through this.
- **Means**: Second, an organization must have the wherewithal to turn that desire into reality. This may take the form of:
  - **expertise**: to establish the detailed case for digital preservation, define the organization's requirements, and oversee their implementation and future operation
  - **financial resources**: to fund staff, services and infrastructure
  - **infrastructure:** to underpin an operational digital preservation capability.

Of the three, either expertise or financial resources are the most critical: expertise can make best use of limited resources and help to secure more resources in future, while money can be used to buy in expertise. The minimum infrastructure required is very variable but, as will be demonstrated later in this book, should be within the reach of most organizations.

1.4 Some digital preservation myths

There are a number of widespread myths and misconceptions about digital preservation, which together serve to foster the image that it is too scary, complex and difficult to be contemplated as a practical proposition by smaller organizations. In particular, it is often perceived that digital preservation:

- can only be tackled by national bodies
- requires huge budgets
- requires deep technical knowledge
- can be left until next year to tackle.

This book serves to counter those myths with some digital preservation realities:

Digital preservation can only be tackled by national bodies

While such institutions have undoubtedly taken the lead in developing digital preservation as a discipline, the existence of mature, affordable, practical tools and services means that it is now not only realistic, but also imperative, for organizations of every size and type to address the issue.

Digital preservation requires huge budgets

You can spend as much or as little on digital preservation as resources allow. While the US National Archives and Records Administration has spent an estimated $500 million on building its Electronic Records Archive,[2] a working digital repository was developed at the English Heritage Centre for Archaeology at the cost of a few hundred pounds and the author's time (see Chapter 4, 'Models for implementing a digital preservation service'). This book demonstrates how much can be achieved using readily available tools and resources, as well as with more complex systems.

Digital preservation requires deep technical knowledge

While it can undoubtedly lead into very technical territory, especially at the cutting edge of research, digital preservation practice does not require deep technical knowledge. Practitioners today come from hugely varied backgrounds, ranging from traditional library and archives roles and IT, to astronomy and archaeology. Adaptability and enthusiasm are the most important characteristics for any would-be digital archivist. While most have developed their skills on the job, there are now an excellent range of training opportunities to suit all needs and budgets, from online tutorials, through seminars and conferences, to longer training courses and postgraduate qualifications. Digital preservation is also becoming established as a vital professional skill within information management training courses. Couple this with a very supportive and collaboration-minded community, and no one should have cause to fear that digital preservation skills are inaccessible or difficult to acquire. The opportunities for training and professional development are discussed in detail in Chapter 4, 'Models for implementing a digital preservation service'.

Digital preservation can be left until next year to tackle

This is an issue that organizations need to address urgently, if they are to realize the enormous benefits, and avoid substantial legal, financial, operational and reputational risks, as well as the loss of information of great historical and business value. This is not to say that you must do everything at once, or that your requirements will be the same as another organization's – the maturity model introduced in Chapter 4, 'Models for implementing a digital preservation service', and expanded in Chapter 8, 'Preserving digital objects', illustrates how you can develop your capabilities over time, and to a level that suits your needs. However, now is the time to begin tackling digital preservation at a practical level.

1.5 The current situation

So what challenges do small organizations currently face? A survey in 2008 provided an interesting snapshot of the state of readiness across local authority archives in the UK to preserve digital records.[3] There is little to suggest that the situation has changed greatly since, and it is worth looking at the results of this survey in some detail, as they illustrate the challenges faced globally by smaller organizations in general.

Although most archives demonstrated a basic awareness of digital preservation, and knew (74%) about basic sources of support such as the Digital Preservation Coalition, the level of more detailed knowledge dropped off very noticeably beyond that. Around half were aware of the seminal international standard, the Open Archival Information Systems (OAIS) Reference Model, and of key initiatives run by national memory institutions such as the British Library and The National Archives (TNA). Two-thirds were unaware of other key international standards, such as PREMIS or METS, and a similar proportion were unfamiliar with projects of particular relevance to UK local archives, such as the East of England Digital Archive Regional Pilot[4] and Paradigm.[5]

Nearly half (47%) had a digital preservation policy, which conforms to the findings of other surveys before and since (see Chapter 2, 'Making the case for digital preservation'). However, relatively few had taken the next step of introducing detailed standards and working practices, such as guidelines for depositors (16%) or ingest procedures (11%).

Most archives (79%) considered themselves to be reacting to the demands of depositors, rather than proactively building their digital records capability, although almost all held some digital material, and only 5% were actually turning away digital records because of a lack of facilities. Despite their nascent digital collections, they frequently lacked even basic information about the nature of that material, such as detailed volumes or file counts. The information supplied by respondents about the file formats they held is illuminating: in addition to the ubiquitous image formats resulting from digitization initiatives, and the expected Office-type formats, there was a wide range of obsolete formats, such as Lotus 1-2-3 and Claris Filemaker, as well as specialized formats such as computer-aided design (CAD) and genealogy data. Many archives also reported holding digital audiovisual collections. Although unsurprising, given the wide-ranging collecting policies of many local authority archives, this diversity highlights some significant preservation challenges. As a result of fairly minimal information gathering activities at ingest, most archives did not have the information necessary to undertake any form of preservation planning.

The majority had some form of backed-up, server-based storage, although 87% also had some material on optical media such as CD or DVD; 42% simply stored the data on its original media, although around half did at least perform basic checks on ingest, such as testing whether the media could be read. Only a tiny proportion was undertaking more sophisticated actions, such as generating checksums or normalizing formats. Only one respondent had use of a content management system, and one was outsourcing its storage.

Access is a fundamental requirement for any archive, but two-thirds of respondents were relying on purely *ad hoc* arrangements, rather than any formal user access system. Such online delivery facilities as did exist were mainly limited to image galleries, and therefore did not support access to other types of digital material.

Interestingly, less than half of respondents reported close involvement in the implementation of electronic records management systems, even though these are likely to be one of the principal sources of digital records for such archives in the future.

A particularly noteworthy aspect of the survey was the section on barriers to digital preservation, in which respondents were asked about the main perceived obstacles. The report identified three groups of these from the responses: cultural, resource and skills. Perhaps unsurprisingly, funding was seen as the main barrier, followed jointly by IT support and skills, then political support. On the other hand, staff motivation, leadership, time and strategic partnerships were all seen as less significant barriers. While one should be cautious about drawing too many conclusions from this, it does suggest that costs and skills are at least perceived as the major obstacles – the spirit is willing but the funding is weak.

Those respondents who suggested how these barriers might be overcome were most concerned with gaining institutional buy-in, and developing and embedding policies and procedures. These essential steps are discussed in detail in Chapter 2, 'Making the case for digital preservation'.

More detailed questions about the skills gap yielded a range of development requirements, from generic management and IT skills to very specific digital preservation knowledge. These highlight the importance of access to practical and affordable training.

Another key issue highlighted was the disconnect between archivists and information and communications technology (ICT) support services, with relationships in some cases being described as poor or antagonistic. Allied to a lack of budget provision for, and experience of managing, major IT projects, this means that although most archives have access to ICT support services, including developer resources, few are in a position to take advantage of these facilities to develop digital preservation capabilities.

There was remarkably little consensus among archivists when asked what their preferences were for providing digital preservation services in future. Although an in-house repository or regional consortium was preferred by the greatest number of respondents, almost as many ranked the in-house solution their least favoured. The only point of consensus was a general rejection of outsourcing to a commercial provider, although it was unclear whether this was motivated primarily by perceived budget constraints, a paucity of plausible commercial services, or as a point of principle.

So what can we conclude about the situation faced by smaller organizations today? First, the main barriers to developing digital preservation capabilities are practical – money, skills, leveraging available resources – rather than the more fundamental obstacles of awareness and will, although the latter may still apply to parent bodies and other funders.

Second, most organizations have some of the basic building blocks of a capability in place, and are not allowing the lack of a more comprehensive capability to stop them from beginning to collect digital material. While such an approach needs to be taken cautiously – it would be irresponsible to accept material that one is fundamentally unequipped to preserve – it must also be encouraged: trying to develop a complete and perfected solution in one step can only lead to disappointment, and practical experience is essential for learning.

1.6 A very brief history of digital preservation

Interest in the longevity of digital information and curatorial approaches to its management have been evident since the early years of the digital information age, and can be traced back at least to the 1960s, when the first data archives were established. Designed to manage scientific research data, and make it accessible to the scholarly community, archives such as the Inter-University Consortium for Political and Social Research (1962)[6] and UK Data Archive (1967)[7] laid much of the groundwork for digital curation as we know it today.

The advent of personal computers and the internet triggered an explosion in the creation and use of digital information, which started in earnest in the early 1980s, gained enormous momentum in the 1990s as a result of the emergence of the world wide web, and continues unabated to the present day. Suddenly, the world was producing a plethora of new types of digital information – from office documents to multimedia, web pages to 3D models, e-mails to e-books – in hitherto unimaginable quantities. Digital information had moved from being the preserve of big business and major research institutions to a fact of everyday life for billions of people.

Concerns about the fragility of digital information crystallized in the formation in 1994 of the Task Force on Archiving of Digital Information. After two years of deliberation, this US group published a seminal report,[8] which laid the foundations for most subsequent work in the field, and continues to shape the agenda even today. Concepts and concerns such as certification of trusted digital repositories, format registries, cost models, and integrity and authenticity – which this report first articulated as a coherent set of challenges – remain the focus of daily discussion within the digital preservation community today, at conference, in blogs and on Twitter.

This should not be taken to indicate that the discipline has failed to progress since the report was published, or to find answers to the searching questions that it posed. Far from it: digital preservation today is the focus of an enormously vibrant, active and collaborative community. Indeed, it is instructive to look briefly at how far that community has come in such a short period of time. In 1996, when I first began developing a digital archiving programme at the English Heritage Centre for Archaeology,[9] it was possible to assemble and read virtually everything of note written on the subject in a few pages of bibliography;[10] 16 years later, even maintaining awareness of developments in the field is a constant challenge, reading all their published outputs an impossibility.

As with any emerging discipline, two strands of activity are required to progress: the development of strong theoretical underpinnings and standards, and the establishment of a diverse and active pool of practitioners, who can advance and expand the theory through practical application.

The publication of the OAIS Reference Model has proved to be one of the seminal moments in the development of a coherent conceptual framework for digital preservation. Originally developed by the space science community in the 1990s, and released as a draft recommendation by the Consultative Committee for Space Data Systems in 1996, it rapidly became accepted as a *de facto* standard. It was formally published as a full recommendation in 2002, before being issued as an international standard (ISO 14721: 2003), and most recently updated in 2012.[11] It sets out a detailed model of the functions and processes required of a digital repository, as well as introducing a set of terminology that has become established as the *lingua franca* of the digital preservation community.

Another key area of standardization has been in relation to metadata. Thanks to the emergence of internationally recognized schemes such as METS (2001) and PREMIS (2003), the community is well served by a range of standards tailored to the needs of digital preservation (these are discussed in detail in Chapter 7, 'Describing digital objects').

While OAIS provides a conceptual model for what digital repositories should do, the widespread development of operational digital preservation services has led to much discussion about the detailed standards to which they should adhere in practice. From this has emerged the concept of 'trusted digital repositories'; this trend is examined in Chapter 4, 'Models for implementing a digital preservation service'.

The more practical development of the discipline has been driven equally by the efforts of individual institutions in building their own preservation solutions, and through collaborative research. Projects such as CEDARS (CURL Exemplars in Digital ARchiveS) in 1998,[12] and the Dutch Nationaal Archief's Digital Preservation Testbed (2000),[13] were highly influential, applying rigorous scientific principles to the development and testing of practical digital preservation methods.

The first major digital preservation repositories were built by national cultural memory institutions, such as the National Library of Australia (2001), the Koninklijke Bibliotheek, the National Library of the Netherlands (2002) and the UK National Archives (2003). Today, they are no longer the exclusive province of such institutions, with repositories proliferating among many other types and scales of organization, including university libraries, local archives and business archives.

This has been enabled by the emergence of production-quality digital repository systems, which provide the technological platforms on which to build digital preservation services. A number of open-source solutions have emerged, of which Fedora (1997), EPrints (2000) and DSpace (2002) are the most widely adopted examples today. In parallel, commercial products such as Safety Deposit Box (2003) and Rosetta (2008) have been brought to market, often borne out of initial funding from national memory institutions. Most recently, cloud-based services such as DuraCloud (2011) and Preservica (2012) offer a new paradigm for providing digital Preservation-as-a-Service (PraaS), which may be of particular interest to smaller organizations. These technologies and the options for building digital repositories are discussed in detail in Chapter 4, 'Models for implementing a digital preservation service', and Appendix 3.

Alongside repository software, the emergence of widely available, practical preservation tools and services such as the PRONOM technical registry (2002), JHOVE characterization tool (2003) and DROID format identification tool (2005) has played an essential role in making digital preservation a practical proposition for many organizations.

The specialized discipline of web archiving has a history almost as long as the Web itself. From the foundation of the Internet Archive (1996) and the Nordic Web Archive (1997) to the wealth of local, national and international web archiving programmes we see today, the huge volumes of data acquired have spurred the development of digital repositories capable of managing and preserving them.[14]

Since the early 2000s, many advances have come as a result of major research projects, such as those funded through the Library of Congress' National Digital Information Infrastructure and Preservation Program (NDIIPP) (2000),[15] and the European Commission's various research funding programmes.[16] While space does not permit a detailed account of these, projects such as ERPANET (2001), DELOS (2004), DigitalPreservationEurope (2006) and Planets (2006) have all had a huge impact on the development of the state of the art, and this momentum is being carried forward in the current crop of projects, which are discussed in Chapter 10, 'Future trends'. Similarly, NDIIPP has funded the development of major tools and services, including JHOVE2, LOCKSS and the MetaArchive.

We have also begun to see the emergence of organizations dedicated to the advancement of the discipline, such as the UK's Digital Preservation Coalition (2002)[17] and Digital Curation Centre (2004),[18] the Dutch Nationale Coalitie Digitale Duurzaamheid (2008)[19] and the international Open Planets Foundation.[20] This last, together with projects such as SPRUCE (Sustainable PReservation Using Community Engagement),[21] signals a growing movement towards the development of nationally and internationally based practitioner communities. Agile and enthusiastic, and centred more around community activities such as hackathons, rather than traditional project and institutional structures, these have the potential to advance the discipline in new and exciting ways (as discussed in Chapter 10, 'Future trends').

An excellent visual overview of the history of digital preservation, alongside key IT developments, is provided by the timeline developed by Cornell University Library, as part of its online tutorial on digital preservation management.[22]

1.7 A note on terminology

Digital preservation provides a fertile breeding ground for new terminology, as well as finding new uses for that which is established. As a young discipline, its specialist nomenclature has yet to mature and settle – in some cases, a number of alternative terms have been applied to the same, or similar, concepts. Furthermore, it bridges a number of long-established fields, each with their own unique vocabularies. All of this can appear calculated to confuse newcomers and seasoned practitioners alike. I have therefore attempted to be clear and consistent in my own use of terminology, and have provided a glossary in part to clarify the sense in which I have chosen to use it.

Two terms in particular appear constantly throughout the book, referring to the subject and means of preservation respectively: *digital object* and *digital repository*. These are so fundamental as to justify exploring them in a little more detail now.

What is a digital object?

In this book I am using the term 'digital object' to signify the thing that we are seeking to preserve, but what does this phrase really mean? It is worth taking a moment to consider the nature of these 'digital objects', to really understand what they are, and how they compare with their analogue counterparts.

Indeed, the analogue world is a good place to start. We have little difficulty identifying and understanding the nature of physical collection objects, whether they be printed books, parchment rolls or stone sculptures. Their very physicality provides a natural structure for describing and arranging them. For example, it is easy to see that there is a different relationship between the individual pages of a book and the book as a whole, as opposed to that between two different books by the same author; the volume provides a natural atomic point of reference. Of course, even in the physical world it is important to acknowledge differences in approach between the curatorial disciplines. The hierarchical nature of archival description, for example, is very different from the more discrete, unitary world of the library catalogue. However, the physical nature of the material does impose structures that are much more clearly and rigidly defined than in the digital realm.

This may not be immediately apparent. If we consider a PDF version of a paper publication, there is a straightforward one-to-one correspondence between the digital and physical object. However, this represents the simplest possible case, and conceals a frequently overlooked complication. At one level, the digital world has a very obvious and simple atomic unit: the file, but in reality the file is a purely technological artefact, having no direct relationship with the structure or nature of the information content.

This can be illustrated by considering the varying ways in which the same information object might be technically represented. We can simplify this by taking an example that is analogous to an object in the physical world – a book. An electronic book could exist in a plethora of forms (I deliberately avoid referring to 'formats', for reasons that should become apparent). There might be the author's finished 'manuscript' version, in Microsoft Word 2000 format. Depending on authorial practice, this might comprise a single Word file, or multiple Word files – one for each chapter. The Word 2000 files might subsequently be updated to Word 2007 format. This is a fundamentally different creature – each file is actually a container format, comprising a series of separate XML documents. The printed version of the book might be digitized, resulting in a set of TIFF image files, one for each page. These might then be amalgamated into a single PDF file, for ease of access. An e-book version could be created for use on devices such as the Kindle, in specialized formats such as EPUB or Amazon's KF8. Finally, we might envisage a web version of the book, where each page or chapter of the book becomes a separate web page. In this case, the book is represented as a series of HTML files, together with a range of additional files, such as cascading stylesheets and images, which are required to render the pages in a web browser. These representations are summarized in Table 1.1.

Table 1.1 Alternative representations of a book	
Version	**Technical representation**
Physical	1 printed volume (comprising 12 chapters and 700 pages)
Word 2000	12 DOC files
Word 2007	12 DOCX files (each containing various XML files)
Digitized masters	700 TIFF files
Digitized access copy	1 PDF file
e-Book	1 EPUB container file (containing various XML, XHTML and image files)
Web	12 HTML files, 1 CSS file and 15 GIF images

We can therefore see that our digital object is much more complex and variable than its physical analogue, which has a very clear cut, discrete existence. It can comprise one or many files, in the same or different formats; it can comprise files contained within other files; even the relationship between the constituent files varies – in some cases, such as with individual Word documents for chapters, each file serves an equivalent function; in others, such as the website, a single stylesheet file might be used by every HTML file, and has a very different function.

And this represents the simpler end of the spectrum; something like a

Geographic Information System (GIS) is a very complex entity, with many component parts in sophisticated and dynamic relationships, and no real-world counterpart.

My use of the term 'digital object' therefore serves as shorthand to cut through some of this complexity. Chapter 8, 'Preserving digital objects', delves deeper into the fascinating implications of the digital information environment, and examines how we can manage these complexities through the separation of digital objects into information objects (representing the underlying entity, such as a book) and data objects (the technical components of that entity, such as files), and the use of concepts such as multiple manifestations.

What is a digital repository?

The term 'digital repository' conjures visions of vast, complex, expensive and forbidding IT systems, only viable for major institutions to consider building. This is very far from the case: as this book will demonstrate, a digital repository is a concept, capable of being realized in many different forms, to suit all levels of budget and expertise. For the purposes of this book, the following definition will be applied:

> A digital repository is a combination of people, processes, and technologies which together provide the means to capture, preserve, and provide access to digital objects.

In general, the term is therefore used in this book to refer to the body providing the digital repository function, rather than just the systems employed at a given point in time to help realize this. In the cases where it is employed in the narrower sense, this should be apparent from the context.

As previously mentioned, there is a detailed, formal definition of what is required to provide those means: the OAIS Reference Model. However, although widely cited, and undoubtedly of great value, especially in providing a common vocabulary for expressing these concepts, the complexity and terminology of OAIS can be off-putting. Fundamentally, the core functions of a digital repository are the same as any memory organization, and can be expressed very simply: it must be able to acquire control of new content, make that content available to its designated user community, and perform the various preservation and management activities required to continue doing so for as long as required. This is illustrated in Figure 1.1.

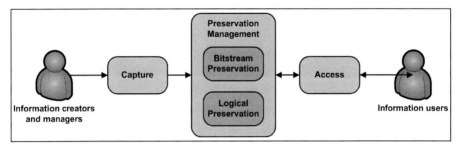

Figure 1.1 Functions of a digital repository

This book describes in detail how smaller organizations can develop the practical means to perform each of these functions, with relevant case studies throughout. It begins by looking at what is involved in building a digital preservation capability, from making the case and securing the necessary mandate and resources (Chapter 2, 'Making the case for digital preservation'), to defining your requirements (Chapter 3, 'Understanding your requirements'), and identifying an appropriate model for turning them into reality (Chapter 4, 'Models for implementing a digital preservation service'). It then examines in detail the core repository functions:

- **Capture**: A repository must have a means to capture new content, and bring it within its control. This is discussed in Chapters 5, 'Selecting and acquiring digital objects'; 6, 'Accessioning and ingesting digital objects'; and 7, 'Describing digital objects'.
- **Preservation management**: The repository must be able to manage its content so that it remains available in an accessible and authentic form. This is addressed in Chapter 8, 'Preserving digital objects'.
- **Access**: Any repository must provide a means for its users to discover and access its content. Chapter 9, 'Providing access to users', covers this.

Digital preservation is a fast-moving world, with practitioners and researchers continually evolving new ideas, techniques and tools. The final chapter therefore takes a look at how some of these may develop over the next few years (Chapter 10, 'Future trends'). Lastly, the appendices include a number of useful templates, as well as examples of a wide range of tools and services which may be of value to digital archivists, with links to further information.

1.8 Getting the most from this book

Even when focusing on smaller organizations, the diversity of resources, skills, needs and organizational contexts represented there make it very difficult to offer practical guidance useful to all: what might seem simplistic or familiar for one may be overly technical or simply irrelevant to others. I have therefore tried to provide guidance which is sufficiently detailed to provide genuine substance for the more technically minded, but which can also be dipped into by those requiring an overview. At the end of each chapter, a series of key points summarizes the main recommendations.

No single book can hope to offer a comprehensive account of such a vast and varied subject. The present volume is no exception, and claims to be no more than a starting point, an initial guide to the strange, compelling and rewarding world of digital preservation. However, it includes pointers to further information at every turn, with links to online sources wherever possible, so that readers can explore particular subjects in much greater depth, according to their inclination.

I have also included a large number of case studies throughout, for two reasons: first, I firmly believe that practical exposition is the best form of explanation, and second, I hope that demonstrating how smaller organizations of all kinds have built practical digital preservation solutions will reinforce my central thesis – digital preservation is a practical proposition for all.

1.9 Notes

1 Waller and Sharpe (2006) provide further information about these and other examples.
2 US Government Accountability Office (2010).
3 Boyle, Eveleigh and Needham (2009).
4 MLA East of England and East of England Regional Archive Council (2006) and MLA East of England (2008).
5 See www.paradigm.ac.uk/.
6 See www.icpsr.umich.edu/icpsrweb/landing.jsp.

7   See www.data-archive.ac.uk/.

8   Garrett and Waters (1996).

9   Brown (2000).

10 See, for example, the bibliography in Brown (2002a).

11 Consultative Committee on Space Data Systems (2012).

12 Two snapshots of the project website are preserved in the UK Web Archive at www.webarchive.org.uk/ukwa/target/99695/.

13 See, for example, Potter (2002) and the Testbed website, as archived by the Internet Archive at
http://wayback.archive.org/web/*/http://www.digitaleduurzaamheid.nl.

14 For an overview of the history of web archiving, see Brown (2006), 8–21.

15 See www.digitalpreservation.gov/.

16 See Strodl, Petrov and Rauber (2011) for a detailed history of EC-funded digital preservation research.

17 See www.dpconline.org/.

18 See www.dcc.ac.uk/.

19 See www.ncdd.nl/en/index.php.

20 See www.openplanetsfoundation.org/.

21 See www.dpconline.org/advocacy/spruce and http://wiki.opf-labs.org/display/SPR/Home.

22 See www.dpworkshop.org/dpm-eng/timeline/popuptest.html.

2

Making the case for digital preservation

2.1 Introduction

Building a digital preservation service requires resources, including staff time and skills, budget and technical infrastructure. More fundamentally, it requires an understanding from the organization that digital preservation is a high priority, and a commitment to the principles and practice. Securing such a mandate is therefore critical: with it, you have taken a crucial first step towards delivering a successful service; without, it will be an uphill battle to achieve anything.

This chapter describes the drivers for implementing a digital preservation service, and strategies that you can adopt for making an effective business case to secure senior management buy-in and resources. It advocates the development of a digital preservation policy as a first step in building this case, including a discussion of techniques for quantifying the financial and non-financial benefits of implementing a successful preservation solution, and introduces the concept of a digital asset register. Finally, it considers the essential elements of the business case itself.

Building an effective business case may initially seem daunting, but can be broken down into a series of simple steps, as illustrated in Figure 2.1.

This chapter considers each of these stages in detail, illustrated with examples, from understanding the fundamental arguments to use, to developing a comprehensive business case.

2.2 Understanding the drivers

A good understanding of the drivers for digital preservation is obviously a prerequisite for developing a compelling business case. Every organization has its own unique imperatives, but there are many generic arguments which should be considered.

Collection development

The growing ubiquity of digital ways of working in our business, cultural and social lives is reflected in the increasing desire by many organizations to acquire digital content. Whether it be the library moving from print to electronic journals, or the gallery displaying new forms of digital art, digital information is becoming a fundamental aspect of collection development.

Corporate memory

Most organizations retain information as part of their 'corporate memory', in the form of institutional archives and libraries. Besides the obvious historical purpose, these have a wider role in maintaining the accumulated knowledge and expertise of the institution. This may be especially important if highly specialized knowledge is critical to the organization over long time periods, for example in the fields of aerospace engineering or pharmaceuticals. It may also be crucial if an organization is restructured, or in the commercial environment when companies merge or are acquired. Needless to say, in a digital world, the long-term viability of corporate memory depends on digital preservation.

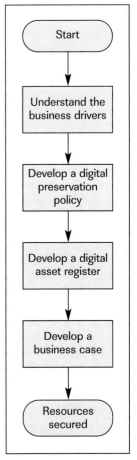

Figure 2.1
Making the case

User access

Many organizations besides libraries and archives provide information access to specific groups of users, whether internal staff, specialist communities or the general public. Those users require the information to be available in an accessible form, and have expectations about its longevity. If that information access is dependent on technology, digital preservation facilities will be required to ensure that those expectations can continue to be met over the long term.

Information reuse

Organizations are increasingly expecting to reuse and add value to the digital information resources which they have invested so heavily in creating, whether public bodies opening up their data to be exploited by third parties, academic institutions publishing research data, or oil exploration companies reanalysing old geophysical survey results in the light of modern extraction technologies. Maintaining these resources in accessible forms is a prerequisite for such reuse, and a digital preservation service provides the capability and confidence to achieve this.

Reputational protection

The reputation of an organization may be hard to quantify or value, but damage to it can have catastrophic consequences. The loss of digital assets entrusted to its care, or on which its business depends, can have reputational implications which far exceed the operational impact. Organizations may also care about how their digital preservation policies and practices compare with their peers or competitors. For example, many national libraries and archives, together with universities, have already implemented digital repositories, and this has undoubtedly provided the impetus for others to follow suit. While there are advantages to not being at the cutting edge, not least because those institutions can then benefit from the experiences of others, there are significant reputational risks in being seen to be failing to adopt current good practice.

Legal and regulatory compliance

All organizations are subject to legal and regulatory regimes, which require them to manage their digital information appropriately, and to sustain that information for as long as required. For example, freedom of information and privacy legislation require relevant information to be maintained in an accessible form, while corporate transparency and accountability measures such as the Sarbanes-Oxley Act, 2002 in the USA and the international Basel III Accord, as well as financial and health and safety laws, determine how long public and private organizations are required to retain certain types of information, and whether such information must be publicly disclosed. In some cases, such as pension information or asbestos records, retention will be required for many decades. Enabling legislation for cultural memory institutions, such as libraries and archives, may create detailed statutory obligations for preservation, which may or may not explicitly reference digital materials. As an example, the Legal Deposit Libraries Act, 2003 in the UK includes provision for future regulations governing the deposit of non-print publications; such regulations are currently being developed for websites and electronic journals. Equally, intellectual property legislation may circumscribe the preservation strategies available to collecting bodies, for example by preventing the creation of copies or migration to new formats.

There is a very high risk that without proactive intervention to implement a digital repository and associated digital preservation processes, digital information will become inaccessible and the organization will be unable to meet its statutory and regulatory obligations.

Business continuity

The risk of losing access to vital digital information assets is a very real, if often overlooked, threat to business continuity in the modern world, and appropriate digital preservation facilities should feature as a vital part of any business continuity plan. A frequently cited statistic is that 90% of businesses suffering a major data loss go out of business within two years.[1]

Efficiencies and savings

Digital preservation can support more efficient ways of working, and therefore provide attendant savings. This can be particularly important for smaller organizations needing to make the most effective use of limited resources. As part of a comprehensive information management strategy, it can minimize duplication and maximize ease of access; if the authoritative version of a digital asset is preserved and accessible in a digital repository, the duplicate copies that tend to proliferate in any organization's systems can safely be deleted, reducing storage costs and the scope for confusion for users. Very significantly, it can avoid nugatory expenditure as a result of data loss, and enable reuse.

Protecting investment

Organizations may invest very significant resources in the creation and acquisition of digital information. Many libraries and archives have been allocating substantial budgets to the digitization of their collections, in order to broaden access and, potentially, generate additional income. In the private sector, digital information assets may have huge commercial value. These investments are at risk, unless protected by active preservation intervention. Any loss or damage to that information is likely to incur substantial future costs to either re-create it, or engage in expensive 'digital archaeology' to rescue it. In the worst cases, assets may be irreplaceable or unrecoverable, in which case the investment would be lost forever.

The future costs of preserving digital information are substantially reduced, the earlier sustainability is addressed; indeed, for new information, it should be factored in from the point of creation. This will allow the organization to minimize future preservation costs – it is much more expensive to retrofit systems to meet preservation requirements than to incorporate these standards from the outset.

Supporting digital ways of working

The implementation of a digital repository and other preservation services is a fundamental prerequisite for any organization to manage its information electronically; without the assurance that we can organize and preserve digital information into the future as effectively as we can paper, we can never fully realize the benefits of digital ways of working. Digital preservation may support the future realization of benefits and savings from other activities. For example, many public sector bodies, which currently publish large amounts of information on paper, are looking to make substantial savings by moving to online-only publication. Such a transition must be supported by the digital preservation policies and procedures necessary to ensure that the electronic publications can be maintained in accessible form. Equally, these are required to underpin activities such as digitization, or the implementation of new information management systems, such as corporate Electronic Document and Records Management Systems (EDRMS) or Enterprise Content Management Systems (ECMS). Within the wider context of electronic records management, digital preservation can also support transparency and accountability within public administrations.

Rationalizing data storage and implementing shared services

Digital preservation may enable existing arrangements for the storage of digital resources to be rationalized, for example by replacing a plethora of niche storage areas with a single repository, realizing efficiency savings in storage costs and in how solutions are implemented for disaster recovery, refreshing storage media, and technology migration. It can do so by:

- eliminating unnecessary data duplication
- ensuring that data is not retained for longer than required
- ensuring that data is stored in the environment most suited to its management requirements.

Archival information has different storage requirements to information in current business use. While the latter typically demands high-availability, high-performance storage, the former has much lower requirements in both of these areas, emphasizing integrity and reliability instead. This can allow information of long-term value, but limited demand, to be moved to lower-cost storage environments.

Not all of the drivers discussed above apply in every case, and the detail varies from organization to organization. A little time spent considering which drivers are most relevant to a given situation, with concrete examples, will be amply repaid when it comes to framing first the policies, and subsequently the business case for implementing a practical digital preservation solution.

2.3 Developing a policy

Any organization with a serious desire to address digital preservation should aspire to developing a digital preservation policy as soon as possible. Not only does this provide a basis from which detailed requirements can then be identified, and a solid, consistent intellectual foundation for practical solutions, it also forms an important step in securing organizational buy-in to the principles and practice. The following section provides guidance on how to develop an effective, realistic digital preservation policy.

The need for a policy

A 2005 survey, carried out on behalf of the Digital Preservation Coalition, found that only 18% of organizations surveyed in the UK had a digital preservation policy or strategy document.[2] It is tempting to make a direct correlation between this and another finding of the survey – that only 20% of organizations had provided adequate funding for digital preservation. This is confirmed by a contemporaneous survey by the Museums, Libraries and Archives Council (MLA),[3] which found that only 23% of respondents had a digital preservation policy; the survey report went on to note that '[organizations were] asked specifically about whether there was funding allocated for ongoing maintenance of the digital materials created. The reply was almost unanimously "no".'[4]

Today, the situation has undoubtedly improved, as illustrated by a much larger survey (with more respondents and a greater breadth of geographical coverage) conducted by the EU-funded Planets project in 2010.[5] This surveyed over 200 organizations from around the world, the majority European, and found that 48% had a policy, with 47% having the corresponding budget to begin implementing their policy. The Planets survey is particularly relevant in having investigated the impact of a policy in some detail. It is worth quoting its conclusions in full:

> There exists a digital preservation divide between the policy haves and the policy have-nots.
>
> Organizations with a digital preservation policy are more likely to include digital preservation in their operational, business continuity and financial planning. They are three times more likely to have secured a budget for digital preservation, four times more likely to be investing in a solution now and three times more likely to have a long-term solution already in place.
>
> By contrast, organizations without a digital preservation policy are four times more likely to have no experience or be unaware of the challenges presented by digital preservation, three times more likely to have no plans for the long-term management of digital information, and more than twice as likely to put off investing in a digital preservation solution for more than two years. The existence of a digital preservation policy is therefore a vital first step towards implementing a solution.[6]

Getting started

While having a policy is therefore a fundamental building block for building practical solutions, developing one may seem a daunting prospect. Fortunately, there is a wide range of very useful recent guidance – as well as some excellent examples of actual policies – available to draw on, and some of these are discussed later in this chapter.

Furthermore, a standard approach to developing a policy can be adopted by any organization, as illustrated in Figure 2.2.

The individual steps are discussed in more detail below.

Analyse what already exists

The policy cannot and should not exist in a vacuum; it needs to fit within an existing organizational context, and take account of current resources and practice. Before embarking on policy development it is therefore necessary to review existing policies and strategies within the organization and externally. These might include business plans, IT strategies, information management policies, and corporate finance and staffing policies. Some will be specific to particular kinds of organization: for memory institutions, these might include collection policies and user access policies, whereas higher education institutions may have research strategies, and teaching and learning strategies.

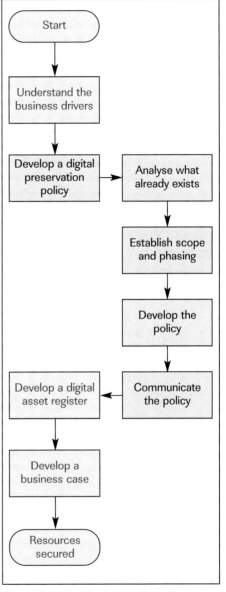

Figure 2.2 Developing a policy

It is also necessary to consider the existing information and IT infrastructure; although the policy should be technology-independent, being a statement of principles rather than tied to specific IT products, it does need to take account of current and planned IT provision and information management systems. For example, if your IT is outsourced, you need to consider what services can be called on, and what constraints this imposes.

Establish the scope and phasing

It is essential to be clear about the scope of the policy – which information resources will be collected and preserved. Consideration should also be given to the required level of detail, and the timetable for implementing the policy. For example, a 'big bang' approach, where all the different, interdependent elements of the solution need to be implemented at the same time, is not only expensive but also complex, and therefore risky. Rather, a staged approach may be better, starting with a high-level policy, and gradually adding more detail over time, as part of a phased programme of implementation. It may be more effective to begin with some 'quick wins', which can then build a momentum for introducing more radical or wholesale changes. For example, the UK Parliamentary Archives introduced a programme to archive its websites periodically as a means to acquire important content, gain practical experience, and raise awareness of digital preservation within Parliament in advance of work to build a digital repository.

Develop the policy

See 'What should go into the policy?' below for a discussion of what to include when writing your policy.

Communicate the policy

A policy which is not adopted is worthless. It is therefore essential to plan, implement and review the means by which the policy will be communicated to those who need to be aware of it. Having such a plan is key whatever the size of the organization: larger organizations have a range of formal communication channels to be considered, while in smaller organizations, where informal communication may be the norm, important information and lines of responsibility may be lost or unclear without a more formal communication plan. It may be helpful to begin by assessing the current level of awareness among stakeholders. This assessment might be undertaken formally as a survey, or through informal soundings among colleagues. A clear plan for how the policy will be disseminated should then be developed. This should identify everyone who needs to know about it, bearing in mind that this may include people not directly involved in information management, and indeed possibly outside the organization, such as end-users and peers. Approaches to communicating with stakeholders are considered in more detail in the next chapter.

The process of raising awareness will then continue throughout the development of the policy and beyond. As part of this process, the effectiveness of the communications strategy should be reviewed periodically. This might be measured directly (for example through a periodic survey) or indirectly (for example, by looking at changes in the volume of content submitted for preservation).

What should go into the policy?

The exact content of a digital preservation policy is dictated by the particular organizational context, but many elements are common to all policies, and it is therefore possible to consider a generic model.

First, there are some common principles to consider:

- **Longevity**: It is to be hoped that a digital preservation policy will remain relevant and in use for many years. A process of periodic review and revision is required to ensure this but, to minimize the need for constant updating, it is desirable that the policy should be as future-proof as possible. This should be supported by ensuring that the policy is focused on *principles* rather than specific *implementation details*; the policy should be a statement of 'what' and 'why', rather than 'how'.
- **Effectiveness**: The policy must demonstrate the benefits it will provide, and the risks it will mitigate.
- **Clarity**: The policy should be written in language that is accessible to its intended audience, avoiding unnecessary jargon, and should be well organized and logical. Its requirements should be unambiguous.
- **Practicality**: Implementation of the policy must be achievable, given the resources and expertise available to the organization. It is pointless and counterproductive to develop a policy that cannot be achieved in any realistic timeframe. This is especially important for smaller bodies, which typically work with tighter budget and staff constraints.

A standard digital preservation policy might include the following sections:

- purpose
- context
- scope
- policy principles
- policy requirements
- standards
- roles and responsibilities
- communication
- audit
- review
- glossary.

These are considered in more detail below.

Purpose

The document should begin with a clear statement of purpose, establishing the function of the document.

Context

The background and context to the policy should be described. This should align the policy with organizational objectives and other relevant policies, strategies and initiatives, as identified through your initial analysis. This is also an appropriate place to provide some background, summarizing relevant previous work within the organization, such as digitization or electronic records management programmes, and anticipated next steps.

Scope

It is essential to clearly establish the scope of the policy. For example, does it relate only to internally produced content, or material acquired from external sources? Does it cover born-digital material, digitized documents, or both? Does it apply to records, publications or other types of digital resource? It may also be helpful at this point to highlight the diversity of content which may be covered; this can help to counter misconceptions that the policy applies more narrowly than is in fact the case, e.g. only to 'office' documents such as e-mails, spreadsheets and word processed text.

Policy principles

The detailed requirements of the policy should be prefaced by the underlying principles that inform them. This should state the key commitments which the policy supports, including statements about archival authenticity and accessibility, define the organization's preservation objectives, introduce any key preservation concepts, and discuss acceptable preservation strategies.

The policy must make clear the custodial status of archived content – who owns it, and who is legally responsible for management, preservation and providing access. This is essential for supporting legislative and regulatory compliance (e.g. defining responsibilities under data protection and freedom of information laws), and is becoming an increasingly complex issue in a world where some or all of an organization's digital information management and preservation services may be contracted out, and where its data may be hosted externally, for example in the Cloud (see Chapter 8, 'Preserving digital objects', and Chapter 10, 'Future trends').

Policy requirements

Perhaps the single most important section of the policy is a statement of the underpinning policy requirements for digital preservation. The following areas are likely to be standard:

- **Creation and management**: Where this is within the control of the institution, the policy should define principles governing the creation and management of digital information before preservation. In particular, it is essential to underline the importance of addressing sustainability from the outset, for example by making informed choices about file formats, and setting minimum documentation standards for creators. The document should refer to any relevant standards, such as records management policies.
- **Appraisal, selection and acquisition**: The policy should reference any relevant appraisal, selection and acquisition policies and procedures, or records disposal schedules. It should also refer to procedures for transferring custody from creator to archive, and effecting the physical ingest of content into a repository. For organizations that acquire external content, this may include standards for depositors, specifying acceptable formats, transfer media, documentation etc. (see Chapter 5, 'Selecting and acquiring digital objects').

- **Preservation**: The policy must set out the high-level requirements for achieving preservation. This can usefully be subdivided into requirements for bitstream and logical preservation, which are discussed in more detail in Chapter 8, 'Preserving digital objects'.
- **Access and reuse**: The policy should state the kinds of access that are required. Will there be public access, or will it be limited to internal users? Is networked or online access required? Does access need to be integrated with other business systems, such as an electronic document and records management system? How will online access integrate with any wider organizational website? What degree of reuse must be supported: is the emphasis on providing human-readable versions, editable versions or machine-readable data? What access restrictions apply, including copyright implications?
- **Infrastructure**: Sustainability requirements need to inform the design, procurement and management of an organization's IT infrastructure, for example, when deciding which office software product to move to next; the policy is a useful place to assert this principle. There is also a more specific requirement that the infrastructure required for digital preservation, such as a digital repository, must itself be sustainable for as long as the digital resources it manages. This has an impact on the IT architecture adopted. For example, rather than building systems where the component parts are heavily dependent on one another, it is preferable to keep them loosely coupled, with well defined, standard interfaces between them; this can reduce the impact on the overall system when individual components need to be replaced or upgraded.

Standards

The policy should identify all internal and external standards that will apply. These may include formal international standards, such as OAIS, *de facto* standards such as PREMIS or METS, sector-specific standards such as MARC or ISAD(G), or internal documents such as technology standards.[7]

Roles and responsibilities

The clear assignment and acceptance of roles and responsibilities is critical to achieving an effective policy. The document should therefore define where responsibility lies for all aspects of the policy. This will certainly include the organizational units responsible for curation, IT provision and content creation. It may also cover external suppliers and service providers.

In smaller organizations, individual staff may need to combine a number of different roles, and it may not be possible to have dedicated posts with responsibility for digital preservation. This is not an issue, provided responsibilities are clearly defined, and sufficient time allowed within job descriptions to undertake them.

An organization must ensure that its digital preservation activities are carried out by sufficient staff with the appropriate skills. The document should therefore identify how the organization will provide training opportunities to allow staff to develop, maintain or enhance their digital preservation expertise. This may include participation on courses, self-directed learning, attendance at national and international seminars, workshops and conferences, study visits, internships and working exchanges with other institutions and professionals. The benefits of joining advocacy organizations such as the UK's Digital Preservation Coalition[8] and the Nationale Coalitie Digitale Duurzaamheid in the Netherlands[9] should also be considered. Roles and training are discussed in more detail in Chapter 4, 'Models for implementing a digital preservation service'.

Communication

It is essential to describe the methods that will be used to communicate the policy, as discussed earlier. The policy may also commit to raising awareness of, and providing training in, digital preservation issues within the wider organization and its user community.

Audit and certification

A policy is only as effective as the extent to which it is followed. It is therefore important to set up some form of audit mechanism to monitor adoption. This should be seen as a constructive process, intended not only to measure levels of compliance, but also to solicit valuable feedback, which can be used to improve the policy. Audits can be used to assess the effectiveness of a policy's implementation identify future priorities, and inform future reviews of the policy (see below). The formality of the audit process will vary considerably from organization to organization; while larger bodies may well have existing internal audit teams which can be drawn on, smaller organizations may take a more *ad hoc* approach. In all cases the principles remain the same. There are a number of emerging certification standards for digital repositories, which offer a range of audit regimes, including self-certification. These are discussed in more detail in Chapter 4, 'Models for implementing a digital preservation service'.

Review

Any policy document requires periodic review, to ensure that it remains up to date and relevant. It is therefore important to define the frequency of review and a mechanism by which this will be achieved. As discussed above, a policy should not be subject to very frequent change; as a guide, a review frequency of every two years would be typical. Reviews will also be required as a result of major organizational or technology changes.

Consideration should be given to how the review will be undertaken. Who should be involved? Is external participation desirable? It may be extremely valuable to invite professional colleagues from other institutions to assist with this.

Glossary

The policy should be easily understood by non-specialists. In a technical, jargon-laden field such as digital preservation, a glossary is therefore always helpful. If intended for an external audience, any organization-specific acronyms and terms should also be included.

Models and sources for digital preservation policies

The ERPANET project published a policy tool in 2003,[10] while a 2008 study commissioned by the Joint Information Systems Committee (JISC) in the UK[11] looks at what should go into an effective digital preservation policy, and provides very useful practical guidance. Although focused on the UK higher and further education sectors, it draws widely on policies and implementations from other sectors and countries and is therefore much more widely applicable. It provides a model policy and framework, which organizations can easily adapt to their own circumstances. It considers both high-level policy, and implementation issues, and includes exemplars of individual clauses.

The UK's Digital Curation Centre has published a template for digital preservation policies,[12] which includes example policy statements for each section. It has also developed an online tool for creating the data management plans required by research funding bodies of their grant-holders.[13] While specific to the higher education research sector, the tool includes much that is relevant to the development of digital preservation policies more generally. A US equivalent of the tool is also available.[14] The Inter-University Consortium for Political and Social Research (ICPSR), based at the University of Michigan, has also developed an outline for a policy framework,[15] which is intended as a model for any organization to use.

The international OpenDOAR directory of open access repositories website includes a tool for creating repository policies (Figure 2.3).[16] Specifically, it provides support for creating metadata, data, content, submission and, most relevantly, preservation policies. It is worth noting that

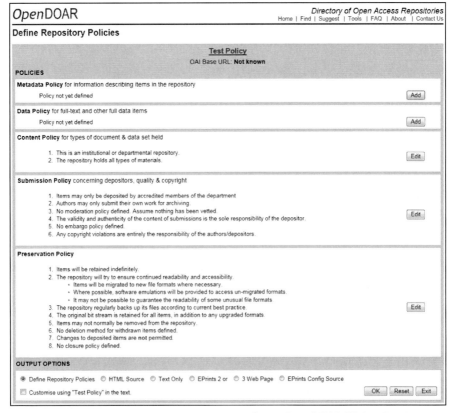

Figure 2.3 Web form for creating a repository policy in OpenDOAR (University of Nottingham)

OpenDOAR uses a very narrow definition of 'preservation policy' – in the context of this discussion, all five of the policy types covered by the tool would be relevant to a digital preservation policy. The tool provides a simple web user interface for creating policies. For each type of policy, a range of options can be configured, using check boxes. For example, the preservation policy covers retention periods, functional (logical) preservation, file (bitstream) preservation, withdrawal of items, version control and closure of content; each of these can be customized to individual needs. Once the policies have been defined, they can be saved in HTML format for the web, plain text, and even as a configuration file for the EPrints digital repository software, enabling automated execution of the policies. Although OpenDOAR is aimed specifically at the open access repository community, the tool is more widely applicable, and could certainly be helpful as a starting point for any organization that is planning a policy.

A number of institutional digital preservation policies for libraries, archives and other kinds of organization are available online, and may be helpful as models. A very non-exclusive list, biased towards smaller organizations, includes:

- **Archives**:
  - Hampshire Record Office (2010)
  - Swiss Federal Archives (2009)
  - UK Parliamentary Archives (2009)[17]
  - West Yorkshire Archive Service (2007)
- **Data services**:
  - Arts and Humanities Data Service (2004)[18]
  - ICPSR (2007)[19]
  - UK Data Archive (2011)
- **Libraries**:
  - Columbia University Libraries (2006)
  - National Library of Australia (2013)
  - Yale University Library (2007)
- **Museums and galleries**:
  - National Museum of Australia (2012)
- **Multi-disciplinary organizations**:
  - Guildhall Library Manuscripts and London Metropolitan Archives (2008)
  - Libraries and Archives Canada (2008)

    □ Wellcome Library (2007)[20]
- **Commercial services**:
    □ Online Computer Library Center (OCLC) (2006).

Once created, the policy needs to be ratified and adopted. The process for this will vary from organization to organization, but the policy should be endorsed by a group with sufficient seniority and influence to carry real weight; if at all possible, it should be approved at board or equivalent level. This also provides an excellent opportunity to publicize and promote digital preservation within the organization, and to begin to engage with data creators and owners, helping them to understand their responsibilities. For example, the policy could be published on the organization's website, and highlighted in relevant promotional materials, presentations and literature.

Having a digital preservation policy provides a firm foundation for beginning to develop a practical service, and demonstrates organizational commitment to the *principles* involved, but it is not usually sufficient in itself to secure the resources required to put the policy into *practice*. For this, a more detailed plan of action and business case will typically be needed. The remaining sections of this chapter examine how to build such a case.

2.4 Developing a digital asset register

The most powerful arguments are usually those which are supported by concrete evidence. The case for digital preservation is undoubtedly strengthened if real examples of digital assets that are important to an organization and at risk of loss can be found; the benefits of ensuring their preservation, and the consequential impact arising from their loss, can then be measured in terms that will resonate most strongly with the organization. For example, in developing its business case for digital preservation, the Parliamentary Archives quantified the creation cost and usage of a number of important digital collections, including Historic Hansard[21] and conservation photographs of works of art,[22] to illustrate the value – financial and otherwise – of the assets that would be protected by a digital repository.

A digital asset register can be a very useful tool for illustrating tangible risks and benefits. In essence, it is a list of an organization's digital assets that analyses the risk of loss, and the impact of that loss, in each case. It should:

- identify digital assets requiring long-term access

- identify the threats to future accessibility
- quantify the risks of those threats materializing
- quantify the costs and other impacts that would be incurred if the threats materialized
- quantify the benefits to be derived from continued access
- determine a priority for action.

Methods for doing so are described below.

The level of detail applied can be varied to meet individual requirements, and the work involved in developing and maintaining a register can be as great or little as the situation demands, and resources permit. Even a very high-level register, however, describing assets in the broadest terms, can provide tremendous support when making the case for preservation. This value is multiplied by the variety of uses to which a digital asset register can be put, once created – some of these are considered at the end of this section.

The register should include:

- basic information about the asset, such as its name, a brief description, and an identified business owner
- a basic categorization of the type of asset (e.g. digitized images, database, office documents, or a website); this will help to inform some of the generic risks that may need to be considered
- volume information, including the current volume of the asset and, where applicable, estimates of future growth rates; this helps to give a sense of scale
- identification of the main vulnerabilities; it is essential to identify the key threats to the future accessibility of the resource
- identification of the benefits of continued access, and the potential for reuse; for example, if a particular set of documents is heavily used by researchers, or a dataset could have future commercial value, this should be highlighted
- identification of the likely impact if the asset were to be lost or damaged; this might be reputational, operational or commercial impact
- an estimate of the financial value or other economic impact of the asset; this might be calculated in a number of ways, including:
  - the original cost of creation of the asset
  - the cost of rescuing the asset, if damaged
  - the cost of re-creating the asset, if lost

    ☐ the potential revenue from its commercial use
- a risk assessment, which should use a numeric assessment of the probability, impact and proximity of the risk of loss to calculate an overall risk score. The probability and proximity will be informed by the vulnerability assessment, while the impact can be determined from the financial value and non-financial impacts. Although a degree of subjectivity remains in any risk assessment, this can be minimized through the use of a standard scoring mechanism.

An example template for a digital asset register is shown in Appendix 1. Once the register has been created, it can be used in a number of ways. First, it should provide as comprehensive and accurate a list of assets requiring preservation as possible. This is not only a practical tool for the digital archivist, but also provides concrete evidence of the reality of the threat and its likely impact; this will prove invaluable in putting together a business case. Its other functions can include:

- helping to prioritize content for preservation, using the risk score; in the first instance, this may be used to identify any assets requiring urgent treatment, in advance of a full digital preservation solution; once a digital repository has been implemented, it can then form the basis for a programme to ingest content
- helping to prioritize the development of future preservation strategies
- providing the basis for calculating savings that will accrue from implementing a digital repository, and the costs of doing nothing; for example, it can be used to calculate a profile of the opportunity costs for re-creating or rescuing the identified assets over the life of the project; for each asset, a proportion of the re-creation cost can be included, based on the probability of loss; the year(s) in which these costs are assigned can then be based on the proximity of the threat; this method is explained in more detail in Appendix 1
- predicting demand for future storage growth
- identifying new potential for reuse of digital assets
- illustrating the breadth and depth of content requiring preservation for stakeholders, including potential suppliers and users.

2.5 Developing a business case

The final step in the process of making the case for digital preservation is to secure a concrete commitment from senior management, and the necessary resources to establish a functioning service. Within most organizations, this will require a formal business case of some description.

Organizations have their own procedures and templates for business cases. In addition, the level of detail required may vary considerably. Nonetheless, any business case needs to address certain standard questions. This section describes a generic template for a business case, and examines how this can be applied to the specific challenge of digital preservation. Much of the information from the policy and digital asset register can be reused here. The SPRUCE project is developing a generic business case for digital preservation, which may also prove useful.[23]

A typical business case includes the following sections:

- executive summary
- introduction
  - □ objectives
  - □ deliverables
- strategic intent
  - □ benefits and risks
  - □ critical success factors
- context
- options assessment
- dependencies
- project organization
- project risks.

These are considered in more detail below.

Executive summary

The main document is likely to be long and detailed, and will need to be reviewed and approved by a diverse audience, from senior management to technical staff. A succinct statement (no more than one or two pages) of why the project is required, what resources are being requested, and what it will deliver in return is therefore invaluable.

Introduction

The opening section of the business case should establish the background to the project, and define its *raison d'être*. This is the place to include a basic introduction to the challenges of digital preservation, and why they matter to the organization – the analysis of the organizational drivers, discussed at the beginning of this chapter, can be used to inform this. It should also clearly define the fundamental objectives of the project, and concrete deliverables which will be produced. Example objectives and deliverables for a generic digital preservation project are given below.

Objectives

- 'Take urgent action to safeguard the organization's most vulnerable digital information.'
- 'Meet the organization's legal and regulatory responsibilities, e.g. for data protection and freedom of information.'
- 'Ensure that access to digital resources is maintained, throughout their planned life cycle, preserving both active business information and information of permanent historical value for future users.'
- 'Ensure that processes are implemented across the organization, to ensure that newly created information adheres to digital preservation standards.'
- 'Safeguard the organization's investment in the creation and maintenance of digital resources, enabling full benefits realization and avoiding wasted expenditure in the future (e.g. on expensive digital archaeology).'
- 'Provide input to other information-related projects to ensure that digital preservation issues are considered in their planning, thus avoiding or reducing future costs.'
- 'Support and underpin all the organization's activities, programmes and projects which create or receive material in digital format by ensuring that access to it can be guaranteed for as long as is needed.'
- 'Contribute to the reduction of data storage costs by using the most efficient archival storage technologies.'

Deliverables

- 'Establish a digital repository for content identified for long-term preservation, including work flows for ingest of content from a range of

environments, and a baseline for user access to archived content.'
- 'Implement a technology watch and preservation planning process to identify and mitigate threats to future access.'
- 'Introduce technology standards and policies to support the sustainability of future information.'
- 'Develop and deliver a range of training and guidance for stakeholders.'

Finally, it will be helpful to summarize any progress to date, including any 'quick wins' already achieved.

Strategic intent

This section sets out why the proposed work is necessary to the organization at a strategic level. It needs to put forward the case for why the work is required now, and cannot be deferred to some future date. It must explain how the work would fit into the broader strategic context. If possible, the relationship to corporate objectives, business plans or strategies should be defined. This definition should draw on previous work to define the context for the digital preservation policy.

This section should also analyse the benefits that the project will bring and the risks it will address, together with the 'critical success factors' for the project. These are considered in more detail below.

Benefits and risks

It is essential to identify and quantify the benefits of digital preservation from the outset. Clearly, these will be central to building a case for action. More broadly, they will provide a basis for defining detailed requirements, and a benchmark against which to assess the success of any solution. These benefits may take many forms and will differ between organizations.

You should also clearly state the risks to the organization that will be mitigated by carrying out the work. In many cases, these will be the inverse of a benefit. Although it is usually preferable to emphasize the positive reasons for taking action, it is important to recognize that there are also powerful arguments to be made from the risks of *not* taking action. Whether it is more effective to emphasize the risks or the benefits is a matter of judgement, and will depend on the culture of the organization in question.

Both risks and benefits derive from the business drivers, discussed at the beginning of this chapter. Thus the imperative to maintain a corporate memory would give rise to a benefit – ensuring that the organization has persistent access to its digital resources – and mitigate a risk – damage or loss of corporate information.

Some benefits may give rise to savings, e.g. from more efficient use of electronic storage or improved working practices, and also avoided future costs, such as having to rescue or re-create lost data. It helps to be as specific as possible in defining these financial benefits, while remaining realistic – over-promising savings is never a good idea. It is also useful to include details of how the figures have been calculated. If a digital asset register is being used (see above) it can provide the basis for detailing avoided costs.

The JISC-funded project Keeping Research Data Safe (KRDS) in the UK has developed a toolkit which can help organizations to understand and demonstrate the benefits, value and impact of digital preservation. This may prove very helpful when it comes to articulating this part of the business case.[24]

Critical success factors

The business case should define the critical success factors for the project. These are the main criteria against which the success of the project can be measured, and should be framed as statements describing what a successful outcome would look like. These are examples of typical critical success factors:

- 'An affordable, flexible and scalable digital preservation solution is implemented to enable persistent access to the organization's current digital resources and those which will be created in future years.'
- 'Content owners can deposit historically significant data for preservation easily, and users can access archived data effectively.'
- 'Users trust the organization's preserved digital assets as being authentic and reliable.'
- 'Organizational change is managed and staff are supported as they develop new skills in creating, managing and accessing digital resources.'

Context

The document should describe the context for digital preservation within and beyond the organization, including the types of digital resources that need to be preserved, and reference to other relevant internal and external projects and programmes. Ideally, it should also provide an overview of the current market for digital preservation solutions. This will provide a good introduction to the detailed assessment of the options.

Options assessment

An assessment of the available options, together with a recommended approach, is one of the crucial elements of any business case. In seeking management approval for a project, it is essential to demonstrate that all realistic options have been considered, and to show the basis on which the recommended option has been selected. A 'do nothing' option should always be included, to provide a comparison for all the positive options.

Each option should be analysed in detail, with a description of the option, and an assessment of the advantages, disadvantages and predicted resourcing implications, including staffing and non-staff costs. The range of options that are typically available to an organization is discussed in depth in Chapter 4, 'Models for implementing a digital preservation service'.

As part of this, you need to assess potential sources of funding. These may include internal funding, partnership funding, or external grants from bodies such as funding councils or the EU. It is important to include any proposals for revenue generation, such as charges for depositors or end-users, which may offset the start-up and running costs.

It may be helpful to provide some form of sensitivity analysis for the options. This is a way of showing how susceptible each option is to changes in external factors. It requires two steps: first, identify the key factors that might vary, for example changing timetables for the project (e.g. to balance the needs of other projects), variations in the available resources (e.g. arising from cuts in government funding) and different levels of demand to ingest content into the repository. Second, identify the implications of these changes for each option. For example, using an external service provider might enable you to cope better with changing levels of demand, but offer little flexibility on budget. An in-house solution might offer the reverse.

The final part of this section should be a clear statement of the recommended option for which the business case is seeking approval. It should clearly and simply set out the rationale for choosing the favoured option, and rejecting the others.

Dependencies

It is essential to identify any dependencies with other projects or operational activities. Dependencies can go in either direction. For example, having an operational digital repository might be a dependency for enabling future content creation projects, such as digitization, to proceed. Equally, a digital repository project might rely on another project to redesign the organizational website, to enable public access to archived content. When describing dependencies, it is important to define the nature and the timing of the dependency.

Project planning

It may be helpful to give some indication of the approach that will be taken to structuring the programme of work, if known. For example, the project may naturally divide into a number of discrete work streams. An outline timetable is also useful, together with an indication of any governance structure, such as a project board and the composition of the project team. It is often helpful to adopt some form of project management methodology. This should very much be tailored to the time and expertise you have available, and the size of the project – it is very counterproductive to impose over-elaborate project management processes on a simple project – but it is always useful to employ a project management mindset: plan the tasks that need to be undertaken, and the order in which they must occur, identify the people and resources required to achieve them, and monitor how events actually unfold in relation to that plan.

Project risks

The business case should identify the key risks to the success of the project. These are entirely separate from the risks of not undertaking the project, discussed above. At this stage, it may only be possible to identify high-level risks – developing and maintaining a detailed project 'risk register' will be a standard project management task once the project itself gets under way, but these risks can still be expressed in similar form at this stage. Typically, this includes the following elements:

- a description of the risk
- a risk score
- a risk owner: the person or group responsible for managing the risk
- a summary of the proposed mitigation for the risk.

Appendices

The appendices can be used to provide supporting information. This might include a copy of the digital asset register, and a detailed options investment appraisal, analysing the proposed budgets for each option, with costs, revenues and savings, and discounted cash flows to assess the true value of the investment over time.

2.6 Next steps

The combination of a clearly defined policy for digital preservation, and a well argued business case for the resources necessary to implement that policy, should secure an organization's commitment in both principle and practice. The time and effort which may be required to achieve this must not be underestimated; however, the reward will be a practical, achievable route to developing a digital preservation solution appropriate to the needs of the organization.

With that mandate secured, you can move on to the next step: defining your detailed requirements for a digital preservation solution. This process is described in the next chapter.

2.7 Key points

- **Understand the drivers for your organization to undertake digital preservation**: Understanding the risks and benefits that apply to your particular circumstances will help you to build a compelling argument for action.
- **Create a digital preservation policy**: This provides the intellectual framework for developing your business case and understanding your requirements.
- **Build a digital asset register**: This provides the evidential basis for your business case.
- **Develop a detailed business case**: This represents the culmination of

your argument, and is intended to secure your mandate.
- **Reuse what others have done**: There are many excellent examples of policies and business cases available, which you can draw on.

2.8 Notes

1 Despite its frequent citation, it has proven difficult to confirm the source for this statistic. While it should therefore be treated with caution, there does appear to be good evidence to support it.
2 Waller and Sharpe (2006).
3 Simpson (2005).
4 Simpson (2005, 14).
5 Sinclair (2010).
6 Sinclair (2010, 9).
7 A wide range of relevant standards is discussed elsewhere in this book, and listed in the bibliography.
8 See www.dpconline.org/.
9 See www.ncdd.nl/.
10 ERPANET (2003).
11 Beagrie et al. (2008).
12 See www.dcc.ac.uk/webfm_send/236.
13 See https://dmponline.dcc.ac.uk/.
14 See https://dmp.cdlib.org/.
15 See www.icpsr.umich.edu/files/ICPSR/curation/preservation/policies/dp-policy-outline.pdf.
16 See www.opendoar.org/tools/en/policies.php.
17 Parliamentary Archives (2009).
18 See James (2004) for the preservation policy, although the full range of policies available at www.ahds.ac.uk/about/reports-and-policies/index.html are of interest.
19 McGovern (2007).
20 Checkley-Scott and Thompson (2007).
21 See http://hansard.millbanksystems.com/.
22 See www.parliament.uk/about/art-in-parliament/.
23 See http://wiki.opf-labs.org/display/SPR/The+SPRUCE+Business+Case+for+Digital+Preservation.
24 See www.beagrie.com/krds.php.

3

Understanding your requirements

3.1 Introduction

This chapter provides guidance on how to identify and understand your requirements for digital preservation services, from high-level needs to the detailed documentation necessary to enable systems to be developed or procured.

The importance of understanding your requirements as a precursor to implementing any kind of solution cannot be overstated. To omit this step should be as unthinkable as attempting to build a house without detailed architectural plans. Taking the time to do this properly will improve the quality of the end result. This is even more critical for smaller organizations with limited resources, where maximizing value for money is vital; understanding what matters most ensures that those resources can be invested to achieve the greatest possible impact.

This chapter begins by examining how to develop a set of requirements, including identifying and engaging with everyone who can and should contribute, modelling business processes, and drawing on existing work. It then considers how requirements should be articulated and documented, and the types of requirement that need to be considered. Finally, it looks at how the resulting requirements can be applied in practice, as a basis for developing actual systems and services.

3.2 Identifying stakeholders

An organization's requirements for digital preservation will not derive from any individual or single group; a wide variety of parties will have an interest. These may be key individuals, or those representing the interests of wider groups with whom it is not possible to engage directly. They may also be decision makers, who need ultimately to authorize the adoption of those requirements as a basis for implementation. Identifying these various stakeholders, and what role they need to play, is therefore an essential first step in understanding one's requirements. They will, of course, vary considerably from case to case, but a number of common categories of stakeholder should be considered:

- **Content creators and managers**: The people who actually create or manage the content to preserve are clearly an essential group. These may be internal staff or external depositors and publishers, and this distinction will be a major factor in determining by what means, and indeed to what extent, they can be identified in advance and consulted. Understanding the nature of the content that needs to be preserved and the processes by which it is managed prior to archiving is essential to inform the design of any solution. Equally, you almost certainly need to influence this group to adopt working practices and technology standards which are as conducive to preservation as possible.
- **Information managers**: Those with responsibility for information management and curation within the organization are of self-evident importance as stakeholders. This is the group that will have responsibility for managing a future digital preservation service, and be accountable for its successful operation. Defining a solution that meets their needs should be a given. This may also be the group that will be required to undergo the most significant and fundamental changes to their working practices and expertise; managing that change successfully is therefore vital.
- **IT providers**: The IT function within an organization will be a key stakeholder. IT providers will need to understand, and be happy with, the technical impact of any proposed solution, including its effect on other systems, and its support needs. They will almost certainly be required to provide key resources during the design and implementation of the solution, which may include project managers, architects and analysts; where an in-house route is being taken (see Chapter 4, 'Models for implementing a digital preservation service'), they might also include developers. In many cases they will also be expected to support any solution, once it is operational. They will almost certainly play a major role in defining the technical architecture of the solution, and setting any technology standards which will need to be followed.
- **End-users**: The people who will eventually use the preserved content can

arguably be considered the most important stakeholders of all, at least in the long term – they represent the ultimate motivation for undertaking digital preservation. Like data creators, these end-users may be internal or external. Their interests will lie principally in the use and reuse of archived content, and should shape requirements for how that content can be discovered and most usefully made available to them.

- **Decision makers and funders**: Those who ultimately make decisions and control budgets are clearly a key stakeholder group. It is vital to understand what information they will require to enable them to make these decisions, and what arguments are likely to prove most persuasive. Ideally, a sponsor within this group should be found, who can champion the cause of digital preservation at a senior level as well as advising on how best to manage communications with this group.
- **Potential suppliers**: In many cases, the future solution will rely at least in part on external suppliers, such as software vendors or other organizations offering tools or services. While it may be difficult, or indeed inappropriate, to enter into detailed dialogue with potential suppliers, and care must be taken not to compromise any future procurement exercise, some consideration must be taken of their capabilities. The market for digital preservation solutions is still small (see Chapter 4, 'Models for implementing a digital preservation service'), and an understanding of the current state of the art is important to inform one's requirements. At this stage, engagement with suppliers might be limited to desktop research into the market, and perhaps talking to them informally at events such as conferences.

There may be additional, or more specific, groups of stakeholders in particular organizational contexts, but the categories above should provide a good starting point. Having identified the relevant categories of stakeholder, these should be translated into actual groups, whether individuals or teams. Ultimately, named individuals need to be identified and approached. Care should be taken to ensure that the identified stakeholders are genuinely representative. For example, a local archive may have a very large number of external depositors, and it becomes important to strike a balance between limiting numbers to a manageable level and adequately covering likely variations in requirements. It is also essential to make sure that personalities or politics do not dominate, to the detriment of requirements.

3.3 Talking to stakeholders

The appropriate means of communicating with stakeholders varies, depending on who they are and what information needs to be elicited from, or communicated to, them. Some types of stakeholder, such as data creators, users, IT staff and information managers, may need to be involved in detailed discussions about requirements, while others, such as decision makers, may only require periodic, high-level updates on progress. For each of your stakeholders, you should identify the kind of communication required.

It is essential to remember that communicating with stakeholders is a two-way process – you must think not only about what you need to find out from them, but also what you want to tell them. Depending on this, a number of strategies can be used, including:

- questionnaires and surveys
- structured interviews
- workshops
- collaborative authoring of documents (for example using an institutional wiki)
- informal conversations.

Table 3.1 illustrates the types of communication that are typically needed with different types of stakeholder. It shows both the types of information which may be required from them, and which should be communicated to them.

3.4 Modelling your processes

Many requirements relate to business processes. For example, ingest is a process (see Chapter 6, 'Accessioning and ingesting digital objects'), and the requirements for ingest functionality in a digital repository derive from the sequence of activities that make up that process. Analysing the processes required can therefore be a useful tactic for defining requirements. Processes themselves derive from policies, and requirements can therefore be seen as the final expression of organizational will, which is defined at the highest level in policy and strategy documents, distilled from these into specific processes and standard operating procedures, before finally being articulated as requirements for the systems that will support and implement those processes (Figure 3.1).

Table 3.1 Stakeholder communications

Stakeholder types	Communication	
	Ask them about...	Tell them about...
Content creators and managers	• what content they create • formats, systems and processes for creation and management • data volumes • business use	• information management standards • progress reports
Information managers	• descriptive standards • information management standards • working practices • hybrid collections	• potential changes in practice • progress reports
IT providers	• technology standards • IT strategy • storage • infrastructure requirements	• technical requirements • data volumes • information management standards • progress reports
End-users	• what content they use • formats, systems and processes for use • reuse • frequency of use	• progress reports • content availability
Decision makers and funders	• formal approvals • funding decisions	• business case • resource implications, including costs • milestone achievements
Potential suppliers	• capabilities • outline costs	• procurement process • agreed requirements

The following example illustrates how this sequence might be put into practice. We might start with a statement in a digital preservation policy as follows:

> All ingested objects will be in acceptable formats, accompanied by metadata which meets the repository minimum standard, and free from viruses.

Figure 3.1 From policies to requirements

This might be expanded into a series of processes such as:

- validate formats
  - ☐ identify formats
  - ☐ check against acceptable list
- validate metadata
- virus check
  - ☐ perform initial virus check
  - ☐ quarantine
  - ☐ perform second virus check.

This in turn might yield the following requirements:

- The repository must provide an automated means to identify the formats of all files submitted for ingest, to compare the results against a configurable list of acceptable formats, and reject any files in non-preferred formats, generating an explanatory message for the administrator.
- The repository must provide an automated means to validate all metadata submitted for ingest against a defined repository schema, for accuracy and completeness. It must report any validation errors to the administrator.
- The repository must provide a means to check all files submitted for ingest for malicious software. This check must be performed before and after a quarantine period of configurable duration, using the latest available malware definitions on each occasion.

If possible, it may well be fruitful to undertake some detailed modelling of the underlying business processes; this can range in sophistication and complexity from the use of simple flow diagrams to formal methodologies such as the Unified Modelling Language (UML).[1] To get the most from this requires the specialist skills of an experienced business analyst, but it can still be a valuable exercise without access to such expertise. Though it may sound daunting, the principle is simply to identify each process involved in operating a digital preservation service, and then to break it down into its component activities, analysing in each case who (or which system) performs the task, where in the sequence that task occurs, and any prerequisites or outcomes it may have. A process model for the virus check element of the example above is shown in Figure 6.3 (p. 135).

The resultant models can greatly simplify the task of defining requirements, as well as provide a means of checking their consistency and completeness. Each activity in a given process will have an associated requirement; this might be for a system to undertake an automated step, such as virus checking, or to enable human input, such as approving a preservation plan. If the models are complete, and requirements defined for each step in those models, it is reasonable to assume that the requirements have been fully captured.

In future, the definition of formal process models or rules may become even more significant. A growing area of research within the digital preservation community is the use of rules to automate preservation processes. The premise is simple: if we can derive explicit, unambiguous rules from our policies, those rules can then be implemented in software. If policies change, these changes are articulated as new or modified rules.[2]

3.5 Learning from other people's requirements

Many organizations have already been through this process, and documented their requirements, and these can therefore provide good examples to draw on. The following is a non-exhaustive list of examples that may be helpful:

- Rosenthal et al (2005) offers an interesting introduction to defining requirements from the bottom up.
- In 2009, the EU-funded SHAMAN project published an analysis of requirements for three user communities: memory institutions, industrial design and engineering, and e-science.[3]
- The US National Library of Medicine issued a statement of requirements for a digital repository in 2007, structured around the classic OAIS functions.[4]
- In 2010 the US National Archives and Records Administration published the requirements document for its Electronic Records Archive programme.[5]
- Between 2008 and 2010, the Wellcome Library issued a number of invitations to tender, including detailed statements of requirements, for its digital repository[6] and an associated workflow tracking system.[7]

- The JISC-funded Repositories Support Project in the UK issued a briefing paper in 2008 called 'Specifying repository requirements'.[8]
- The various standards for trusted digital repositories (discussed in the next chapter) provide a useful basis for thinking about requirements.

These examples cover organizations of all sizes. While it may be useful to start by looking at those most similar to your own context, you should not be limited by this; for example, a small organization can very usefully adapt requirements from a national body. Fundamental requirements for digital preservation are very similar at all scales – most differences appear only in the detailed implementation. For example, repositories of all sizes have requirements for virus checking and quarantine.

3.6 Documenting your requirements

Having consulted with stakeholders, looked at what analogous organizations have done, and analysed the underlying business processes and policies, you should be well placed to begin formulating a set of requirements. This process may be best delegated to a small group, with the necessary time and expertise available.

Getting the right level

When defining requirements, it is important to focus on the desired result, rather than the means of achieving it. This is sometimes referred to as an 'outcome-based' approach.

One of the most difficult aspects of analysing your requirements is to select the correct level of detail. If requirements are defined at too high a level (e.g. 'the system must preserve digital objects') then they become meaningless. If they are defined at too low a level (e.g. 'the system must perform integrity checking with the SHA-1 algorithm, using the *SHA-1Generator 1.2* software') then they begin to stray into the realms of system design, placing a straitjacket on potential solutions.

Although highly subjective, a requirement can be considered to be defined at the right level if it articulates the outcome that needs to be achieved with enough detail for a potential supplier to suggest a concrete solution, but doesn't actually specify how the solution might be provided. A good requirement defines the problem, but leaves the solution open. Thus, an integrity checking requirement might be expressed as follows:

- The solution must provide a facility to automatically monitor the integrity of digital objects and their metadata, including audit trails. The frequency of integrity checking should be user-configurable.
- The method of integrity checking must be modular, configurable, and capable of being changed without impact on the wider solution. The integrity monitoring solution must be scalable, in accordance with the rate of growth of the repository.
- The solution must detect and repair data integrity errors, and maintain an audit trail which records the date/time and method used for all integrity checks, any errors detected, and the date/time, method, and success or failure of any repair.

Types of requirement

Requirements for systems are usually subdivided into 'functional' and 'non-functional'. Functional requirements describe the desired functionality of a system – they define what it should do. These are usually accompanied by non-functional requirements, which define the overall characteristics of the system, and any constraints or standards that apply to its design. For example, a functional requirement might state that the system needs to provide a means to characterize the formats of all digital objects during ingest. A non-functional requirement might be that the system must support 100 concurrent end-users.

In some cases, organizations also define 'service' requirements, for services required to support the system, such as user training. In other cases these may be incorporated within the non-functional requirements.

In addition to the requirements themselves, it is helpful to provide background information to place them in their context. This might briefly describe the organization and its goals, and the background to the project, and set out the overarching approach and philosophy that the requirements reflect.

Developing a requirements catalogue

The ultimate expression of your requirements will be a requirements catalogue, a document that collates and describes the requirements in a consistent, detailed manner. Many approaches to documenting requirements are possible, ranging from the narrative to the highly structured. This is largely a matter of choice and organizational preference. The following information will always be required:

- a unique identifier for each requirement, for ease of reference
- a description of each requirement
- a statement of whether each requirement is mandatory, desirable, optional or for future development
- a statement about the source or derivation of the requirement; this is important for tracing a requirement back to the underlying processes and policies from which it arose (see above).

What is essential is to be precise in the phrasing of requirements, so they are unambiguous. In particular, the following points should be borne in mind:

- **Consistency**: Be consistent in the use of words such as 'must', 'may' and 'shall'. The convention[9] is that 'must' or 'shall' are used for mandatory requirements, and 'may' for optional ones, with 'must not' or 'shall not' used to define prohibited behaviour.
- **Precision**: Be as precise as possible in the language used. Try to avoid ambiguity, or vague statements, unless you expect to clarify them at a later stage.
- **Level**: Frame each requirement at the right level (see above).
- **Clarity**: Define all specialist terms and acronyms using a glossary. Be especially aware of those that can have well understood but very different meanings to different audiences. Classic examples include 'file' and 'archive', which are very differently understood by archivists and IT professionals.

Functional requirements

The functional requirements for any digital repository will be complex, and it is important to structure them in a way that aids understanding. Requirements are normally organized into thematic groups, relating to specific areas of repository functionality. One approach might be to use the OAIS functional areas:

- ingest
- data management
- archival storage
- preservation planning
- administration
- access.

As these may not be entirely self-explanatory, especially beyond the digital preservation practitioner community, some organizations have opted for a simpler approach. As an example, the Parliamentary Archives divided its functional requirements into the follow headings:

- ingest
- cataloguing and metadata
- bitstream preservation
- logical preservation
- access
- administration
- capacity.

Whatever structure is used, it should provide a logical place to fit every requirement – if you find you have lots of 'miscellaneous' requirements, this is probably a sign that the structure is not quite right.

Non-functional requirements

These cover requirements that are not directly related to the capabilities of the system. They tend to be similar for any IT system, and typically include areas such as:

- **Usability and accessibility**: This may include any web accessibility or user interface standards to be followed, and any requirements to meet disability legislation. It might also include specifying meaningful error reporting.
- **Desktop infrastructure**: This defines requirements relating to any desktop client provided by the system. Typically, this will need to be compatible with the organization's standard desktop operating system, or be browser-based.

- **Server infrastructure**: This describes any server architecture on which the system would operate. This may define requirements not only for the server environment, including standard operating systems, but also for any database components, and for storage and network infrastructure. It may include any constraints or requirements around the use of technologies such as virtualization, the Cloud, or grid computing.
- **Performance**: This defines how quickly the system must perform certain tasks, such as ingesting data, or providing access.
- **Resilience**: This sets the expected resilience of the system, including availability, and recovery times in the event of failures.
- **Operational**: This covers a range of features which may be required to support day-to-day operation and administration of the system. These might include supporting a test environment, back-up, storage management, and upgrade and patch management.
- **Application integration**: This defines generic features required to support integration with other systems, such as provision of an Application Programming Interface (API) or Software Development Kit (SDK).
- **Enterprise search**: This details any requirements to support enterprise search – a single means for users to search across multiple systems.
- **Sustainability**: This covers requirements to ensure that the system is itself sustainable. This is essential for future-proofing the repository, and might include specifying a modular architecture with clearly defined interfaces and the ability to export the complete content of the repository, including all metadata in open formats.
- **Compliance**: This defines any legal and regulatory requirements that the system must support, for example on the processing of personal information.

Non-functional requirements are typically much more detailed when procuring a fully fledged repository software platform; for more basic implementations they can be fairly simple.

Service requirements

These describe requirements for services to support the implementation and use of the system, rather than the system itself. They also tend to be generic, and typically include:

- **Consultancy**: This defines any specialist consultancy services which may be required. These might include creating new ingest workflows, integrating with other systems, or adding additional preservation tools such as format converters or characterization utilities.
- **Implementation**: This describes how the system will be implemented, including the project management approach in use. This may include defining key points of contact with suppliers, and arrangements for reporting progress and issues.
- **Ongoing support and maintenance**: This defines the required arrangements for supporting the solution, including technical support. A supplier's support systems will need to integrate with any in-house IT support. For example, first-line support may be provided by an in-house helpdesk, with more technical support calls being passed to the supplier. As many solutions may make use of third-party tools, it will be essential to clarify how these will be supported.
- **Change management**: This describes changes to culture and working practices within the organization which are required for the successful adoption of the system, and identifies any support for this expected from a supplier.
- **Training**: This defines any training needed, for example for IT staff, curators or end-users, including any that a supplier will be expected to provide. This should include start-up and ongoing training; it may be useful to specify a train-the-trainer approach, to reduce future costs and dependence on a supplier.
- **Documentation**: This defines the documentation required, such as user guides, maintenance guides, technical documentation and training materials. It should also cover rights to use and modify documents provided by suppliers, and how they will be updated.
- **Design and configuration**: This describes how the supplier will be expected to contribute to any system design, and to configure the system for operational use.
- **Testing**: This covers all types of testing required before a system is ready to go live, including system testing and user acceptance testing. This should include any documents that a supplier will be expected to provide, such as test scripts.

3.7 How to use your requirements

The requirements catalogue forms the basis for identifying, designing and implementing an appropriate solution. The range of options for this are discussed in detail in the next chapter; however, all will require either the procurement of products or services, in-house development, or some combination thereof. As the formal articulation of an organization's needs, the requirements catalogue provides an invaluable tool for communicating those needs to suppliers, developers, funders and others, and a benchmark against which the developing reality of a system can continually be tested. The next section shows how it can be applied in either scenario.

Procurement: developing an invitation to tender

If systems or services are to be procured, the requirements catalogue will form a key part of the formal documentation needed for this. Specifically, it will be the centrepiece of a 'call for bids' or 'invitation to tender' (ITT), detailing the requirements against which potential suppliers will be evaluated and selected. An ITT typically adds two things to a requirements catalogue: first, it includes information about the tender process, and detailed terms and conditions that will apply to the resultant contract; second, it includes evaluation criteria for every requirement, so that tenderer's responses can be assessed consistently. These essentially turn the requirement into a question: if there is a requirement for x, the accompanying evaluation criterion might be 'The tenderer should explain how it will achieve x'.

The actual procurement process is described in Chapter 4, 'Models for implementing a digital preservation service'. Once a supplier has been selected and awarded a contract to supply the solution, the implementation stage will begin with the development of a detailed design for the solution, followed by development, installation, integration and configuration, testing and, finally, deployment of the live system. The requirements catalogue should be referred to throughout the design stage, to ensure that the final system design actually meets all the requirements. It normally also forms the basis for 'user acceptance testing' – the process by which the customer satisfies themselves that the finished solution really does fulfil the requirements they originally specified. The implementation stage is discussed in more detail in Chapter 4.

Developing an in-house specification

The requirements catalogue is no less important if a solution is to be developed in-house. The only difference is that there will be no need to incorporate it into an ITT, or go through a procurement exercise. However, a similar evaluation process could still be used to consider alternative options. The requirements catalogue can then be used directly to guide the design, building and testing of the system.

3.8 Conclusion

Defining a set of requirements is a fundamental prerequisite for developing a digital preservation capability. Given its importance, it is essential to take the time necessary to ensure that the requirements catalogue is comprehensive, sufficiently detailed and – most crucially of all – accurately reflects the individual needs of the organization. Having such a statement of requirements will contribute immensely to the likelihood of developing a useful, practical and sustainable digital preservation capability.

3.9 Key points

- **Take time to develop your requirements catalogue**: Don't rush this step, or try to second guess requirements. Consult as widely as possible, and use process modelling to drill down into the detail.
- **Don't reinvent the wheel**: Your requirements catalogue should be based on your policies, rather than standing in isolation. In addition, you can draw on the wealth of readily available requirements documents which other organizations have developed.
- **Think about outcomes rather than solutions**: Requirements say what you need, not how to achieve it.
- **Use your requirements catalogue to its full advantage**: Having invested so much time and energy in its creation, you should seek to extract every last drop of value from it. Use it to choose the best solution, help build that solution, and verify that the results really do fulfil your needs.

3.10 Notes

1 For more information on UML see www.uml.org/.
2 Examples include the iRods system (see https://www.irods.org/) and the

SHAMAN project (see http://shaman-ip.eu/).

3 Innocenti et al. (2009).

4 National Library of Medicine Digital Repository Working Group (2007).

5 Electronic Records Archives Program Management Office (2010).

6 Wellcome Library (2008).

7 Wellcome Library (2010).

8 Repositories Support Project (2008).

9 Bradner (1997).

4

Models for implementing a digital preservation service

4.1 Introduction

Many different models are possible for operating a digital preservation service – there are options to suit every size and type of organization, from national bodies with substantial dedicated budgets and teams, to the smallest organization seeking to achieve something practical at minimal cost, and without specialist skills. This chapter analyses the range of possible options, including bespoke, in-house and outsourced solutions. It assesses the pros and cons of the alternatives, and considers which elements of a service may be most suited to certain approaches, and under what circumstances. It also considers the current and developing market for providing these solutions. Next, it looks at the process of implementing the chosen solution, and some of the practicalities of operating a digital repository, including the roles required, and availability of suitable training. It then examines the notion of 'trusted' digital repositories and proposes a 'maturity model' for digital preservation, which enables organizations to assess their capabilities and create a realistic roadmap for developing them to the required level. The alternative models are illustrated by a series of case studies.

4.2 Options

Digital preservation is a comparatively new discipline, and models for good practice, including the technologies and services required to support them, therefore exist at varying levels of maturity. Approaches to providing the fundamental elements of a digital repository are now well established, but some of the techniques and technologies required to deliver advanced preservation functions, especially for newer and more complex types of digital content, remain in their infancy.

This section analyses the available options in detail, assessing the respective strengths and weaknesses of each.

Do nothing

Any analysis of options should always include the *status quo* – not only does this provide a baseline against which other, more positive, options can be assessed, but it also allows a true comparison of the implications of not taking action. The costs of doing nothing include the continued burden of maintaining archival data on inappropriate storage infrastructure, and the costs of re-creating, or failing to preserve, digital resources that would be lost as a result of inaction, as described in Chapter 2, 'Making the case for digital preservation'.

This option assumes no development of digital preservation services, including zero investment and staffing. Table 4.1 sets out the pros and cons of the do nothing option.

Table 4.1 The do nothing option	
Pros	**Cons**
• no investment required • no organizational change required • keeps options open for future investment	• does not meet any of the business objectives for digital preservation, or the expectations of key stakeholders • loss of digital resources in the short to medium term, and therefore the failure to provide users with the information they need • loss of corporate records in digital form, with the associated reputational, governance and heritage damage that would result, including failure to comply with legislative, regulatory and information security requirements • additional cost of continuing to manage archival data on high-cost storage infrastructure • loss of investment in digitization projects which it may not be possible to replicate for financial or conservation reasons • additional costs incurred by undertaking digital archaeology to recover lost resources or in repeat digitization to replace them • additional costs incurred as individual IT systems reach obsolescence and valuable content needs to be preserved in a reactive, *ad hoc* fashion
Costs	
Although the cost of investment is obviously zero, the net costs are potentially very high, especially over the longer term – the costs and other impacts of repairing, re-creating or losing information are generally much higher than those of preserving it.	

The minimal repository

It is possible to build a functioning digital repository without any elaborate tools or systems, and indeed this will be the most realistic option for many smaller organizations. Such a repository will typically use simple, readily available tools and existing infrastructure:

- **Ingest**: This could be a manual, or semi-manual, process, using a variety of free tools (as described in Chapter 6, 'Selecting and acquiring digital content', and Appendix 3).
- **Metadata**: All or part of this might be stored in a simple spreadsheet or database. Alternatively, descriptive metadata could be stored in an existing catalogue system, with technical metadata stored as text files alongside the content.
- **Storage**: This might use existing network storage space, with some form of back-up, or removable media.
- **Preservation**: This will also typically be a manual, or only partially automated process, using free tools and services of the kinds described in Chapter 8, 'Preserving digital objects', and Appendix 3.
- **Access**: This will typically be provided on demand, via a terminal in the reading room, or remotely on removable media.

The 2012 Future Proofing project, carried out by the University of London with JISC funding, explores the possibilities of such a minimal approach in detail, using open-source tools to perform a variety of ingest, preservation, access and other repository management workflows;[1] an OCLC report of the same date[2] and a series of blog posts by Chris Prom[3] provide further recommendations for implementing a basic repository. The case study of the Centre for Archaeology at the end of this chapter provides an example of this approach in practice. Table 4.2 sets out the pros and cons of the minimal repository option.

Table 4.2 The minimal repository option

Pros	Cons
• low cost • begins to develop the infrastructure, skills and experience needed for digital preservation within the organization • flexible and customizable to local need • can be developed incrementally • allows action to be taken in the short to medium term, providing a flexible solution, which can be adapted over time to take advantage of maturing markets and service providers, and advances in digital preservation research • there is no reliance on a single company or service provider	• may be difficult to provide the full range of functionality • not scalable to large volumes – entails a comparatively high level of manual input • may require technical skills to set up • minimal or no support is available for many of the tools
Costs	
By using only free and existing software, and existing hardware, the costs of this approach should be minimal, with staff time and training likely to be the most significant elements.	

Developing a bespoke solution

Some organizations develop their own bespoke repositories, either using in-house development teams of programmers or by commissioning external software developers. The result will be a solution tailored to your precise requirements, but this is likely to be the highest-cost option – software development is expensive. In addition, developing a digital repository platform from scratch is a complex exercise, and is likely to require several generations of the technology to achieve a mature, stable product. This approach was quite common among large memory institutions in the early days of digital preservation, when third-party solutions were not as readily available; today, it is unlikely to be appropriate unless you have very unique requirements which cannot be met by current technologies. Even then, in most cases it is more economical to adapt existing tools than build something entirely new.

As an example, when the UK National Archives (TNA) began developing its digital repository in 2001, the only viable option to meet its requirements was to procure a bespoke solution, and it commissioned a commercial software developer accordingly. The resultant product was successful, winning the inaugural Digital Preservation Award in 2004 and the 2011 Queen's Award for Enterprise in Innovation, but required substantial investment. TNA subsequently licensed the technology back to the developer, to use as a basis for creating a commercial product – Safety Deposit Box (SDB) (discussed later in this chapter and in Appendix 3). Table 4.3 sets out the pros and cons of the bespoke option.

Table 4.3 The bespoke option	
Pros	Cons
• offers most flexible solution, tailored exactly to the organization's needs	• very expensive and time consuming to develop • very complex • very high risk – technology is unlikely to be stable or mature for several generations • less opportunity to collaborate or learn from others
Costs	
This is a very expensive option in terms of development and ongoing support costs.	

Using open-source software

Repositories can be developed entirely using existing open-source tools (as described later in this chapter and in Appendix 3). Such tools are typically free to use, but this does not mean that this approach is without cost: you are likely to require some development resource (either in-house or external) to adapt, configure and support the tools. Your organization will also bear the entire risk, rather than sharing it with suppliers. This approach is widely adopted in universities and the larger cultural memory institutions, which typically have access to in-house developers. The case studies of the LSE Library and Burritt Library at the end of this chapter provide good examples of using open-source software, albeit within hybrid solutions. Table 4.4 sets out the pros and cons of the open-source software option.

Table 4.4 The open-source software option	
Pros	Cons
• offers a very flexible solution, adapted to the organization's needs • hands-on experience develops organization's ability to act as an intelligent customer • there may benefits to be gained from becoming part of a user community for the chosen solution with the potential for shared service developments, training, support and recruitment in future	• potentially costly in terms of staff • can require a significant element of bespoke software development and enhancement • high risk, because of the immaturity of some technologies • minimal or no support is available for many of the products • substantial management overhead • organization may not have expertise in, or currently support, many of the technologies involved
Costs	
Highly variable, depending on the availability and cost of system development and support resources.	

Procuring a commercial solution

A common option is to procure a commercial off-the-shelf digital repository solution, with contracted-out support, and services. The small, but growing market for such products is discussed later in this chapter. This can be characterized as a high cost, low risk option, and much of its success depends on the development of a strong relationship with the supplier. An example of this approach is given in the case study of the Wellcome Library at the end of this chapter. Table 4.5 sets out the pros and cons of the commercial option.

Outsourcing the service

This approach involves contracting a third-party provider to supply a full digital preservation service to meet your requirements. This is potentially a low risk option, since it places all responsibility for implementation with

Table 4.5 The commercial option

Pros	Cons
• flexible and customizable • provides all functionality in a single, supported package • high level of support available • may provide access to an established user community, whereby you can benefit from others' experience	• typically high cost • commercial products may not meet all requirements 'out of the box', and may require configuration or customization • creates a dependency on an external supplier • may introduce proprietary aspects to the repository • may require a lengthy procurement process

Costs
Commercial products are likely to come with a comparatively high price tag. You typically need to pay a one-off licence fee and annual support costs. On top of this, you should expect the supplier to charge for customization and configuration of the product to suit your requirements – in some cases, this may account for the single largest cost element.

the service provider. At the same time, it may introduce risks associated with the lack of direct control over the repository. Customers are wholly dependent on the supplier for the service; for institutions where preservation is a core business, this may be undesirable. Services may also be provided under very short-term contracts, with equally brief notice periods on either side; if the supplier chooses to terminate the contract, or indeed to leave the market, their customers may have very little time to source an alternative provider. In a still very new market, there is a real danger that there may not even be any credible alternative suppliers, which could leave an institution in a very difficult situation.

At present, this is perhaps the least mature sector of the market, except in specialist areas, such as web archiving. However, more comprehensive Preservation-as-a-Service (PraaS) models are also beginning to emerge; some of the early players in this market are discussed later in this chapter, while the development of this trend is addressed in Chapter 10, 'Future trends'. Outsourcing is more commonplace for providing elements of the repository infrastructure. For example, many organizations host their servers in third-party data centres, or outsource their storage to a managed service, or the Cloud. The implications of the latter are considered in more detail in Chapter 8, 'Preserving digital objects'.

This option minimizes the direct impact on the organization, insulating it from the changes required for implementation, and the need to support particular technologies. It also has a very low barrier to entry, making it particularly attractive to smaller organizations; however, it does require the organization to have the capacity to oversee management of the contract, which may require new resources and expertise, for example within the ICT and information management functions.

A good example of a widely used outsourced service, albeit one which only addresses the capture and hosting of a single type of content, is Archive-It, a web archiving facility provided by the Internet Archive, and described in Chapter 5, 'Selecting and acquiring digital content'. This is used by a wide variety of small organizations from around the world to carry out web archiving, as exemplified by the case study on the Greater Manchester Archivists Group at the end of this chapter. Table 4.6 sets out the pros and cons of the outsourced option.

Table 4.6 The outsourced option

Pros	Cons
• outsourcing accesses specialist skills and experience which may not be available within the organization, and allows action to be taken pending the development of internal capability • defers or avoids the need for the organization to develop or manage infrastructure for digital preservation • for specific activities, such as web archiving, contractors can offer excellent value for money • outsourced services can be very quick to set up, and potentially very easily scaled up or down to meet changing demands • outsourcing to a service provider who is actively undertaking research in the field means that the organization could benefit from that innovation without incurring additional development costs • as future demand grows, further service providers may well appear	• service providers may not be available to fulfil all the organization's requirements • the market is immature, with a small number of potential service providers • it would be difficult for the organization to maintain an intelligent customer capability without practical experience • outsourcing may not be an option for sensitive content • the costs of contracting out may be higher in the medium term than implementing a service in-house • there is a danger of losing or failing to develop the skills base within the organization • a lack of adequate exit strategies may result in being locked into a contract for longer than is desirable • risk of overdependence on a single supplier until the market develops further • services are often offered on very short-term contracts, with limited notice periods • governance arrangements are likely to be more complex
Costs	
Outsourcing requires no up-front capital investment, operating either on an annual charge or a pay-per-use basis. Unless the unit costs of the service decline over time at a similar rate to alternative options, this can prove an expensive option over the long term, but it can also significantly lower the financial barrier to entry.	

Partnership approaches

Another option is the collaborative approach, whereby a number of organizations with a common set of requirements establish a partnership to develop and share services. These partnerships may be set up in various ways, with different degrees of formality:

- **Informal arrangements**: At the least formal end of the spectrum, there might be a simple understanding, without any written agreement, perhaps based on a long-standing existing arrangement. However, such an approach is unlikely to be suitable as a basis for the long-term preservation of digital material, since it offers no guarantees or safeguards for future preservation or access.
- **Formal agreements**: There are various kinds of formal written agreement which can be defined between two or more parties. These include memoranda of understanding (MoUs) and letters of agreement, which usually stop short of forming a legally binding contract, the consortium agreement, which is normally legally binding, and a formal contract. An example model for consortium agreements from the UK is provided by the Lambert Toolkit, intended for universities and companies that wish to undertake collaborative research projects with each other.[4]
- **Establishing a separate legal entity**: Perhaps the most complex form of partnership is to establish a new legal entity which represents the shared interests of the partners. This might take the form of a non-profit entity, such as a charity, trust, foundation or private company limited by guarantee. The precise forms of non-profit organization allowed vary from country to country, but most enjoy tax exempt status. An existing legal entity might also play host to a partnership entity which has an independent existence from its members, but is not itself legally constituted. An example of this approach is the MetaArchive Cooperative, discussed in detail in a case study at the end of this chapter.

Partnerships can also operate in different ways:

- The partners may jointly procure a service from a third party, using any of the other options discussed in this section.
- They may establish a distributed infrastructure. This might involve each partner hosting a copy of all, or part, of the system, using technologies

such as LOCKSS (see later in this chapter), or partners providing
different services, according to their skills and resources.
- One partner may operate the service on behalf of the others.

Table 4.7 sets out the pros and cons of the partnership option.

Table 4.7 The partnership option

Pros	Cons
• economies of scale • greater leverage with suppliers • pooling of resources • sharing of best practice and expertise • potentially sustainable beyond the life of individual partners • potential for distributed infrastructure, improving resilience	• misalignment of partners' objectives • withdrawal of partners • lowest common denominator applies • exit strategies may be more difficult • formal agreements may be complex to negotiate
Costs	
Because of the economies of scale, a partnership approach should result in lower costs per partner to achieve a given result than a single partner could achieve in isolation.	

Hybrid approaches

In many cases, a hybrid approach may actually be the most appropriate option.
In this scenario, various elements of the solution are developed in-house,
procured as commercial off-the-shelf products, or outsourced as appropriate.
This can provide the most flexible and cost-effective solution, but may be
complex to develop and operate, requiring careful planning and integration to
ensure that the components work together correctly. The case studies on the
LSE Library and Burritt Library at the end of the chapter exemplify this
approach. Table 4.8 sets out the pros and cons of the hybrid option.

Table 4.8 The hybrid option

Pros	Cons
• As for individual options above	• As for individual options above
Costs	
Highly variable, depending on the mix of elements used, but offers the opportunity to create the most cost-effective long-term solution.	

4.3 The current market

The market for digital preservation solutions is still comparatively new, but
also growing and evolving rapidly. There has been relatively little analysis of

the sector, although the Planets project published a white paper based on a survey of vendors in 2009.[5] The potential size of the market was estimated in 2011 as being worth in excess of $1 billion,[6] which supports the view that this growth will continue.

There are already a large number of solutions available, capable of fulfilling a wide range of requirements, and suited to a variety of scenarios. Many of these have released a number of stable, production-quality versions, and can be considered mature tools; some have been available for over a decade.

It is not the role of this book to recommend particular products, commercial or otherwise. Nonetheless, it is instructive to mention some of the solutions currently available, with the proviso that inclusion here does not constitute an endorsement. The range of available tools is described in much more detail in Appendix 3.

Commercial products

There is a small, but well established community of commercial suppliers, offering customized off-the-shelf solutions. In many cases, these represent commercial versions of systems originally developed for specific national libraries and archives. With a comparatively small amount of integration and customization, these can offer a generic digital preservation solution, which can then be extended through further development to provide whatever additional functionality the customer may wish. Increasingly, these solutions are being enhanced to comply with developing international standards, and to use emerging third-party services. It is also possible to contract the majority of support and administration to the supplier, minimizing the impact on in-house IT support, and other IT-enabled programmes. The main commercial products, including Rosetta from Ex Libris, and Tessella's SDB (Figure 4.1), are discussed in more detail in Appendix 3.

Open-source products

A number of open-source technologies have been developed, primarily within the higher education community. Although few of these individually provide a complete digital preservation solution, some institutions are using them as the building blocks to develop their own systems. Open-source tools can also be used to complement commercial solutions.

Figure 4.1 Safety Deposit Box (Tessella Ltd)

A number of complete open-source digital repository management systems are available, although these vary in the level of preservation functionality which they offer directly. The most widely used systems include DSpace, EPrints, Fedora and LOCKSS, but a number of new platforms, offering more advanced preservation functionality, are now emerging. A more detailed description of all of these is provided in Appendix 3.

In addition to these repository systems, a number of toolkits and individual utilities have been developed, either by individual organizations, or under the auspices of collaborative projects. These can potentially be used to add preservation functionality to existing repository systems. They include characterization tools such as DROID and JHOVE, ingest tools like the Curator's Workbench, forensic tools, including BitCurator, metadata tools such as Archivists' Toolkit, and migration tools like Xena. Again, a wide range of current tools are discussed in Appendix 3.

Service providers

A nascent community of providers is beginning to offer a range of digital preservation services on both a commercial and a free to use basis. These services vary considerably in scope and maturity, and this area of the market is subject to particularly rapid development (trends in this space are discussed in Chapter 10). Some services, such as the UK National Archives' PRONOM registry,[7] have become widely adopted as *de facto* standards, and are likely to form part of many solutions. Service providers may specialize in one particular service, or type of content, or may offer more comprehensive preservation services, which seek to provide all the functions of a digital repository. Others provide consultancy services tailored to the needs of individual clients. These permutations are discussed below.

Specialist services

Perhaps the largest range of suppliers can be found providing services relating to specific types of content, such as web archiving and audiovisual material. They also tend to specialize in certain types of activity, such as capture or format migration. For example, non-profit organizations such as the Internet Archive and Internet Memory Foundation, and commercial entities such as Hanzo Archives all offer services to capture, store and provide public access to web content (see Chapter 6, 'Selecting and acquiring digital objects'). Other services focus on particular repository functions, exemplified by technical registries such as PRONOM and the Library of Congress Digital Formats site.[8]

Comprehensive services

A growing number of suppliers are beginning to offer a full range of digital repository services. In some cases, suppliers have emerged to meet the needs of specific communities. For example, the UK Data Archive (UKDA)[9] and the ICPSR[10] provide data archive services to the international social sciences community. Furthermore, UKDA is part of a network of specialist data services established to support the archaeology, history, literature, performing arts and visual arts communities within UK higher and further education.[11] The international library community is served by services such as Portico, which preserves e-journals, e-books and digitized historical collections on behalf of publishers and libraries,[12] and the OCLC Digital Archive, which is primarily designed to preserve the outputs from library digitization projects.[13]

More generic services are also now appearing. For example, Chronopolis is a digital repository service provided under the management of the San Diego Supercomputer Center.[14] For a standard annual charge ($2,200 per terabyte in 2012), Chronopolis provides ingest, validation, replication to three sites within the USA, integrity monitoring, reporting and transmission of content back to the data provider when and if needed.

A number of cloud-based commercial services have also emerged. DuraCloud is provided by DuraSpace, the non-profit organization which also maintains the DSpace and Fedora Commons repository technologies (see above), and provides ingest, storage, integrity checking and online access, including image serving and media streaming for audiovisual content.[15] DuraCloud uses multiple cloud storage providers, acting as a broker on behalf of customers, and offers four service plans, with annual pricing (as of 2012) starting at $1,500 per terabyte. In 2012, the Preservica service was launched by Tessella. Preservica offers PraaS, built on the SDB platform and hosted in the Cloud on Amazon's S3 service.[16] It is offered on a pay-as-you-go model, although pricing details have not been made public at the time of writing. The Preservica literature suggests that customers will be able to specify which territory their data will be hosted in, which will mitigate some of the legal and governance issues raised by the Cloud. However, the use of a single, US-headquartered cloud provider may still be problematical for some potential customers. Preservica is unusual in providing SDB's logical preservation functionality, including preservation planning and format migration – most other service providers leave this to the customer, although they may offer some support at extra cost.

Consultancy services

A number of providers offer consultancy services to assist organizations with their preservation needs. Typically, these involve targeted projects, for example to audit existing holdings, elicit requirements, develop policies and procedures, or advise on standards. To benefit from consultancy – which can be a costly option – it is essential to have a very clear, focused brief and to choose both the project and the consultant with great care. However, at its best such consultancy can bring an impartial and expert perspective to issues.

Partnerships

There are some excellent examples of the partnership model in practice, many based on LOCKSS technology (see Appendix 3). To illustrate:

- Eight US universities, which form part of the Association of Southeastern Research Libraries, are collaborating to preserve each others' electronic theses and dissertations using a private LOCKSS network.[17]
- CLOCKSS (Controlled LOCKSS) is an international, not-for-profit community partnership between libraries and publishers, which uses a private network based on LOCKSS technology to provide a distributed archive for electronic scholarly content.[18] As of 2012, CLOCKSS has over 150 participating libraries, and provides 12 archive nodes, hosted by libraries in Asia, Australia, Europe and North America. Content is harvested from over 100 publishers and stored across the archive nodes; when a 'trigger event' occurs, such as the publisher going out of business, or ceasing to provide access to a title or its back issues, the CLOCKSS network makes that content freely available to everyone. CLOCKSS is funded through the annual subscriptions paid by participating libraries and publishers, but is seeking to raise an endowment, which would secure its long-term operation.
- The Alabama Digital Preservation Network (ADPNet) provides a low-cost distributed digital preservation service for cultural heritage organizations in Alabama. Founded in 2006, and using a private LOCKSS network, it is operated by seven higher education institutions.[19]
- Between 2004 and 2006, two UK local authorities (Bedfordshire and Hertfordshire) worked with the UKDA on a pilot project to investigate the issues involved in establishing a regional archive and records management service for digital records.[20] This aimed to identify possible solutions, and establish the basis for a business case for a digital preservation strategy in the east of England. It was followed in 2007–8 by a second phase of work, to survey the use of digital media by organizations regularly depositing records with the Bedfordshire and Luton Archives and Records Service (BLARS).[21] The studies provided a useful analysis of the challenges of collaborative approaches in the UK archival sector, but have not so far led to any operational partnerships.

Another partnership initiative, the MetaArchive, is considered in detail in a case study at the end of this chapter.

4.4 Approaches to procurement

If your preferred option entails purchasing a commercial product or service, it is likely that you will need to undertake some form of procurement exercise. Public sector organizations are likely to be more constrained in their procurement options than the private sector. For example, within the EU, public bodies are required to comply with a number of EU directives, most notably Directive 2004/18, which covers contracts for public works, public supply and public service.[22] In the USA, federal procurement is principally governed by the Federal Acquisition Regulation.[23] Other countries typically have equivalent legislation.

Private sector organizations are free to approach procurement in whatever manner they wish, within the bounds of the law, but most still have clearly defined procurement policies, which share many of the features of public sector procurement. It is beyond the scope of this book to describe in detail the procurement rules that may apply in particular circumstances or jurisdictions. However, it is possible to make some general observations about the kinds of approach that may be considered.

Your requirements catalogue (see Chapter 3, 'Understanding your requirements') should be your starting point. The procurement process is then essentially a case of asking potential suppliers to define how they would meet those requirements, and evaluating their responses. Depending on the rarity of the service or product being procured, it may be necessary either to take steps to ensure that as many potential suppliers as possible respond, or to limit the respondents to a manageable number. It is common practice to issue some form of prior notice, alerting suppliers to an upcoming procurement. Where the number or quality of suppliers may be an issue, an initial pre-selection stage may also be taken to restrict the number of bidders; since the evaluation of full tenders is the most complex and time-consuming part of the process, this can considerably reduce costs and simplify the overall process.

The main phase of procurement involves the issue of an ITT – a formal and detailed definition of the service or product required, the format and nature of responses required, the process by which tenders will be evaluated, and the terms and conditions under which a contract will be awarded. At the core of this is therefore the requirements catalogue. Bidders respond by submitting tenders, which are evaluated against the statement of requirements, including a financial evaluation of the cost of each proposal.

At the conclusion of the tender evaluation, a preferred supplier will be identified. It will also often be necessary to provide feedback to unsuccessful suppliers.

4.5 Implementation

Having selected an option and, if appropriate, undertaken any necessary procurement, the final step is to actually implement the chosen solution, which typically involves the following stages:

- **Detailed design**: As discussed in Chapter 3, 'Understanding your requirements', the requirements which formed the basis for choosing a solution should not themselves constitute the design for that solution. Consequently, once a solution has been chosen, it is usually necessary to undertake some degree of design to finalize the details of how it will work in practice. This is necessary even if using an off-the-shelf product, since this still needs to be configured to your particular circumstances, and may require a degree of customization. In many cases, design will be undertaken by your chosen supplier, or your IT support function. The design stage may not be required if the service is to be entirely outsourced, since the shape of that solution may either be predefined or have been satisfactorily specified in the supplier's response to any procurement exercise.
- **Development**: Almost every option requires some activity to put in place the relevant tools and structure. This may be as simple as installing some simple tools and setting up some folder structures, or as complex as undertaking software development and configuration.
- **Testing**: No system works exactly as planned from the outset, and thorough testing is a critical stage of implementation. Your requirements catalogue should once again be central to this process: you need to test whether or not each requirement identified has been successfully met by the solution. Such testing can be relatively informal, or fairly elaborate, involving written test scripts; however you approach it, you should at least document whether or not each requirement has been successfully tested, and how this was achieved. This testing against user requirements is often referred to as user acceptance testing (UAT). For IT systems, additional system testing may be required to ensure that any new hardware and software will operate correctly within your IT environment, and will not have an adverse impact on other systems.

- **'Go live'**: Once the solution has passed testing, it is ready to be put into operation. Precisely what this entails depends on the nature of the solution, and the organizational context: for many small organizations this may simply be a decision point, but if you have a supported IT infrastructure any change to it is likely to require some kind of formal process.
- **Review**: It is important to remember that going live is not the end of the story – you should also plan to review how well the operational system is performing at regular intervals thereafter. The purpose of such reviews is twofold: at a practical level it is a means to identify issues, suggest and make improvements, and learn lessons; strategically, it is an opportunity to demonstrate the practical benefits being achieved to stakeholders (as identified in Chapter 3, 'Understanding your requirements'). This is crucial to ensuring their continued support.

The benefit of managing the whole development of a digital preservation service, from initiation to implementation, as a project has already been discussed in Chapter 2, 'Making the case for digital preservation'. Such an approach is likely to prove its worth most especially during the implementation stage, since this is the point at which it will be most crucial to marshall staff and resources in order to achieve tasks to specific deadlines.

4.6 Operating a digital repository

You need to prepare for the practicalities of going live by putting in place the procedures and staff required to operate the digital preservation service. The detail of what is likely to be involved in this occupies most of the remainder of this book. One of the most critical considerations is to ensure that you have identified the staff and roles required, and that those staff have the necessary skills.

Staff roles

While the exact nature and number of staff roles required to operate a digital repository, and how you choose to provide them, will be very specific to your particular circumstances, there are a number of generic role types which you are likely to need:

- **Ingester**: Manages individual accession and ingest processes from start to finish, including any necessary liaison with depositors. This role is usually performed by librarians or archivists with suitable training.
- **Cataloguer**: Ensures that descriptive metadata is created and captured to appropriate standards, either during or post-ingest. This role is usually undertaken by existing cataloguing staff. In some cases, it may be combined with the ingester role.
- **Repository manager**: Manages the repository function, including ingest, preservation and access. This is usually the most specialized repository role, and may be filled by suitably trained curatorial staff, or a specialist digital archivist.
- **System support**: Supports users of the repository. This is normally referred to as first-line support – more complex issues may be referred to system administrators or suppliers. Where possible, this should be integrated with any existing IT helpdesk support but, in a small organization, it might be combined with the repository manager role.
- **System administrator**: Manages the IT systems and infrastructure on which the repository depends. Tasks may include second-line support, database administration, and managing storage and user accounts. This role is normally performed by IT staff.

Training

The widespread availability of high-quality, affordable training in digital preservation theory and practice, at a variety of levels, is essential to organizations of all sizes, but especially for smaller bodies with limited training budgets and a particular need to develop existing staff with new skills. While the provision of such training varies greatly from country to country, it is becoming ever more widely available.

Graduate and postgraduate training

Digital preservation is increasingly addressed to some extent in graduate and postgraduate information management training courses. Long considered a marginal element, there is now growing recognition that digital preservation awareness and techniques are a core element of the modern information management professional's skill set, and one which employers expect when recruiting new staff.

The majority of postgraduate library and archives courses now explicitly cover digital preservation and digital information management in some depth. Courses with a focus on digital collections management are also beginning to appear. For example, the Humanities Advanced Technology and Information Institute (HATII) at Glasgow University specifically addresses digital preservation as part of its undergraduate degree in digital media and information studies, as well as postgraduate courses in computer forensics and e-discovery, information management and forensics, information management and preservation, and museum studies,[24] while the University of Arizona's Graduate Certificate in Digital Information Management includes a specific course on digital preservation.[25] There are also increasing opportunities to research digital preservation at a doctoral level, such as King's College London's doctoral programme for digital humanities research.[26]

In-career training

Substantive training courses are also required for existing staff who need to develop new expertise. A number are available, typically lasting between two and four days, which provide a thorough introduction to the principles and practice of digital preservation, and are highly recommended for anyone seeking to develop their practical skills and knowledge.

These may include online teaching materials which are accessible to all, and very valuable for those unable to attend the face-to-face teaching. Notable training courses include:

- **Digital Preservation Management Workshops and Tutorial**: Currently hosted by MIT Libraries, but based on the seminal training programme developed by Cornell University and subsequently ICPSR, this offers a combination of three-day workshops, an online tutorial, and supplementary one or two-day topical workshops. While the workshops will primarily be of interest to US institutions, the award-winning online tutorial, which is available in English, French and Italian, is highly recommended for all.[27]
- **The Digital Preservation Training Programme (DPTP)**: The DPTP is one of the longest-running digital preservation training courses. Operated by the University of London Computer Centre, the two or three-day course is usually taught twice a year, at a variety of locations around the UK.

Centred on the OAIS model and modular in form, it uses a mixture of lectures, practical exercises and discussions to provide a thorough grounding in the basics. The Digital Preservation Coalition frequently offers a limited number of scholarships to support its members in attending the course.[28]

- **Digital Preservation in a Box**: An online training toolkit, developed by the US National Digital Stewardship Alliance's Outreach Working Group, this acts as a portal to a wide range of training resources.[29]
- **Data Intelligence 4 Librarians**: Designed primarily for librarians, this new course is operated by the 3TU.Datacentrum, a Dutch scientific data archive, in conjunction with a number of Dutch universities. The four-day course covers data management, technical skills, and acquisition and selection through a combination of online and face-to-face teaching.[30]

Short (one or two-day) introductory courses are also available for staff requiring a basic familiarity with the concepts, but not the in-depth knowledge provided by longer courses, or for those wishing to develop their knowledge in particular areas. These are often run by advocacy and training bodies such as such as the UK's Digital Preservation Coalition[31] and Digital Curation Centre,[32] the Dutch Nationale Coalitie Digitale Duurzaamheid[33] and the international Open Planets Foundation.[34] The Library of Congress maintains an online calendar of digital preservation training opportunities[35] as part of its Digital Preservation Outreach and Education programme. Within this initiative, it has also developed a baseline curriculum and is building a train-the-trainer network.

4.7 Trusted digital repositories

The concept of 'trust' has assumed a position of critical importance for many in the digital preservation community, and the notion of trusted digital repositories is widely used and, perhaps on occasion, abused. It is therefore useful to understand how this concept is being applied, and what its practical implications may be.

Digital repositories provide services in two directions – to those who deposit content with them for preservation, and to those who consume that preserved content. Both communities rely on the repository to fulfil certain obligations, which may be explicitly stated or implicitly understood, in order to provide those services; the effectiveness of a repository depends on the extent to which it is trusted by those communities to do so. A repository that is not trusted by potential depositors to manage their content responsibly and effectively will receive little material to preserve; one which users don't have confidence in to provide access to usable, reliable records will not be consulted.

The debate on trusted digital repositories is therefore about what organizations must do to develop and maintain that trust.[36] It is concerned with those attributes of a repository on which trust is built. A repository has no control over the extent to which it *is* trusted – all it can do is to take steps that are likely to engender that trust. It is, therefore, more meaningful to talk about trust*worthy* repositories.

The concept of trust is not unique to the digital world; cultural memory institutions have always relied on it. However, digital information brings it into especially sharp relief: the ease with which it can be published, copied, altered and destroyed has led many organizations to take a much more proactive and self-conscious attitude to trust than may previously have been the case.

In its seminal 1996 report, the Task Force on Archiving of Digital Information referred frequently to the importance of trust in the archival process, noting that 'a critical component of digital archiving infrastructure is the existence of a sufficient number of trusted organizations capable of storing, migrating, and providing access to digital collections.'[37] It went on to suggest that 'a formal process of certification, in which digital archives meet or exceed the standards and criteria of an independent certifying agency, would serve to establish an overall climate of value and trust about the prospects of preserving digital information.'[38] The Task Force recognized that there were two models for certification – one based on third-party inspection, the other on users' validation of a repository's stated adherence to standards – without advocating one over the other. It recommended that a dialogue be instituted between relevant organizations as to how such a certification process might be developed.

Perhaps understandably, over the next few years such a dialogue took second place to the need to develop a sound theoretical and practical basis for digital preservation. Such a basis was provided by the publication in 2002 of the OAIS Reference Model,[39] which also foresaw the need for follow-on standards, including those for certification of archives.[40] The next major step forward took place in the same year, when OCLC and the Research Libraries Group (RLG) published a report on the attributes and responsibilities of a 'trusted digital repository'.[41] Since then, a number of substantive initiatives have emerged, including:

- **TRAC**: The Trustworthy Repositories Audit & Certification Criteria and Checklist (TRAC) was published in 2007 by the Task Force on Digital Repository Certification, and has subsequently become an international *de facto* standard.[42]
- **nestor**: At the same time, the German nestor (Network of Expertise in long-term STORage) project[43] was developing its catalogue of criteria for trusted digital repositories.[44] Although co-ordinated with the TRAC standard, the work of nestor is focused on the particular requirements of libraries, archives and museums in Germany. It has now been published as a standard by the German National Bureau of Standards (DIN 31644).
- **DRAMBORA**: Also published in 2007, the Digital Repository Audit Method Based on Risk Assessment (DRAMBORA) toolkit provides a risk-based methodology for repository audit developed by the UK's Digital Curation Centre, and the EU-funded DigitalPreservationEurope project.[45] While drawing on, and intended to complement, the work of TRAC and nestor, DRAMBORA focuses on the practical application of audit methodologies, based on self-assessment. It was developed in part to address perceived difficulties in the practical application of the existing schemes, such as the lack of metrics for measuring and comparing an organization's compliance.
- **PLATTER**: The PLATTER toolkit was published in 2008 by the DigitalPreservationEurope project.[46] This provides a checklist and guidance to help repositories plan their objectives, including the achievement of 'trusted' status. It provides a means for repositories to classify themselves, in order to be able to compare their policies and practices with similar repositories; defines a series of 'strategic objective plans' within which a repository can codify its objectives; and proposes a planning cycle, whereby organizations can define, realize, review and refine their objectives.
- **Data Seal of Approval**: The 2010 Data Seal of Approval (DSA) is intended to provide a comparatively lightweight assessment process, aimed primarily at repositories of structured research data, and comprising 16 criteria. The repository assesses itself, and this is subject to external review by the DSA Board.[47]

Since 2007, work has been under way in various quarters to formalize these initiatives as *de jure* standards. ISO 16363, published in 2012, provides an audit and certification standard, primarily based on TRAC and broadly equivalent to DIN 31644, while ISO 16919, which is still under development, will define requirements for audit and certification bodies. Both have been developed under the auspices of the Consultative Committee on Space Data Systems (CCSDS).

In 2010, a MoU sponsored by the European Commission was signed between the three groups currently working on standards for trusted digital repositories – CCSDS, DIN and DSA – to develop a co-ordinated approach within Europe. This established a European Framework for Audit and Certification of Digital Repositories, with three levels of certification:

- **basic certification** for repositories which obtain DSA certification
- **extended certification** for repositories which obtain basic certification, and additionally perform an externally reviewed and publicly available self-audit based on ISO 16363 or DIN 31644
- **formal certification** for repositories which obtain basic certification, and additionally obtain full external audit and certification based on ISO 16363 or DIN 31644.

A series of test audits using the framework were undertaken in 2012 by the APARSEN project, leading to recommendations for refinements.[48] The framework should go a long way towards unifying the various strands of certification activity, at least within Europe, although practical approaches to external review and audit are still evolving. In the meantime, the DRAMBORA self-assessment method, drawing on the standards within this framework, is most likely to be helpful to smaller organizations considering a suitable implementation model.

The relationships between the main certification schemes are illustrated in Figure 4.2.

The various trusted digital repository schemes can serve a number of practical purposes, including:

- articulating the benefits of digital preservation in a business case (see Chapter 2)
- informing the development of your requirements (as discussed in the previous chapter)

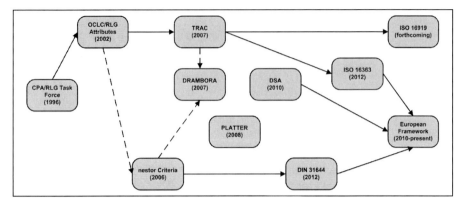

Figure 4.2 The relationships between the main certification schemes for digital repositories

- measuring the success of your repository, once operational, and demonstrating this to your stakeholders.

4.8 A digital preservation maturity model

Maturity models provide a means for organizations to assess their capabilities in a particular area against a benchmark standard. A good example of this is the UK Office of Government Commerce's Prince2 Maturity Model (P2MM),[49] a framework for assessing an organization's project management capabilities. This defines a five-step scale of 'maturity levels', corresponding to the sophistication of an organization's processes, and seven 'process perspectives', which define the areas of business function being assessed, such as financial management or organizational governance.

This chapter proposes a maturity model for assessing an organization's digital preservation capabilities, which draws on the P2MM methodology, together with the various emerging standards for trusted digital repository certification.[50] It then discusses how you can use such a model to review and plan your organization's approach to building its own capability.

Maturity levels for digital preservation

The development of any new capability within an organization usually follows a similar path (illustrated in Figure 4.3): it begins with a developing awareness of the need for that capability and the steps required to acquire it, and ends with the realization of that capability, which may potentially be at

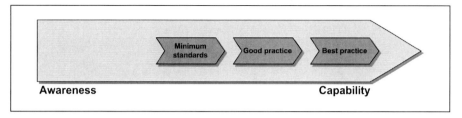

Figure 4.3 Developing capability

varying levels of sophistication, ranging from the achievement of minimum standards to best practice.

With any process, it is possible to envisage a baseline, minimal version, a fully developed version, and an optimal version, in which the process includes proactive steps to monitor its performance and identify required improvements.

This path can be broken down into a series of discrete maturity levels, as shown in Table 4.9.

Table 4.9 Maturity levels		
Stage	**Maturity level**	**Description**
Awareness	0 No awareness	The organization has no awareness of either the need for the process or basic principles for applying it.
	1 Awareness	The organization is aware of the need to develop the process, and has an understanding of basic principles.
	2 Roadmap	The organization has a defined roadmap for developing the process.
Capability	3 Basic process	The organization has implemented a basic process.
	4 Managed process	The organization has implemented a comprehensive, managed process, which reacts to changing circumstances.
	5 Optimized process	The organization undertakes continuous process improvement, with proactive management.

For any given process, in any given organization, we can measure which maturity level applies. We can also use this scale to define the level to which the organization should aspire. It is not a given that everyone should strive for Level 5 in every process – this might well be excessive in certain situations.

Digital preservation process perspectives

Having defined our generic maturity levels, we can now identify the set of processes that constitute a digital preservation capability. There are many ways in which we might choose to do this. A good starting point is provided by the various standards, discussed in the previous section, which are emerging to define best practice for digital preservation, by identifying the attributes that make a 'trusted digital repository'. Although each standard may arrange and define these attributes in slightly different ways, they can all be mapped to a common set of requirements.

Table 4.10 distils these core requirements into a set of ten process perspectives.

Table 4.10 Process perspectives	
Process perspective	**Definition**
A Organizational viability	Governance, organizational structure and resourcing of the repository, including financial and staff management
B Stakeholder engagement	Processes to engage with stakeholders within and external to the repository, including content depositors and users
C Legal basis	Management of contractual, licensing, and other legal rights and responsibilities
D Policy framework	Policies, strategies, and procedures which govern the operation and management of the repository
E Acquisition and ingest	Processes to acquire and ingest content into a repository
F Bitstream preservation	Processes to ensure preservation at the bitstream level of all stored content over time
G Logical preservation	Processes to ensure the continued accessibility of the logical content over time
H Metadata management	Processes to create and maintain all metadata required to support management and use of the repository
I Dissemination	Processes to enable discovery and dissemination of stored content within the designated user community
J Infrastructure	Physical and technical infrastructure, including security, required to support the repository

Together, these process perspectives define the set of resources, policies, processes and systems that are required to provide a digital preservation capability. A more detailed definition can be defined for each maturity level of every process perspective: to illustrate the principle, we can consider what might constitute a 'basic' level of maturity (e.g. Level 3) for each of these processes (Table 4.11).

Table 4.11 A basic preservation capability

Process	Level 3 definition
A Organizational viability	• Staff have assigned responsibilities, and the time to undertake them • A suitable budget has been allocated • Staff development requirements have been identified and funded
B Stakeholder engagement	• Key stakeholders have been identified • Objectives and methods of communication have been identified
C Legal basis	• Key legal rights and responsibilities, together with their owners, have been identified
D Policy framework	• A written, approved digital preservation policy exists
E Acquisition and ingest	• An acquisition policy exists which defines the types of digital content which may be acquired • A documented accession and ingest procedure exists, including basic guidance for depositors • Some individual tools are used to support accession and ingest
F Bitstream preservation	• Dedicated storage space on a network drive, workstation, or removable media • At least three copies maintained of each object, with back-up to removable media • Basic integrity checking performed • Virus checking performed • Existing access controls and security processes applied
G Logical preservation	• Basic characterization capability exists, allowing at least format identification • *Ad hoc* preservation planning takes place • *Ad hoc* preservation actions can be performed if required • Ability to manage multiple manifestations of digital objects
H Metadata management	• Documented minimum metadata requirement exists • Consistent approach to organization of data and metadata implemented • Metadata stored in a variety of forms using spreadsheets, text files or simple databases • Capability exists to maintain persistent links between data and metadata • Persistent unique identifiers are assigned and maintained for all digital objects
I Dissemination	• Basic finding aids exist for all digital content • Users can view or download data and metadata, either online or on-site
J Infrastructure	• Sufficient storage capacity is available, and plans exist to meet future storage needs • IT systems are documented, supported and fit for purpose

This might be considered the minimum standard for any organization to provide a genuine digital preservation service. For many, this may be an entirely appropriate target, sufficient to meet their objectives. Others may wish to achieve greater levels of capability in particular areas. Example definitions for all three capability levels (Levels 3–5) within each process perspective are provided in Appendix 2.

An organization can then be assessed according to which maturity level it has achieved for each process perspective. An example of such an assessment is illustrated in Figure 4.4.

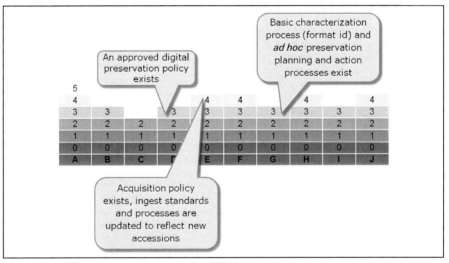

Figure 4.4 Measuring maturity levels for different process perspectives

Organizations may find it helpful to assess themselves against such a maturity model at various points, to understand their current level of maturity, define their aspirations, and review their progress towards achieving those goals. As previously mentioned, it should not be assumed that these aspirations should always be to the highest possible level; in practice, most organizations wish to define different target levels for different process perspectives, and in many cases a relatively modest level may be entirely appropriate. The value of such maturity models lies primarily in providing a framework for thinking about digital preservation as a broad spectrum of acceptable capabilities, rather than a single, and almost certainly unobtainable, ideal of curatorial perfection. By doing so, it should help organizations to think about what 'good enough' preservation looks like, in their own particular circumstances.

The value of maturity models for digital preservation is increasingly being recognized, with a number of other approaches now being mooted. For example, Becker et al. (2011) take an approach rooted in the methodologies of IT enterprise architecture, while Tessella plc (2012) proposes a model focused on assessing the maturity of repository software systems. Meanwhile, the National Digital Stewardship Alliance is developing the concept of levels of digital preservation.[51]

4.9 Case studies

The following case studies illustrate the practical application of each of the models for implementing a digital repository discussed in this chapter.

Case study 1 The minimal approach applied to English Heritage's digital archaeological archives

The in-house archaeological team at English Heritage, which advises the UK Government on England's historic environment, has been generating digital archives since the 1970s, and had evolved a range of procedures for managing them.[52] In the late 1990s, the then Centre for Archaeology (CfA) began to devise a comprehensive digital archiving strategy,[53] and an accompanying programme to put this strategy into practice.[54] Having no dedicated resources, this programme had to be developed and operated with a minimal budget and only a proportion of the time of one staff member (the author). As such, the minimal approach was the only available option.

The Digital Archiving Programme (DAP) had the advantage of an internally generated archive, with a very consistent structure and range of formats. Detailed procedures were developed for appraising new content and preparing it for accession. The digital repository itself centred on a metadata database called CAMS (the CfA Metadata System), developed by the author using Microsoft Access 97. This included custom modules written in Visual Basic to automate key parts of the ingest process. Its underlying information model also incorporated the concept of a digital object possessing multiple technical manifestations, as discussed in detail in Chapter 8, 'Preserving digital objects'. This was prompted by the decision to normalize on ingest to a restricted set of archival file formats, to simplify future preservation management, while also always retaining a manifestation in its original format. The longevity of the CfA digital archives meant that they included a number of obsolete formats, such as word processed documents created using WordStar software. The DAP therefore undertook extensive format migration, using freeware conversion tools.

The first stage of accession was to create a full metadata record for the new content in CAMS (Figure 4.5). Descriptive metadata for the collection and its constituent objects were first entered manually, together with technical information about the extant manifestations of each object, and the migration pathways used to create them. File level metadata was then generated automatically by CAMS. The user selected the folder containing the data to be ingested, and CAMS would automatically capture basic technical information (file name, file size, file date and path name) and generate an MD5 checksum for every file. It also used custom code to automatically identify the format of each file using internal signatures, and extract key technical metadata, such as the pixel dimensions of images – this module relied on a rudimentary internal format registry, and was thus a precursor for PRONOM and DROID. A manual step was then required to associate each file with its parent manifestation.

As the final stage of ingest, three copies of the data were written to

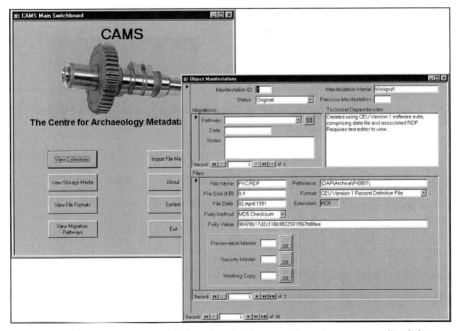

Figure 4.5 The CAMS main switchboard and object manifestations screens (English Heritage)

removable media – a preservation master on digital linear tape, with a security copy and working copy on CD-R – and stored in geographically separate locations. These media choices reflected the available options in 2000, and were designed to avoid using a single media type. At the time, the comparatively high cost and low capacity of network storage also dictated the use of removable media.[55]

The CfA digital archive made only limited provision for public access at the time – this element of its function was being developed in conjunction with the National Monuments Record and the Archaeology Data Service, the bodies with primary responsibility for access to archaeological archives in England – although archival content and metadata could be made available for dissemination on demand. Beyond this, the core functions of a digital repository, including accession and ingest, and preservation management, were all achieved operationally, using off-the-shelf technology (albeit with a small degree of custom development) and minimal resources.

Case study 2 The commercial off-the-shelf approach at the Wellcome Library

The Wellcome Library is part of the Wellcome Trust, an independent charity that funds biomedical research and works to support the public understanding of science. The Library's stated aims are to provide 'insight and information to anyone seeking to understand medicine and its role in society, past and present'.[56] It comprises one of the largest resources for the study of medical history in the world, with more than 38,000 visits each year from users ranging from academics, students, health professionals, consumers, journalists, artists and members of the general public. As well as printed collections the Library holds extensive series of archive and manuscript material, and iconographic, moving image and sound collections. The Wellcome Library has been awarded 'designated' status by the Museums, Libraries and Archives Council, in recognition that its collections are a vital part of the UK's national cultural and artistic heritage.

In 2009 the Library began a five-year programme of transformation, to create a digital library that will enable online open access to its collections, and develop it as a major cultural destination as well as an internationally significant academic research library. It plans to do so through targeted acquisition of new content, strategic digitization of its analogue holdings, and by providing expert interpretation of its holdings. Its digitization plans are ambitious – it intends to digitize over 30 million images in five years. The finished library will comprise a digital repository to manage and preserve its digital assets, systems to support the creation and ingest of diverse types of digitized and born-digital content, and an online public access interface to the collection.[57]

A number of the components required to build the Wellcome's digital library were already in place before the formal programme started, including its catalogues and online search systems. Work to develop a digital repository was also already well advanced. For this repository, the Library opted for a commercial, off-the-shelf solution, and after a procurement exercise selected Tessella's SDB. The initial implementation of the system was launched in 2009. However, as more ambitious plans for the development of the digital library coalesced, it became clear that the then-current version of SDB did not meet all the anticipated requirements for the management of digitized content. After a feasibility study[58] conducted in 2010 concluded that SDB could be extended to meet those requirements, Wellcome commissioned Tessella to deliver a new version, SDB 4, in 2011. The enhanced repository went 'live' in 2012. SDB provides a number of vital pieces of functionality for the production and management of digital content including:

- automated workflows to ingest new content into SDB
- a database to store administrative and descriptive metadata describing the objects stored in SDB
- workflows to characterize digital objects, using tools such as JHOVE, DROID and PRONOM (see Chapter 6, 'Accessioning and ingesting digital objects')
- the ability to share data with other systems, such as the workflow tracking system Goobi
- workflows to undertake preservation planning and format migration, building on the Planets framework
- continuous integrity checking of all stored content
- a programmatic interface to provide access to content, which will be used by the digital delivery system
- a means to automatically export administrative metadata, such as unique SDB identifiers, which is then used by other systems to deliver files to users
- administrative tools to enable library staff to manage the repository.

SDB provides the software to manage the repository, but another key component that had to be developed was its storage system. For this, the Library uses the Wellcome Trust's existing corporate storage infrastructure, a storage area network (SAN) using fast hard disks, which are mirrored between sites to improve data security. Each file ingested into the repository is stored on the main server and mirrored to a second server, as well as being subject to a regular back-up routine. SDB periodically checks the integrity of every file on the main server – in the event of a failure being detected, the damaged file can be repaired from the mirror copy.

One reason for using hard disk as the primary storage medium for the repository is that, in order to reduce the volumes of digitized data being stored, the Library uses a single manifestation of each digital object, in JPEG2000 format, to serve as both the preservation master and access copy. The presentation system requests JPEG2000 format content from SDB and converts it on the fly to JPEG images for presentation. This makes it imperative for the repository to be able to retrieve data as quickly as possible, rather than opting for a potentially cheaper, but also much slower, technology such as tape. For additional speed of delivery a dynamic cache is used that holds and delivers most requested content without the need to query SDB.

Being based on enterprise-grade, commodity hardware the Library's storage technology is also easily scalable, an important consideration when contemplating mass digitization programmes. The choice of storage technology was based on the recommendation of the Trust's in-house IT department, working closely with the Digital Services staff to understand their requirements. Similarly, procurement of the repository software involved a very inclusive project team, representing all interested parties and with a wide range of specialisms. Such a collaborative approach, which secured buy-in from IT and other departments from the outset, is essential to the success of a project of this nature.

Case Study 3 The outsourced approach at Greater Manchester Archivists Group

In 2007, a small group of archivists from archive services within the Greater Manchester area in the UK began investigating digital preservation, and especially solutions for archiving websites of local interest. After consultation with district archive services, it was determined that a number of categories of website should be considered for archiving, including local government websites, community websites, the diocesan website, and sites or pages relating to specific events or topics of local interest.

The group defined its requirements for web archiving, considering issues such as scope, quality control, storage, end-user access and usability. After assessing the available options, the group decided to instigate a pilot project using the Internet Archive's Archive-It service (described in Chapter 5, 'Selecting and acquiring digital objects'). The pilot was undertaken in March 2008, archiving 15 local government and diocesan websites. By virtue of being incorporated within the Internet Archive, each was also made publicly available.

The group found Archive-It to be a user-friendly, flexible, all-in-one solution with good support provided by the Internet Archive and the wider community of users. The cost of a basic subscription would also be affordable if shared between the participating organizations but, without a formal partnership agreement, it proved difficult to establish a sustainable funding model.

Since completing the pilot, the group has instead chosen to work with the British Library's UK Web Archive, which collects sites from across the UK web domain.[59] While the group does not control the archiving process, instead focusing on suggesting sites for archiving and gaining the necessary permissions from the owners, it has found this to be an effective approach: at least 15 sites have been selected for archiving in this way, and the group has also been using social media to encourage community groups to nominate their own sites for archiving. Unlike Archive-It, the UK Web Archive also has the advantage of providing long-term preservation for the content.

In 2011, the Greater Manchester Archivists Group participated in a pilot project led by the UK National Archives (TNA) to explore a web archiving model which could be used to preserve local online resources. As part of this, three websites were archived and made available through the TNA web archive.[60] In 2012, the Greater Manchester Archives and Local Studies Partnership was established, which will provide a framework for collaboration and strategic development between archives and local studies services in Greater Manchester. Underpinned by a formal MoU, this should make it much easier to develop collaborative projects in future.[61]

This case study illustrates the effectiveness of collaborative approaches, and the cost-effectiveness and flexibility possible from using third-party services. It also shows the importance of developing a strong framework for partnership, with the necessary senior management buy-in, and of being adaptable to changing circumstances and opportunities.[62]

Case Study 4 The hybrid approach at the Burritt Library

The Burritt Library at Central Connecticut State University (CCSU) began investigating digital preservation solutions out of necessity in 2009, as a result of embarking on a new digitization programme, which was accumulating large numbers of uncompressed image files.[63] The library wished to implement a solution that complied with OAIS and PREMIS (see Chapter 7, 'Describing digital objects'), and began by surveying a range of available options. The first to be investigated was a commercial service, OCLC's Digital Archive, but this was discounted on grounds of cost, and concerns as to whether it would be suitable for objects not contained within the Library's digital collections management system. Next, the Library considered LOCKSS but, although this was perceived to require much lower direct costs, the Library was unable to find partners for its preferred option of a private LOCKSS network, and did not wish to implement such a solution alone, without the benefit of vendor support.

At this point, the Library decided to investigate an in-house approach, beginning with storage, and was inspired to look at the Cloud as an option. An initial comparison of costs between OCLC and Amazon's S3 cloud storage service suggested that the latter would be less than one-third of the cost of the former.

A custom database was designed to manage archival content, using the open-source MySQL database software. To generate PREMIS metadata, the Library chose Statistics New Zealand's prototype PREMIS Creation Tool, which uses JHOVE, DROID and the National Library of New Zealand's Metadata Extractor. However, in order to increase automation, they are considering moving to the File Information Tool Set (FITS), which integrates DROID, JHOVE and the NLNZ Metadata Extractor with a number of other characterization tools.

The Library of Congress' BagIt tool (see Chapter 7, 'Describing digital objects') is used to package objects and metadata into a standard Submission Information Package (SIP) for ingest. A set of simple scripts was then written to run the metadata extractors automatically, package everything into SIPs (see Chapter 6, 'Accessioning and ingesting digital objects') and run antivirus checks. Standard back-up software is then used to periodically transfer the SIPs to the S3 storage.

The Library reports that the system is operating satisfactorily, although it is seeking greater levels of automation. Staff are also investigating Archivematica as a more fully featured solution (see Appendix 3). The current system lacks any form of preservation planning or action facilities, or end-user access. Nonetheless, it shows that an institution can accomplish much with minimal resources – CCSU's system is based on open-source software, and expertise available in any small IT department, coupled with one commercial service. By doing so, the staff have been able to collect content and gain valuable experience in the operation of a digital repository.[64]

Case study 5 The hybrid approach at the LSE Library

The London School of Economics and Political Science (LSE) is one of the foremost universities for the social sciences in the world. The LSE Library (the British Library of Political and Economic Science) was founded in 1896, as a library for the university as well as a resource for researchers in the social sciences, and is one of five designated national research libraries in the UK.[65] Containing over 4 million books and journals, it collects comprehensively in economics and the other core social sciences, while its special collections include government publications, the publications of inter-government organizations, historical pamphlets and statistics. It also includes the archives of the Fabian Society, the Liberal Party, and the personal papers of individual politicians.

The LSE Library has a growing digital collection, which it categorizes into three types:

- outputs from digitization projects
- born-digital archives
- research outputs.

The composition of these is constantly evolving; for example, within the born-digital category the Library is scoping the acquisition of official publications in electronic format, as well as investigating web archiving. The research outputs are managed in three institutional repositories, running on an EPrints platform:

- LSE Research Online is an open access repository of LSE staff research, including journal articles, book chapters and working papers.
- LSE Theses Online contains completed PhD theses of LSE postgraduate students.
- LSE Learning Resources Online holds electronic teaching materials.

In 2009, the Library launched its Digital Library Management and Infrastructure Development Programme, a major initiative to build the Library's capacity to collect, manage, preserve and provide access to its digital collections. In contrast to the Wellcome Library, the LSE Library chose to build their digital library using predominantly open-source components, but integrated with existing systems, including commercial products. Thus their approach is representative of the hybrid strategy.

The relationship between the established repositories and the new digital library is expected to evolve over time. In the first instance, the Library is exploring how to provide in-place preservation services to them, while retaining existing interfaces and workflows; in the long term, a greater degree of convergence is anticipated.

A notable aspect of the Library's approach has been that although a core team was established to undertake the research and development for the system, its operation is being embedded within existing teams across the Library. Thus, for example, the IT team will support the systems and infrastructure; librarians and archivists will undertake collections management; and, perhaps uniquely, the existing collection care team will assume responsibility for ingest and digital preservation alongside the analogue collections.

The Library began by undertaking an audit of its digital collections, including a risk assessment using the DRAMBORA tool. The Library chose a representative cross-section of risks, ranging from high-level organizational threats, to low-level technical risks. The intent was to capture a snapshot of the overall state of the collections, and identify priority areas for action, rather than comprehensively analyse each risk in every area. The audit process identified ten key risks, which were documented in the form of a risk register.

The Library also undertook an initial analysis of their user requirements, in parallel with an investigation of current best practice within the wider digital preservation community. Based on this work, staff began to draft a detailed set of functional requirements, as well as a draft metadata specification. At the same time, they began development of a set of digital collection policies, including deposit agreements and content licensing policies, which would contribute additional requirements into the latter stages of the programme. Rather than create a standalone digital preservation policy, the Library is planning to update its existing collection preservation policy to cover digital material. This exemplifies its approach to embedding digital preservation operations across the Library, rather than regarding it as a separate, silo activity. It also illustrates how, at least in part, staff are developing and refining policies to reflect the lessons of practical experience. While this book generally advocates working from policy to practice, rather than vice versa, this is an important reminder that policy must always be rooted in, and refined in the light of, practice.

From these activities there emerged an overarching technical strategy, based on the incremental development of a modular digital library architecture. Shared components would be built to provide basic functionality required across the system, such as storage, integrity checking, and managing unique identifiers, while more specific tools would be employed to suit the specialized needs of different types of material in other areas, such as ingest and user access. Such a modular approach would also make it easier to integrate existing systems, such as catalogues. The Library did not wish to undertake new research and development itself, but to make use of current best-of-breed technologies developed by others. Nonetheless, it acknowledged that significant technical resource would still be required to customize, integrate and configure these varied components.

The Library's functional requirements comprised 24 criteria grouped into seven functional areas approximating to the OAIS model, as follows:

- data model
- ingest
- data management
- administration
- metadata
- storage
- access.

Staff undertook a detailed comparison of the three major open-source digital repository platforms available at the time (DSpace, EPrints and Fedora) against these requirements. The latest version of each system was installed on an identically specified virtual machine, tested, and scored on a 'red–amber–green' scale against each functional criterion.

The LSE Library team drew some interesting conclusions from their study. They noted a significant difference in approach between Fedora and the other two systems, concluding that Fedora was inherently more flexible, albeit at the cost of greater work to set up a usable repository. They felt that DSpace and EPrints were focused on the management of open access publications, and would not be suited to preserving born-digital or digitized content without significant modification. On this basis, the project team recommended Fedora as the technology of choice for their digital repository.[66]

The team combined the results of the requirements analysis and comparison with the DRAMBORA risk assessment into a report and set of recommendations for senior management in the Library. This report identified the key risks faced by the collections, and proposed solutions which specifically addressed those risks.

Following approval of these recommendations, the Library moved on to develop an architectural design, based on the functional requirements, and applying three core design principles:

- **Flexibility**: It must be able to cater for a wide range of digital collections.
- **Extensibility**: It must be able to adapt to changing collection types and user needs.
- **Modularity**: It must be possible to replace one component without disrupting others.

The architecture breaks down into four main components:

- **repository core**: digital object storage, identification
- **curation**: ingest and management
- **preservation**: bitstream and logical preservation
- **access**: search and presentation.

The Library planned a phased approach to developing this architecture. Initially, this was envisaged as beginning with preservation, then curation, and finally access, but the development of the access systems was soon reprioritized, as it became apparent that this was instrumental in securing buy-in from external depositors and library staff: it was found that the process of building the access system was an incredibly powerful way of demonstrating the significance to internal audiences, being concerned with concrete collections and users rather than abstract notions of preservation, while having the completed system to show potential depositors really helped them to envisage the value to them.[67]

For each component, the Library has identified and implemented an appropriate technology:

- **Repository core**: As previously discussed, this uses the Fedora Commons platform. In fact, the Library has adopted the Hydra framework (see Appendix 3), which builds on Fedora to create a fully featured digital repository solution, and illustrates their community-based approach to finding and reusing shared solutions to specific problems.
- **Curation**: It was initially envisaged that ingest workflows would be controlled using Archivematica, or LSE-specific digitization workflows. However, the relative immaturity of the former meant that a considerable degree of custom development would have been required, with the risk that this could rapidly be superseded by later software releases. Instead, the Library preferred to invest its development effort into integrating the underlying open-source tools used by Archivematica directly with Hydra. The Library's existing collections management systems – Voyager for library collections, and CALM for archival holdings – continue to perform this function for digital material.
- **Preservation**: Bitstream preservation is based on the Library's standard storage platform (described below), with additional services, such as integrity checking, provided through Hydra. Logical preservation functions will be provided through the Library's overall digital preservation function, and will follow the philosophy of adopting existing best-of-breed tools and services. Those being considered include the Planets framework and the PLATO preservation planning tool (see Chapter 8, 'Preserving digital objects').
- **Access**: The Library offers online access through a custom-built web application (digital.library.lse.ac.uk), which also supports on-site reading room access. An API is also envisaged, which would enable third-party services to access the digital library. Searching of the repository is provided via the Apache Solr search engine, while the Handles service is used to control persistent identifiers (see Chapter 9, 'Providing access to users').

The Library is developing a flexible preservation strategy, based on normalization at ingest to a defined set of preservation formats but, where authenticity or provenance is a key requirement, also retaining the original. This has the benefits of constraining future preservation issues to a minimum set of formats, while leaving future options open: it is expected that a range of longer-term strategies, including emulation, may be used to meet the requirements of specific collections or types of content.

For storage, the Library is using its standard enterprise storage infrastructure, which uses a SAN, but tailored to the specific requirements of digital preservation. The primary copy of every object is stored on the local SAN. Two additional copies are then replicated from this, one to a second off-site SAN, the other to local hard disk. Finally, a tape back-up is taken from the local disk copy. Thus, four copies exist, in two geographical locations, using three different storage technologies. The Library is also investigating taking the tape back-up off-site at intervals, providing a third location.

The development of the web front end for the digital library is described in more detail in Chapter 9, 'Providing access to users'.

The digital library was formally launched in January 2012, as part of celebrations for the 115th anniversary of the LSE Library,[68] and included a core repository to support access and ingest workflows for digitized material. Effort was then switched back to developing the preservation capabilities, with a proof-of-concept preservation workflow and infrastructure being completed in 2012.[69]

Case study 6 The collaborative model as developed by the MetaArchive Cooperative

In 2002, six US libraries joined forces to develop MetaArchive,[70] a community-based digital repository solution for preserving their special collections. Funded through the Library of Congress' NDIIPP programme, the MetaArchive has grown to over 20 members, providing a secure preservation facility for more than 50 libraries, archives and other cultural memory institutions in four countries.

Perhaps the key feature of the community-led model embodied by the MetaArchive is that, rather than outsourcing the repository to a third party, each member actively participates in the preservation process.

Three tiers of membership are available, each running for three years:

- **Sustaining**: The first tier, and commanding the highest membership fee, sustaining members actively develop and maintain the MetaArchive systems, set standards, and sit on the Steering Committee.
- **Preservation**: Members in this tier are primarily beneficiaries of the MetaArchive, rather than leading its development. They have a non-voting representative at annual Steering Committee meetings.
- **Collaborative**: This category allows existing consortia to join, being

treated as a single member, sharing a single server, and nominating a single, non-voting representative at annual Steering Committee meetings. Membership fees are negotiable, depending on the number of institutions represented.

For all membership tiers, in the first year, the member must purchase a server; they also agree to provide staffing as follows:

- 2% of a system administrator
- administrator (acts as member point of contact)
- software engineer (responsible for preparing content for ingest).

Storage is charged on a per-use basis: in 2012 the cost was $1/gigabyte/year. Illustrative costs for preserving 2 terabyte of content in the MetaArchive for three years (excluding staff costs) would be $27,100 for a sustaining member or $19,600 for a preservation member, while an institution forming part of a 20-member collaborative member might pay $7,533.[71]

In addition to the various tiers of membership, the Cooperative also recognizes a number of affiliates – organizations and groups which may collaborate with the MetaArchive on occasion.

The mission and principles, membership structure, organization and governance, and operations of the MetaArchive Cooperative are described in its Charter,[72] while the rights and responsibilities of members are defined in a membership agreement.[73]

The MetaArchive provides bit preservation services for all content, using its integrity management and repair capabilities. It also offers logical preservation services, in the form of format migration, for certain types of content. The underlying technology of the MetaArchive is a secure, private network running the LOCKSS software. Each member hosts a server which is securely linked to that network. When a member ingests new content, it is automatically replicated to seven servers across the network. The size and diversity of membership ensures that servers are available in a wide variety of physical locations, and the system assigns content to servers to maximize that geographical distribution. The content is stored on different members' servers for preservation reasons only, rather than for access by other members. Through LOCKSS, the archive is protected from technical or financial failures affecting any single member, or the withdrawal of a member from the Cooperative, as well as disasters affecting a specific locale. The

MetaArchive maintains a versioning system, retaining previous versions of updated and repaired content. Each server is maintained by a different system administrator, which again reduces the likelihood of a single point of failure in the MetaArchive.

The MetaArchive Cooperative is hosted by the Educopia Institute, a non-profit institution based in Atlanta, Georgia. Educopia also provides a small administrative unit, the MetaArchive Services Group, which is the only element of the cooperative not provided directly by members. This comprises a director (who receives no remuneration), and three part-time posts which are centrally funded, but distributed among member institutions: a program manager, software engineer and system administrator. These internal posts are complemented by a wider set of external technical and managerial staff provided by members, together with a range of consultants contracted by the Cooperative. Strategic direction for the MetaArchive Cooperative is provided by the Steering Committee, made up of representatives from each member. MetaArchive staff support members with the initial set-up of their servers and individual ingests. The MetaArchive provides detailed information for prospective members on the exact staff skills they will be required to provide, and on the technical specifications of the necessary infrastructure. Members commit to maintaining and renewing that infrastructure to a common standard.

Unlike conventional supplier-customer business models, the Cooperative provides cultural memory institutions with a means to control and own the process of digital preservation, to invest in their own infrastructures and develop their own capabilities, but within a supportive network of like-minded peer institutions. This can be a very attractive approach for organizations with a long-term mission to preserve. It allows them to develop and maintain an 'intelligent customer' capability, and to feel that they understand and own not only the outcome, but also the process. It enables them to retain their core functions in-house, rather than becoming marginalized and deskilled by contracting out those functions. It provides some insulation from fluctuations in supplier costs, and allows them to realize economies of scale, maximizing their purchasing and negotiating power through joint procurement. The MetaArchive also leverages its collective nature to provide distributed preservation to all members, achieving greater resilience at no extra cost.

In 2009, the MetaArchive Cooperative undertook a self-assessment using the TRAC audit tool. The resultant report[74] found that the MetaArchive met all 84 TRAC criteria, in other words that it conformed to one norm for expectations of a trusted digital repository. As a result of the assessment, the Cooperative undertook 15 reviews or improvements to its documentation and operations, thus demonstrating the kind of continuous improvement process typical of higher levels of preservation maturity.

4.10 Key points

- **There are many viable models for digital preservation**: There are approaches to suit every size and type of organization.
- **Think about the technical resources and budget available**: These will help determine an appropriate option.
- **Assess the market**: Look carefully at the range of options available for each model before choosing.
- **Implementation is critical**: Plan and execute this stage very carefully – even the best option can go awry through poor execution.
- **Staff are the most important part of any digital repository**: Identify the staff you need and the skills they will require, and invest in their training and development.
- **Be aware of Trusted Digital Repository standards**: Think about how you can use them to your advantage.
- **Analyse the level of maturity you need to achieve**: Use this to inform your approach.

4.11 Notes

1 Pinsent and Good (2012).
2 Erway (2012).
3 See http://e-records.chrisprom.com/recommendations/.
4 See www.ipo.gov.uk/whyuse/research/lambert.htm.
5 Sinclair and Bernstein (2010).
6 Au et al. (2010).
7 See www.nationalarchives.gov.uk/PRONOM/.
8 See www.digitalpreservation.gov/formats/index.shtml.
9 See www.data-archive.ac.uk/.
10 See www.icpsr.umich.edu/icpsrweb/.
11 See www.ahds.ac.uk/.
12 See www.portico.org/digital-preservation/.

13 See www.oclc.org/digitalarchive/default.htm.

14 See http://chronopolis.sdsc.edu/.

15 See www.duracloud.org/.

16 See www.digital-preservation.com/solution/preservica/.

17 See www.aserl.org/programs/lockss-etd-initiative/.

18 See www.clockss.org/clockss/Home.

19 See www.adpn.org/.

20 MLA East of England and East of England Regional Archive Council (2006).

21 MLA East of England (2008).

22 European Parliament and the Council of the European Union (2004).

23 This is formally codified in Title 48 of the US Code of Federal Regulations, see US Government Printing Office (2005).

24 See www.gla.ac.uk/subjects/informationstudies/.

25 See http://digin.arizona.edu/index.html.

26 See www.kcl.ac.uk/prospectus/research/index/name/digital-humanities/alpha/G/header_search/.

27 See www.dpworkshop.org/.

28 See www.dptp.org/.

29 See http://dpoutreach.net/.

30 See http://dataintelligence.3tu.nl/en/home/.

31 See www.dpconline.org/.

32 See www.dcc.ac.uk/.

33 See www.ncdd.nl/en/ .

34 See www.openplanetsfoundation.org/.

35 See www.digitalpreservation.gov/education/courses/index.html.

36 See for example Donaldson (2011).

37 Garrett and Waters (1996, 40).

38 Garrett and Waters (1996, 23–4).

39 Subsequently codified as ISO 14721: 2003.

40 ISO 14721: 2003, 1–5.

41 RLG and OCLC (2002).

42 OCLC and Center for Research Libraries (2007).

43 See www.langzeitarchivierung.de/Subsites/nestor/EN/Home/.

44 nestor Working Group on Trusted Repositories Certification (2006).

45 Digital Curation Centre and DigitalPreservationEurope (2007).

46 DigitalPreservationEurope (2008).

47 Data Seal of Approval Board (2010).

48 APARSEN Project (2012).

49 Williams (2010).

50 This model was first proposed by the author in a presentation at the Oracle-PASIG Conference in London, April 2011 – see Brown (2011).

51 See http://blogs.loc.gov/digitalpreservation/2012/09/help-define-levels-for-digital-preservation-request-for-public-comments/.

52 See Brown (2000) for a detailed case study.

53 Brown (2002a).

54 Brown (2003).

55 A detailed description of procedures, although predating some of the later automation developed using CAMS, is provided in Brown (2002b).

56 See http://wellcomelibrary.org/about-us/.

57 Further information about the Wellcome Digital Library programme is available at http://wellcomedigitallibrary.blogspot.co.uk/.

58 Henshaw, Savage-Jones and Thompson (2010).

59 See www.webarchive.org.uk/ukwa/.

60 See www.nationalarchives.gov.uk/webarchive/.

61 Kevin Bolton, personal communication.

62 Much of the information in this case study is drawn from Bolton (2008).

63 See http://library.ccsu.edu/.

64 Much of the information in this case study is drawn from Iglesias and Meesangnil (2010).

65 See www2.lse.ac.uk/library/home.aspx.

66 Fay (2010).

67 Ed Fay, personal communication.

68 The digital library can be accessed at http://digital.library.lse.ac.uk/.

69 Much of this case study is drawn from Fay (2011) and the LSE Digital Library blog at http://lselibrarydigidev.blogspot.co.uk/.

70 See www.metaarchive.org/.

71 Costs taken from www.metaarchive.org/costs.

72 Educopia Institute (2012a).

73 Educopia Institute (2012b).

74 Schultz (2010).

5

Selecting and acquiring digital objects

5.1 Introduction

This is the first of two chapters that address how digital repositories acquire content. It focuses on the processes of selecting material for acquisition, and of physically acquiring it, including activities that may need to be carried out in advance of transfer. It discusses the principal issues that need to be addressed when developing a selection policy and acquisition process for digital records. It considers approaches to selection, legal and technical issues that may affect selection and transfer, standards and methods for transfer, and transfer agreements. The next chapter investigates the process of accession and ingest, whereby the transferred material is brought within the physical and intellectual control of the repository.

These two chapters describe separate stages within one overall process, as illustrated in Figure 5.1.

In the first stage, the institution makes a decision to acquire a specific collection of material, undertakes any preparatory activities, and performs the physical transfer of that material into its custody. The second stage then consists of the various activities required to ensure that the transfer has been successful, generate all information necessary for the preservation and future management of the content, and ingest it into the digital repository.

Both chapters focus on the practical tools and techniques that smaller organizations

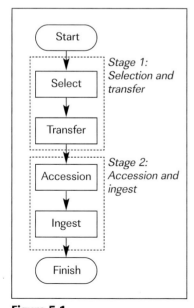

Figure 5.1
Stages of acquiring digital objects:
selection to ingest

can apply when acquiring digital content. Two recent projects, Paradigm[1] and AIMS,[2] have developed detailed guidance for small organizations, with particular emphasis on acquisition. They provide excellent sources for further reading, and are referenced extensively in both chapters.

5.2 The selection and transfer process

The process of selection and transfer can be broken into a number of generic steps, as shown in Figure 5.2.

The applicability and exact form of individual stages may vary between institutions and disciplines, and in some cases may effectively be notional, but the basic steps remain constant:

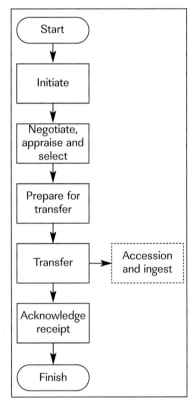

- **Initiation**: There are many different starting points for the transfer of digital material, which are discussed in more detail in the next section. The transfer may be initiated either by a depositor approaching the repository, or vice versa, or it may be triggered through a previously agreed arrangement, such as legal deposit legislation, records retention schedules, or open access agreements with a publisher. In the latter cases, this stage may be little more than notional.
- **Negotiation, appraisal and selection**: After the initial approach, a process of negotiation, analysis or consideration may be required. In an archival setting, a formal appraisal of the prospective transfer may occur, although this may

Figure 5.2
Stages of acquiring digital objects: selection and transfer

not be necessary if sufficiently detailed disposal policies are already in place. In most cases, some form of assessment of the content against a repository collecting policy will be needed, together with consideration of the legal and technical issues, which will culminate in a formal agreement between depositor and repository to accept the transfer.

- **Preparation for transfer**: Once the intention to transfer the content has been agreed, some preparation may be required before it can be enacted.

- **Transfer**: This covers the physical transfer of the digital content and associated documentation from the depositor to the repository. It is important to note that at this stage the content will simply be moved to a storage environment controlled by the receiving institution; accession and ingest into the repository itself comes later.

- **Acknowledgement**: Having completed the transfer, the repository should acknowledge receipt to the depositor. It is unlikely to be feasible or desirable to effect a formal acceptance of custody at this stage: this requires confirmation that the transfer was expected, is complete and accurate, and meets all applicable standards, which will only be possible on the completion of accession (see Chapter 6, 'Accessioning and ingesting digital objects'). Given that this may take some time, it is desirable to provide a preliminary acknowledgement to the depositor that the physical transfer has taken place. It may also be necessary to mark the acceptance by the repository of certain legal obligations (for example under freedom of information or privacy legislation) that may come into effect from the moment it is considered to hold a copy of the information.

- **Accession**: Having received the transfer, the repository can then begin the accession and ingest process, which brings the material under its physical and intellectual control, and is described in detail in Chapter 6. This culminates in formal sign-off and transfer of custody.

5.3 Starting points for selection and transfer

The selection and transfer process can be initiated in a number of different ways, the most common of which are discussed below:

- **Planned deposit**: In most cases, acquisition will be initiated as a planned process, which may originate from either the depositor or repository. Any necessary selection and preparation can then take place in advance of transfer.

- **Periodic transfer**: In some cases, organizations will receive regular transfers from the same source. Examples might include libraries receiving material as a result of subscriptions with publishers, or archives which take periodic deposits or snapshots of records from certain bodies under established agreements or records disposal policies. Such transfers will be especially common for institutional archives. By virtue of their repeated nature, standard processes can be developed for these transfers, and many issues need only be resolved once, at the outset.

- **Self-archiving**: Where collecting bodies are interested in the personal archives of individuals, they may offer services to help those individuals create and use their records in a managed environment, and even to deposit their own material. This is a common approach within institutional repositories in the higher and further education sectors, but very much a developing area beyond this. Under this approach, the depositor plays a much more active role in the transfer process, monitored and assisted by the repository.

- **Internal digitization programmes**: Many cultural memory institutions have programmes to digitize all, or parts, of their analogue collections. The resultant digital surrogates represent a significant investment of time, money and expertise, and may be difficult or impossible to re-create. As such, those institutions usually seek to preserve them as part of their digital collections. These can therefore be considered a special case of either periodic transfer (in the case of ongoing digitization programmes), or planned deposit (where the programme is already complete): the selection decision will be made once, and content will then be transferred as required. Many of the issues that affect other types of transfer can be avoided here, since the institution controls every stage of the process, from creation to transfer and accession.

- *Ad hoc* **discovery and rescue**: In some cases, digital material may be discovered unexpectedly or serendipitously. For example, it is not uncommon for archivists to discover floppy disks within previously accessioned paper files, or for librarians to find CDs within printed volumes. Depositors may also send unsolicited material to an archive, or a repository may be called on unexpectedly to rescue at-risk material, for example as a result of a disaster, such as fire or flood, or the sudden bankruptcy of a local business. In such cases, the physical transfer effectively takes place before selection, but the normal selection process should still occur; if the decision is made not to acquire the material, it can then be returned to the depositor, destroyed, offered to another organization, or otherwise disposed of.

- **Post-custodial approaches**: Where transfer is not likely or possible in the foreseeable future, a repository may try to maintain an ongoing relationship with the content creator, to enable the long-term preservation of the content within their continued custody. This is intended to ensure that it is managed correctly until some future transfer agreement is possible. At this point, the transfer could be treated as a planned deposit.

In some cases you may have to undertake hybrid transfers, which include analogue and digital records. In such circumstances, you will need to ensure that the appropriate standards and processes for both types of material are followed.

5.4 Approaches to selection

Each curatorial domain has its own well defined approach to the selection of content, which applies equally in the digital world, and shares the same fundamental rationale: the institution should have some form of documented collecting policy, which defines the types of material it chooses to collect. Potential acquisitions are then assessed against this in order to determine whether or not they should be selected. Appearing under various guises, including collection development policies, acquisition and disposal policies, and collecting policies, every library, archive and museum should have some kind of policy document that forms the basis for curatorial decisions about which material to acquire.

Existing approaches to collecting decisions should remain entirely valid for electronic material, but collecting policies, which may have been written before the advent of digital collections, might need to be updated to reflect the digital domain. For example, a detailed discussion of appraisal in the context of digital private papers can be found in Thomas et al. (2007, 32–47). In addition, institutions may wish specifically to target collecting digital material, such as e-journals or digital art, as evidence of its developing role within their particular domain.

In practical terms, selection of digital material is likely to prove more complex than analogue, for a number of reasons: the fundamental opaqueness of digital data means that curators are reliant on having access to the correct IT environment in order to view and appraise content, a wider and more rapidly evolving range of technical considerations must be taken into account, and the legal issues may be more involved.

Useful discussions of collection development in the digital environment are provided by the international and interdisciplinary AIMS project,[3] and the Paradigm project workbook,[4] while a wealth of examples of collecting policies that explicitly address digital content can be found online. Representative examples include:

- Dunedin Public Libraries (n.d.) – New Zealand
- Georgia Tech Library and Information Center (n.d.) – USA
- Museum of London (2011) – UK
- Parliamentary Archives (2012) – UK.

As part of the selection process, a relationship should be developed between depositor and repository, through which each party can understand the other's interests and requirements, and establish a basis for mutual trust. It is essential to clarify both what the donor may expect, and what the repository is able to offer, with regard to issues such as long-term preservation, access and ownership. The repository will also wish to obtain as much information about the material under consideration from the depositor at this point, including its background and context. It may be that future transfers are anticipated from the donor, in which case it will be essential to develop a long-term working relationship.

The receiving institution must also determine whether or not it is technically feasible and legally desirable to acquire the material. These aspects are discussed in detail in the next sections.

5.5 Legal considerations for selection

A number of legal issues need to be considered when making selection decisions. It is beyond the scope of this book to look at these in detail, and they are addressed more comprehensively elsewhere.[5] It must also be stressed that, if in doubt, you should always seek professional legal advice. However, the following points require particular consideration when dealing with digital material:

- **Intellectual property**: It is essential to understand the ownership of any content that is being transferred, and to ensure that the repository understands and acquires all the rights it will need for managing, reusing or granting third-party access to that content. This may not be straightforward, even when the ownership of the collection as a whole is well understood. Take the example of a website: the website as a whole and its constituent pages may be the property of the depositor, but it may include images which have been acquired from third parties. These may have been licensed, or used without permission. Even if they have been licensed for use on the original website, this licence may be of limited duration, and may not permit archiving. Establishing the nature of any licensing, whether it covers archiving, and who the true owner is, may be a difficult, if not impossible, task. Institutions need to take a risk-based approach to these difficulties – you may choose to invest less effort in investigating complex issues of intellectual property right (IPR) if the risk of legal consequences is perceived to be low. You should also place the onus on the depositor to identify all IPR in the material. Ideally, the repository should seek to acquire all IPR for transferred content; if this is not possible, as a minimum a non-exclusive copyright licence should certainly be acquired, allowing you to use, copy and redistribute the content as required, and with a duration that matches the expected period of custody (in most cases, this will be perpetual). Comprehensive guidance on IPR in the context of digital preservation can be found in Charlesworth (2012).

- **Content liability**: Repositories need to be aware that they are likely to become liable for the legality of any transferred content. This will most commonly apply to material that might be considered defamatory or obscene, promotes illegal activity, or could infringe someone's human rights. The repository should seek to identify whether any such liability is likely to arise from a particular transfer and, if so, how to mitigate this. Possible responses might range from choosing not to select the material, to closing it or providing limited access.

- **Privacy**: Any content containing personal data will be subject to applicable privacy laws, which the repository will become responsible for applying. It may be difficult to establish the existence of personal data in a large collection, since this can take so many forms (e.g. telephone numbers, e-mail addresses, postal addresses, dates of birth, medical histories and financial information), which may not be easy to detect automatically. Even more problematic to determine can be the effects of 'aggregation'; this occurs when the accumulation of a number of disparate but related data sets reveals information through links between individual data that, on their own, are not personal. For example, aggregated data might link names and addresses to health insurance numbers, and thence to medical records. Privacy can also be a significant issue for web content, and especially for material archived from social networks, such as Facebook or Twitter; it is very easy to capture personal data inadvertently.

- **Freedom of information**: Freedom of information legislation can be a key issue, especially for archives. If an archive takes custody of a collection, it becomes responsible for answering any freedom of information enquiries relating to it which it receives. If some of the material is closed to public access under the terms of the deposit, the archive becomes responsible for making future access decisions, which may place it in a difficult position. It is therefore essential that all closed material has an agreed closure period, rather than simply being closed indefinitely, and that possible exemptions which might be applied in response to access requests have been identified.

The notion of transfer of custody, and its legal implications, requires careful consideration. A repository may be unwilling to accept custody of material until it has had the opportunity to inspect it in detail, which may not be possible for some time after physical transfer has occurred. For example, it will certainly wish to quarantine the material, typically for a month, in order to prevent any malware infection (see Chapter 6, 'Accessioning and ingesting digital objects'). At the same time, certain legal responsibilities are likely to fall on the repository at the moment of transfer, which may be difficult to fulfil until the accession process is complete. For example, by definition, any material under quarantine should be unavailable for inspection, but might be legitimately requested under freedom of information legislation. If these issues are likely to apply, you are strongly recommended to seek legal advice.

To inform your selection decision and subsequent preparations for transfer, you should perform an assessment of the legal implications of that acquisition, in consultation with the depositor. This should:

- identify and resolve any IPR issues
- determine any potential areas of content liability, and appropriate mitigations
- determine the likelihood that personal data is present in the transfer, and identify any steps necessary to comply with relevant privacy legislation
- for closed content, determine a closure period and any potential exemptions that might be applied in response to freedom of information requests.

5.6 Technical considerations for selection

Although not the driving factor, selection decisions must be informed by technical considerations, just as the selection of physical objects must take account of their condition and conservation needs. For example, an archive would need to consider the consequential costs and other impacts of acquiring a collection of records that was severely affected by mould, as would a library which was considering accepting a set of badly damaged books. A digital repository needs to take account of equivalent issues. In particular, it will be important to consider:

- **Content infected by malware**: This will need to be disinfected before it can be ingested into the repository.
- **Damaged media**: If the transfer storage medium is damaged, specialist tools may be required to recover data from it.
- **Obsolete or unusual media**: If the repository lacks the means to read the storage media, it may be necessary to employ a specialist supplier to do so, or to purchase appropriate hardware.
- **Obsolete or unusual formats**: If the repository lacks the means to access these formats, they may require migration to more modern formats, or establishment of an appropriate emulation environment. Alternatively, it may need to purchase new software.
- **Inadequate documentation**: If there is insufficient documentation available at transfer to describe the content adequately, it may need to be recreated *post hoc*, if possible. Be aware that lack of documentation may compromise the authenticity of the material.
- **Large data volumes**: If the volume of data to be transferred is greater than the available storage capacity of the repository, it will be necessary to expand that capacity accordingly. This will certainly incur additional cost, and may also raise technical issues if the required increase goes beyond the original design specifications of the repository, as this may require a fundamental rethink of its architecture. Large data volumes are most commonly encountered in the context of digitization programmes and audiovisual archives.

Some of these issues, such as virus infection, may only become apparent during accession and ingest, but may be grounds for retrospectively rejecting the transfer at that point. Others, such as data volumes, obsolete media or inadequate documentation, should be apparent at the outset and can therefore be taken into account when making the initial selection decision.

The majority of technical issues are solvable, but at a cost. This may arise from the need to purchase additional equipment or software, provide training for staff, or employ the services of specialist consultants or contractors. The question is therefore likely to be whether the desirability of acquiring the material outweighs the associated costs.

5.7 Standards and methods for transfer

Every institution should establish standards governing the acceptability of digital objects which may be acquired. As a minimum, these should cover file formats, minimum documentation, and transfer media and methods.

Formats

Repositories may necessarily vary in their approach to formats. Some may choose to define a very restricted set of acceptable formats. This is attractive because it requires a similarly limited set of processes for ingesting, managing, preserving and accessing content. On the other hand, a rigid approach to formats may limit the content that the repository can take, and might prevent important content from being accepted. Thus, other repositories choose a more open approach, taking the view that they must be responsive to dealing with 'difficult' formats when required to do so to fulfil their collecting mandate. This gives greater flexibility, at the cost of more complexity.

Restrictive approaches are most likely to be effective for organizational repositories, or in other scenarios in which there are a constrained and well understood group of donors. Even if adopting a restrictive approach, it is recommended that you retain the discretion to acquire other formats, if merited by the nature of the content.

Minimum documentation

Setting a minimum standard covering the extent and form of documentation is absolutely essential. You should bear in mind that the documentation provided by the donor may not only be digital but, especially in the case of older data, could also include paper. You need to identify the documentation that exists, or may need to be created by the depositor, what form it takes, and how it will be transferred. You must also be realistic about what documentation can reasonably be expected from the depositor, and focus on what is most essential – for example, most technical metadata can be generated automatically after transfer, but the donor alone may be able to provide information about provenance and context. These are the most critical elements of documentation:

- An inventory or manifest listing the physical content to be transferred, at file and folder level. Such a list can be generated with free tools such as Karen's Directory Printer (see Appendix 3). The inventory should ideally include checksums for each file, to enable the integrity of the transfer to be confirmed. Checksums are discussed in Chapter 6, 'Accessioning and ingesting digital objects'.
- Descriptive information about the deposit as a whole, and its component parts. This might include existing documentation such as data dictionaries and manuals, as well as information prepared by the depositor specifically for this purpose.

Documentation could be provided in the form of word processed documents, spreadsheet, simple text files, or in more sophisticated metadata formats. The development of documentation standards for use by repositories is described in detail in Chapter 7, 'Describing digital objects', including suggestions for a minimum metadata standard.

Transfer media and methods

There are a variety of means by which content can be physically transferred to the repository. This variation arises in part from the differing capabilities of repositories and their depositors, and in part from the nature of the content. It is highly desirable to mandate specific transfer media and methods, and to seek to control as much of the transfer process as possible. This section considers the principal mechanisms that can be used to effect this transfer.

To begin with, you need to understand the environment from which the transfer will originate. This may take a wide variety of forms, including:

- **Removable media**: Content may be stored offline, on removable media such as floppy disks, CDs and DVDs, magnetic tape cartridges, memory sticks, memory cards and portable hard drives.

- **Standalone workstations**: Content may also originate on a standalone PC, laptop or other portable device.
- **Shared drives**: The most prevalent source for transfers is likely to be some form of networked storage, such as shared folders within a network file system.
- **Information management systems**: Content may originate in specialized information management systems, such as:
  - □ web content management systems
  - □ EDRMSs
  - □ digital asset management systems, typically used to manage digital images and multimedia content
  - □ e-mail (and e-mail archiving) systems
  - □ product lifecycle management systems, used to manage the development of designed products, including CAD
  - □ GISs, containing geospatially referenced content, including maps, terrain data and associated multimedia
  - □ casework management systems.

Equally, you need to provide a suitable storage environment in which to receive the transfer. This is usually a temporary working area within which data can be prepared for accession (as described in detail in Chapter 6, 'Accessioning and ingesting digital objects'). Nothing complex is required here – it could comprise a standalone workstation or an allocated area of network file storage – but it should provide the following:

- sufficient storage space for the transfer
- a back-up regime to safeguard the data in the period between transfer and completion of ingest; if the data has been transferred on removable media, it should be sufficient to retain these for the duration
- controls to prevent unauthorized access to the data.

You then need to identify a practical and efficient method for transferring the data. You can take two possible approaches to this: 'push' and 'pull'. The 'push' scenario involves the donor initiating the transfer, whereas 'pull' requires the repository to start the process. A number of options can be considered, as discussed below.

Manual transfer

The most basic method of acquisition is through the manual transfer of content and documentation. Depending on the volume of data to be transferred, as well as the technical capabilities of the donor and the receiving institution, this might take a number of forms. You may visit the donor and perform the transfer in person using a dedicated laptop, or on removable media such as portable hard drives or DVDs. You might supply a set of transfer media to them. The donor could deliver the data in person, or using postal or courier services. Alternatively, some form of online transfer mechanism could be used, such as FTP, or a commercial file transfer service, such as DropBox.[6] Very small volumes might even be sent as e-mail attachments, although this would generally not be recommended.

Automated transfer

Automated transfer is likely to be feasible only in cases where data is being regularly acquired from the same donor or system; it may then become economical to develop an automated process. These are the key features of such a mechanism:

- The transfer process is triggered automatically. The process can be initiated at either the depositor ('push') or repository ('pull') end – which is most appropriate will vary according to circumstance.
- The data transfer occurs via a network connection (e.g. the internet or a local area network).
- The receiving repository automatically validates that the transfer has been completed successfully.
- The transfer requires minimal, if any, manual intervention. A human approval step, for example, may still be required, but manual processing or substantial metadata creation would not be acceptable.

Automated transfer processes are likely to be unique to specific circumstances, and hence require some degree of custom development, but they should be able to use commonplace technologies.

Semi-automatic transfer

Between these two extremes lie a range of permutations which, while still requiring a greater or lesser degree of manual intervention, nonetheless automate portions of the transfer process. For example, the data might be transferred manually on a portable hard drive, but an automated process developed to extract the data on receipt.

Web archiving

Web archiving embraces a range of techniques for capturing web-based information. A subject in its own right, the intricacies of web archiving lie beyond the scope of this book, and have been addressed in detail elsewhere.[7] However, it is worth noting that web archiving is likely to become a commonplace acquisition method for a number of reasons:

- The existence of established service providers means that there is a low barrier to entry for smaller organizations; web archiving can be a very fast and cost-effective means to acquire substantial quantities of digital content.
- For many organizations, their web presence is acquiring an ever greater significance, as a publication channel and a means of providing services; this in turn is leading to a greater awareness of the need to archive web resources, either by institutional archives or external memory institutions.

Many organizations may therefore consider establishing a web archiving programme at an early stage in their digital preservation strategy.

Although some larger organizations operate in-house web archiving facilities, it is much more practical for smaller organizations to use one of the well established specialist service providers. These include non-profit organizations such as the Internet Archive[8] and the Internet Memory Foundation,[9] as well as commercial enterprises such as Hanzo Archives.[10] This avoids the need for in-house expertise or substantial set-up costs, and providers typically host public access to the archive, in addition to undertaking the physical collection. A couple of different business models have emerged:

- **Traditional**: The conventional approach is for the service provider to undertake harvesting on behalf of the customer, to a specified scope, depth and frequency. They will also usually undertake quality assurance of the results, although the customer will almost certainly wish to perform their own quality checks on top of this.

- **Self-archiving**: Under this model, the institution directly manages its own web archiving activities, using the service provider's online tools. The main current example of this approach is Archive-It, a subscription service offered by the Internet Archive.[11] This has a very low barrier to entry, albeit at the cost of limited flexibility. Customers manage their web crawling through an online 'dashboard', by means of which they can control the scope, depth and frequency of harvesting, as well as carrying out quality control of the results and creating descriptive metadata. Archive-It then hosts the resultant collection in fully searchable form, for free public access. As of 2012, Archive-It is used by over 190 organizations in 44 US states and 16 countries worldwide.

The latter model may be most suited to small organizations taking their first steps in this area, as the ease of use, low cost and constrained options provide a simple and safe environment in which to explore the possibilities, gain practical experience, and begin to develop a collection. Over time, the more traditional approach may then be considered if greater flexibility is required.

Although web archiving service providers typically offer harvesting and hosting, they do not tend to provide long-term preservation. If considering using such a service, you therefore need to make alternative arrangements for this. In some cases, institutions choose to do so by acquiring periodic copies of the harvested content to store themselves. This is a particularly attractive option if you have an existing digital repository. For example, the Parliamentary Archives takes an annual transfer of content from its web archiving service provider, which is then ingested into its digital repository for preservation purposes; public access is provided by the service provider, but seamlessly linked to from the Archives catalogue and the main Parliament website.[12]

Alternatively, you may wish to simply ensure that the agreement with the service provider offers contractual and technical provisions for you to acquire a complete copy of the harvested content, in an open format such as WARC, on termination of the agreement. You need to ensure that this covers unforeseen events, such as financial failure of the supplier, as well as planned termination.

Forensic versus logical transfer methods

For manual, semi-automated or automated transfers, two approaches to physically copying the bits from source to target environment are possible. The simplest and most widespread technique is to take a logical copy of the required set of files. This is the method used when copying and pasting files between folders, and works at the level of the file system – it copies the data that is visible to the user and doesn't include deleted files. Logical copying does not require any specialist tools.

The alternative is to use forensic techniques, which acquire an exact bit-for-bit 'image' of the original storage media, including hidden files, or files that have been deleted but not overwritten. As the name suggests, forensic techniques have been developed to secure electronic information for use in criminal investigations and submission in court; thus they place maximum emphasis on preserving the evidential value of the data, and it is this quality which makes them so interesting to digital archivists. Although the motive is different, the requirements are strikingly similar to those for a repository transfer: the sources may be arbitrary and poorly understood IT systems, existing documentation may be minimal, and there may be no recourse to the depositor for assistance. It is also essential to preserve the integrity and evidential value of the data. Creating a forensic image for transfer certainly provides the most comprehensive and authentic copy of the source data, but this comes at the cost of greater complexity and effort – it may take some time and training to learn to use forensic tools successfully, and in many cases this additional effort may not be justified by the material. Forensic techniques can also raise ethical issues, since they may result in the capture of data which the donor did not intend or consent to transfer. A number of forensic tools are available, and some have even been specifically incorporated into digital preservation tools such as BitCurator. Such tools are not limited to software; for example, write blockers are hardware devices that allow the capture of information from a drive while protecting the content of the drive from the possibility of accidental damage, by allowing 'read' commands but blocking 'write' commands. Some of the main forensic tools are listed in Appendix 3.

5.8 Transfer agreements

The outcome of the selection process, as agreed between the depositor and repository, must be clearly documented. Where transfers are governed by established agreements, such as a subscription with a publisher, or a records disposal policy, these are usually sufficient to meet this need. In other cases a formal transfer agreement is likely to be required. As is the case with so much of the transfer process, this is not a particular or unique requirement for digital material, and organizations should be able to use or adapt existing agreements. A transfer agreement should include:

- a description of the transferred materials, including basic details of their content, extent and technical form
- agreed documentation to be provided by the donor
- agreed methods and timeframes for transfer, including details of transfer media, where applicable
- preservation, including any obligations or caveats on the part of the repository; for example, the repository may wish to note the level of preservation it will provide
- ownership, including the right of the repository to dispose of material subsequently
- conditions of use and access, by the repository and its end-users.

Detailed guidance on developing transfer agreements for digital material has been published by the AIMS project[13] and the Paradigm project,[14] both of which provide templates and models. Model transfer guidelines for individuals and corporate bodies are also provided on Chris Prom's blog site.[15]

5.9 Preparing for transfer

Once a decision has been made to select material for transfer, the legal implications assessed and the technical issues, including the appropriate transfer method, reviewed, it will be necessary for the repository and depositor to undertake preparations accordingly. These may include assembling, creating or transforming documentation into acceptable formats, migrating content to approved transfer formats, or setting up and configuring transfer mechanisms, such as FTP sites. Any outstanding points of detail may also need to be discussed and agreed by both parties at this stage.

5.10 Completing the transfer process

The final step is to undertake the actual transfer according to the agreed method and timescale. On receipt, you will need to check the condition of any physical media for obvious damage, and ensure that it is housed in appropriate physical conditions.[16] Once you have completed this you can send an appropriate acknowledgement to the depositor, and the process of accession and ingest begins. In any communication with the depositor at this stage it is essential to emphasize that they should not yet destroy copies of the data they retain, as formal accession has not been completed.

5.11 Conclusion

Selection and transfer are the first stages in the acquisition of new content by digital repositories. Traditional models can continue to form the basis for selection decisions in the digital realm, but need to take account of how creators of digital content work, as well as very different technical and legal considerations. You will need to plan prospective transfers carefully, working closely with depositors wherever possible, to ensure that you receive the content you need, in a form suitable for subsequent accession, access and preservation – effort invested at this stage will be repaid many times over in future.

5.12 Key points

- **Build on existing processes**: All collecting institutions have existing procedures for selecting and acquiring analogue material – use these as the basis for digital transfers.
- **Work closely with depositors**: If at all possible, you should seek to develop a strong collaborative relationship with depositors. This will maximize your opportunities to understand the nature of the material being transferred, and to ensure that it is transferred in the most appropriate form, using the most suitable method.
- **Consider the technical and legal implications carefully**: Don't just base selection decisions on the nature of the content – you also need to understand and take full account of the technical and legal issues, so you can make a fully informed decision.
- **Develop and enforce realistic transfer standards**: Transfers will be much simpler, more efficient, and more likely to be successful if they follow a

common standard, but it is also essential that these standards are realistic and enforceable in practice, and reflect the capabilities of your depositors.

5.13 Notes

1 The JISC-funded Paradigm Project was undertaken by the Bodleian Library at Oxford University, and John Rylands University Library at Manchester University between 2005 and 2007, and investigated the archiving of digital private papers. See www.paradigm.ac.uk/.

2 The AIMS project was funded by the Andrew W. Mellon Foundation between 2009 and 2011 to develop an inter-institutional framework for stewarding born-digital content. The project partners were the universities of Virginia, Stanford, Hull and Yale. See www2.lib.virginia.edu/aims/ and http://born-digital-archives.blogspot.co.uk/.

3 AIMS Work Group (2012, 3–14).

4 Thomas et al. (2007, 10–16).

5 See, for example, Brown (2006, 146–62), Thomas et al. (2007, 247–73) and Padfield (2010).

6 See https://www.dropbox.com/.

7 See, for example, Brown (2006) and Masanès (2006).

8 See http://archive.org/.

9 See http://internetmemory.org/.

10 See www.hanzoarchives.com/.

11 See www.archive-it.org/.

12 See www.parliament.uk/business/publications/parliamentary-archives/web-archive/.

13 AIMS Work Group (2012, 7–8, and Appendix F, 10–12).

14 Thomas et al. (2007, 22–4 and 274–6).

15 See http://e-records.chrisprom.com/recommendations/develop-submissioningest-policies/transfer-guidelines/.

16 See Brown (2008b) for recommendations on physical care, storage and handling of removable media.

6

Accessioning and ingesting digital objects

6.1 Introduction

Accession is the process by which new content is brought within the intellectual and physical control of the repository. It can be divided into three broad types of activity:

- **collating** the content and metadata into a suitable form for ingest
- **checking and enhancing** that content and metadata where necessary, to ensure that it meets all the requirements for ingest
- **ingesting** the content and metadata into the repository.

The accession process is triggered by the conclusion of some form of selection decision and physical transfer, and concludes once the content is under the full control of the repository, and accessible to its user community.

Accession is likely to account for the majority of your activity when operating a digital repository, so it pays to ensure that you have an effective, efficient and robust process. Effort invested in getting this right will yield dividends in future – a good accession process will ensure that new content is securely stored, well documented and error-free, and will greatly simplify its future preservation and access; conversely, even the most effective future management regime may be unable to compensate for mistakes and omissions during accession.

This chapter provides a detailed description of the steps required to accession digital objects into a digital repository. It includes an assessment of the types of tool that are available to support these processes, and practical guidance on 'first aid' procedures for dealing with poorly documented, obsolete or unsolicited deposits. It ends with a series of case studies to further illustrate how these concepts can be put into practice.

6.2 Defining an accession process

Accession involves a standard series of steps or workflow, although every repository is likely to require subtle differences in the detail and order of those steps.[1] A model accession workflow, illustrating those key steps, is shown in Figure 6.1.

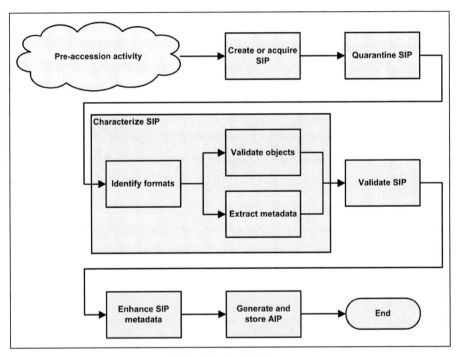

Figure 6.1 Model accession workflow for digital objects

The precursor to this workflow – pre-accession activity – encompasses everything that happens in the lifecycle of a digital collection from creation up to the point at which it is physically transferred to the digital repository. In the first step, a standard package of content and metadata, usually referred to as a SIP, is made available to the digital repository to begin the accession process; this step falls on the cusp of the transfer process, as discussed in Chapter 5, 'Selecting and acquiring objects'. It and the succeeding steps in the accession workflow are described in detail in the following sections, with examples of tools and techniques which can be used to implement them.

6.3 Creating or acquiring a Submission Information Package

Like all workflows, accession is most efficient if its constituent activities can be standardized. Working against this is the fact that the digital curator is likely to be receiving content for accession from a wide variety of different sources, in many different formats, and arranged in varying ways. The solution to this conundrum is to transform all of the incoming material into a single, standard structure for accession, in much the same way as a traditional repository may require items to be boxed and labelled in standard ways.

The first stage of the accession process is therefore to assemble the content and metadata into a standard form or 'package' suitable for accession. The package used by digital repositories at ingest is formally known as a Submission Information Package (SIP), a term coined by the OAIS Reference Model. It is one of three types of information package defined by OAIS, the others being the Archival Information Package (AIP) (the package which is actually stored by the repository), and the Dissemination Information Package (DIP) (the package supplied to an end-user). OAIS defines an information package as:

> A logical container composed of optional Content Information and optional associated Preservation Description Information. Associated with this Information Package is Packaging Information used to delimit and identify the Content Information and Package Description information used to facilitate searches for the Content Information.[2]

Behind this potentially off-putting array of terms lies a rather simple idea: the package is a conceptual grouping of various types of information. At its heart is the actual content to be preserved (the content information), together with the descriptive metadata required for its intellectual control and resource discovery (package description information), and the technical metadata necessary for its preservation (preservation description information). Some additional metadata is then required to describe how the package is itself arranged (packaging information).

Although OAIS defines the idea of a SIP, there is no standard format for these packages, and practice varies considerably among digital repositories. The SIP should be considered a conceptual entity – it may be embodied as some kind of physical package, such as a Zip file, but this is not a requirement. The one necessity is that it must be possible to associate the data objects and their metadata. In practice, the use of a container format is employed by many repositories as an efficient means of managing SIPs.

A number of tools have been developed for creating and manipulating SIPs, although their value is strictly limited by their compatibility with repository systems. For example, several tools are now available to package content according to the BagIt format (described in detail in Chapter 7, 'Describing digital objects', and widely used for creating SIPs), including Bagger, BagIt Library and BagIt Transfer Utilities (these are described in more detail in Appendix 3). However, support for directly ingesting BagIt SIPs into common digital repository platforms is currently limited, and repositories using the format have typically developed custom routines to transform BagIt packages into a form that their repository can ingest. This is likely to change over time: the transformation process is comparatively simple and BagIt is growing in popularity.

On the other hand, commercial systems typically use their own SIP formats, and provide proprietary SIP creation tools (for example, Tessella's SDB provides a SIP Creator application). In the case of repositories which ingest a very narrow range of content, the nature of that content may provide a ready-made SIP, e.g. the WARC format used by many web archives.

A SIP format could be as simple as a standard folder structure and naming convention, as illustrated in Figure 6.2. Here, the SIP is represented by a folder containing two sub-folders: one holds the data, the other the metadata. The data folder should contain the data in its original arrangement, and might therefore contain further levels of sub-folder, if present in the original. The key point here is that the actual form of SIP chosen is much less important than the fact of having one.

The SIP will be created at around the point of transfer to the repository. Precisely how this occurs will depend on the source of the content, and the approach taken by the repository. Two options are possible:

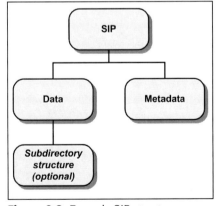

Figure 6.2 Example SIP structure

- **Creation pre-transfer**: It may be possible for the depositor to package the content into the required SIP format prior to transfer. For simple SIP structures using commonplace technologies, such as those based on folder structures or Zip files, this is fairly straightforward, and merely requires specifying the appropriate structure to the depositor. For more sophisticated forms of SIP, such as BagIt, it is only likely to be practical where regular transfers take place from the same depositor. In this scenario, the repository will need to work closely with the donor to devise an appropriate method. This might entail providing a tool, such as one of the BagIt utilities mentioned above, together with appropriate training, or even customizing the export from the source system so that it automatically generates SIPs.

- **Creation post-transfer**: The alternative scenario is for the repository to perform the transformation of the data immediately after transfer. This may be simpler, since it removes responsibility from the donor, but does entail greater work on the part of the repository. However, it is the one approach guaranteed to suit every eventuality, and is therefore the more likely option for many smaller organizations. For more complex forms of SIP, repository staff can either use standalone utilities, or the transformation can potentially be automated as part of the repository accession workflow.

At the conclusion of this step, the incoming content will be in a physical location controlled by the repository, with data and metadata associated and arranged in a standard structure ready for accession.

Some organizations choose to take a photographic record of any storage media at the same time as SIP creation, in order to capture the physical nature and condition of the original media, together with any label information. Decisions also need to be taken about whether or not to preserve the original media as artefacts in their own right – for example, some CD-ROM publications may have interesting screen-printed designs, which could be considered worthy of preservation even after the content has been recovered from them. However, in most cases transit media are destroyed once ingest has been successfully completed. For media containing sensitive information, care should be taken to use secure destruction techniques, including physical shredding of disks and secure data erasure tools.

6.4 Quarantine

The essential next step of any accession workflow must be to quarantine the transferred content. The purpose of quarantine is very simply to prevent any malicious software from being ingested into the digital repository. In a traditional archive, all new accessions are inspected for signs of mould or insect infestation, which could not only damage those documents but also, once inside the repository, spread to other parts of the collection; any such problems which are detected are then treated and neutralized before the documents are allowed into the repository proper. In the digital environment, equivalent threats are posed by viruses, worms, Trojans, and other forms of malware. These too possess the ability to spread, infecting new systems. If malware were to be introduced to a digital repository, it could potentially wreak havoc not only on the files being ingested, but also the entire repository. A thorough quarantine procedure is therefore an essential discipline to maintain, and should always be the first accession activity on receipt of a SIP. It comprises two basic processes:

- detection and containment of threats
- treatment or avoidance of infected content.

Malware detection, and any subsequent treatment, must take place before the content is allowed to come into direct contact with the repository itself, to avoid any possibility of contamination. This requires some form of quarantine environment, which is isolated from the repository. This environment can simply take the form of a dedicated laptop or workstation, physically isolated from other systems. Alternatively, it might comprise storage space allocated on a network fileserver, provided this is separated from the main repository storage space.

You should use standard internet security software to detect and repair malware, the most important consideration being to ensure that it is kept up to date with the latest definitions provided by its supplier. There is something of an 'arms race' between the creators of malware and the antivirus vendors, and there is an inevitable delay between new malware being created, and internet security software being updated to detect and repair it. This creates a window of vulnerability, within which a virus could be introduced to the repository in spite of any antivirus protection. The conventional approach to preventing this is to hold all the files being accessioned in quarantine for a specified time period (typically 30 days), to allow antivirus software definitions to be updated with all the latest threats. The files are then rescanned at the end of this period.

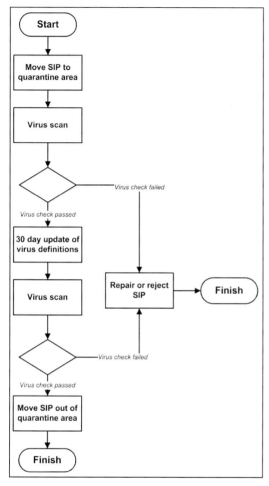

Figure 6.3 Quarantine process for digital objects

Quarantine workflows will typically be configured to a specific duration, but it is advisable to provide some mechanism, such as a manual approval step, to ensure that a virus definition update has indeed taken place within the quarantine period – since updates are released at the discretion of the software vendor, they may not be entirely predictable. A typical quarantine workflow is shown in Figure 6.3.

All files that pass the quarantine period can move on to be ingested into the repository, but the question remains of what to do with any files found to contain malware. Essentially, there are two possibilities: repair the files to remove the malware, or reject the files and request uninfected replacements from the depositor. Clearly the latter option is preferable if at all possible, but the former may be the only choice if no other copies of the data exist. Either way, details of the infection, including the precise type of malware discovered, the antivirus tool (including the specific software version), the date or version number of the antivirus definitions used, and the action taken (including the method of repair, if applicable), should be recorded within the technical metadata associated with the relevant object. If repair or replacement proves impossible, you will have no choice but to reject the SIP.

The only circumstances in which it may be possible to omit the quarantine period and second scan (although never the initial scan) is where the content has already been stored in an environment in which there is no risk of malware infection for at least 30 days. An example might be removable media discovered in paper files that have been stored in a secure environment for a known period. In this scenario, you can be confident that any viruses present will be detectable through the initial scan.

6.5 Characterization

It is essential that all content ingested into a repository be sufficiently well understood to allow it to be properly managed, preserved and accessed. In practice, this requires metadata describing the content in enough detail. In an ideal world, this might all be provided by the depositor, but in practice it is unrealistic to expect this. The types of metadata required by a digital repository are likely to be detailed and highly technical, and the tools required to create it can be very specialized. Most depositors will lack the wherewithal and knowledge to provide it. The process of characterization is required to fill this gap.

Characterization refers to the varied processes that may be used to understand in detail the nature of digital objects, at a technical and logical level. At its simplest, this might entail determining the format of a file; at its most advanced, it might include the automated extraction and construction of metadata for the object. Characterization is a key part of the preservation cycle, and is discussed in Chapter 8, 'Preserving digital objects'. Its specific application to the accession and ingest process is addressed below.

Characterization is usually considered to include three activities (Figure 6.4):

- **identification** of the format of each object
- **validation** of each object to confirm that it is a correctly formed example of its type; validation may take place at the level of individual files, or for higher-level logical entities, such as an entire website
- **metadata extraction** to acquire additional descriptive and technical information about each object.

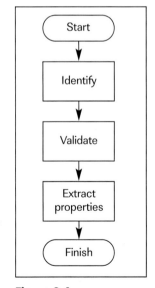

Figure 6.4
The characterization workflow for digital objects

Identifying the format of a file is the key to establishing a means to read the content, and therefore a fundamental requirement for preservation. A modern operating system such as Windows will attempt to do this automatically, but it is not foolproof, and unlikely to help with older or more unusual formats. The file extension (the suffix, usually three or four characters, which follows the 'dot' in the filename, e.g. '.pdf') provides an indication, but this is neither reliable nor necessarily sufficiently granular. For example, the .doc extension usually indicates Microsoft Word format, but does not tell you which of the many versions of the format it is, and therefore which versions of Word software will be able to open it. Furthermore, it might not be a Word document at all; early word processors such as WordStar did not use standard file extensions, and users frequently created their own extensions to indicate types of document, e.g. .doc for a document, .let for a letter.

The only reliable means of identifying the format is to look at the bitstream itself for the characteristic patterns and structures that uniquely identify particular formats, and versions thereof. Fortunately, there are a number of freely available software utilities to do this, discussed later in this section.

Validation is a slightly more specialized task, requiring tools specific to individual formats and object types. It entails checking that the structure and content of a digital object complies with some external specification – it is a valid example of the type of object it claims to be. Examples include validating a file against the formal specification of the format, validating an XML-based document against the appropriate schema or document type definition (DTD), or confirming that a snapshot of a website has captured the complete set of content. While not as critical as format identification, validation can help to identify potential preservation problems at an early stage.

One potential issue can arise from over-zealous validation; in the real world, many IT systems tolerate a degree of variance from formal specifications, and it is therefore unnecessary to validate beyond this. PDF is a case in point – the format specification is very complex, and may be interpreted in subtly different ways by the various tools available. As a result, PDF validation tools may highlight errors (or even disagree as to whether or not an error exists) that PDF rendering tools will gracefully ignore. In such circumstances, the pragmatic approach may be to note the error, but accept the file anyway.

Metadata extraction is an equally specialized process, and involves the automatic capture of additional information about the object, which may be useful for its preservation management or use. This might include extracting technical information about a digital photograph, or records management metadata about a document from an EDRMS.

While characterization is predominantly concerned with discovering the properties of the SIP that are relevant to its longer-term management, it can also identify issues of immediate concern. For example, digital objects may be received which have been compressed, encrypted or password-protected. Each of these represents a barrier to preservation, and needs to be reversed if possible, which may require the co-operation of the depositor, or may even be grounds for rejection of the SIP. Characterization tools can identify such cases and flag them up for attention.

Characterization relies on automated tools, and fortunately there is a wide, and growing, range available, of varying sophistication and maturity. Many of these are either free or very inexpensive to purchase. Some of the most common tools are mentioned below, while a more comprehensive list is provided in Appendix 3.

There are a number of format identification tools to choose from, many of them specifically developed for the purposes of digital preservation, including DROID (Figure 6.5), Apache Tika, FIDO and Unix File. Validation

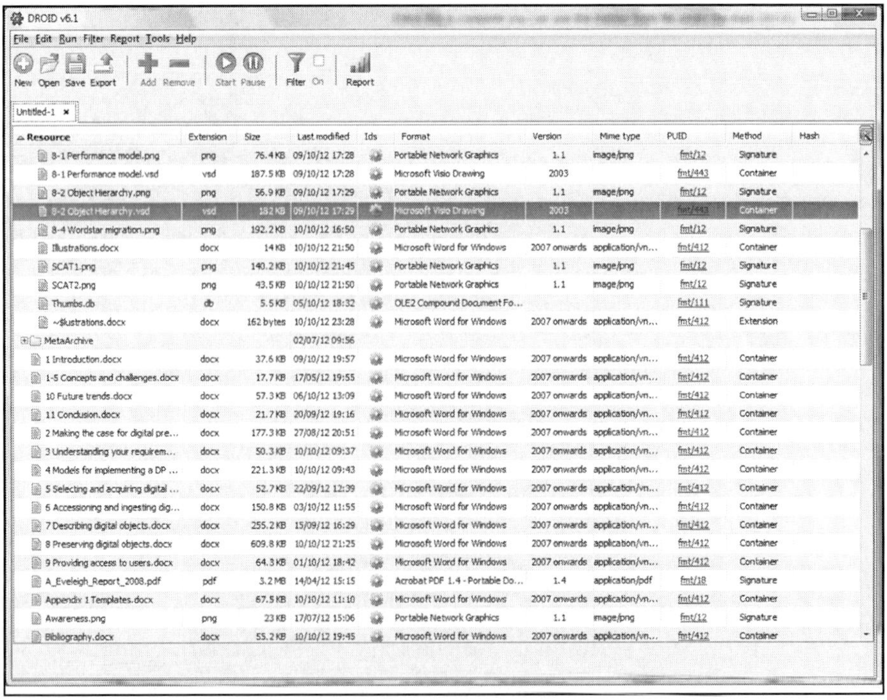

Figure 6.5 Format identification results in DROID (The National Archives)

and metadata extraction tools tend to be more specialized, applying only to a specific format or type of object, but more broadly based examples include JHOVE, JHOVE2 and the NLNZ Metadata Extractor. Other tools have been developed that combine a number of individual utilities for ease of use. For example the FITS format identification tool includes DROID, JHOVE, NLNZ Metadata Extractor, Unix File, ExifTool and FFIdent.

In principle, tools are available to identify, validate and extract metadata from the majority of commonly encountered formats, but they vary considerably in terms of ease of use, performance and reliability. Some, like JHOVE and DROID, have been in existence for many years, have released multiple versions, and are widely adopted; others remain at the prototype stage, and are not yet really suitable for production use. While some tools are designed to be used directly by a human operator, and offer user-friendly interfaces, others are intended to be embedded within automated workflows behind the scenes, and provide only command-line interfaces that require a much greater degree of technical knowledge to operate.

Nonetheless, there are a sufficient number of free, mature, robust, user-friendly characterization tools available to allow even the smallest organization to undertake this activity with confidence.

6.6 Validating the SIP

Although characterization includes validation of individual objects within the SIP, it is also essential to validate the SIP as a whole – to confirm that it contains the expected content, is what it claims to be, and meets the repository's minimum requirements for an accession. SIP validation should test four things:

- **Completeness**: Does the accession include everything which is expected and, equally, not contain anything extraneous?
- **Accuracy**: Does the metadata accurately describe the content?
- **Conformity**: Does the SIP conform to repository requirements? Is it arranged in the correct structure, does it include at least the minimum metadata in the correct format, and are the file formats in accordance with any defined restrictions?
- **Integrity**: Is the integrity of the SIP intact following transfer – has no corruption or loss occurred en route from the donor to the repository?

For small accessions, validation may be a manual process, undertaken through visual inspection, supported by one or two easily available software utilities. However, it is desirable to automate as much as possible, and essential in the case of large accessions. Fortunately, validation lends itself to automation: checking structured information against a clearly defined set of rules is a task at which computers excel.

Completeness will normally be assessed by checking the SIP content against an inventory or manifest prepared before transfer (see Chapter 5, 'Selecting and acquiring digital objects').

Validating metadata is also easily automatable: most metadata standards use XML, and publish schemas against which metadata can be validated using any XML authoring tool. Specific tools are also available for validating certain key metadata formats, including METS, PREMIS and BagIt, and are listed in Appendix 3.

Any exceptions to file format restrictions can easily be screened using the results of characterization; the reports generated by file format identification tools such as DROID can be checked for non-permitted formats by eye, and this process also lends itself to easy automation.

Integrity can be simply and automatically tested using checksums. A checksum is a value based on the content of a file and calculated through some form of mathematical algorithm. The checksum algorithm is designed in such a way that changing a single bit within the file will result in a completely different value. If a checksum value is calculated for every file within a SIP before transfer, then the integrity of that file can be tested at any future date by recalculating the checksum and comparing it to the original value: any difference will demonstrate that the file has been altered in some way. Even if it is not possible to generate checksums before transfer, creating them during accession is essential to provide a baseline for managing their future integrity. Commonly used checksum algorithms include MD5 (see Rivest, 1992) and SHA-1 (see Eastlake, 2001), and there are many free utilities for creating and comparing checksums, some of which are listed in Appendix 3.

6.7 Enhancing SIP metadata

Metadata is considered in detail in Chapter 7, 'Describing digital objects', but the specific role of metadata for accession and ingest merits separate consideration.

Metadata forms an essential component of any SIP. Although some metadata should be present from the outset, it will tend to accumulate throughout accession. Documenting the processes that occur during the life of a digital object to create an audit trail is an essential archival function, supporting its authenticity and future use. The accession process is no exception, and all the key events in the workflow should be recorded within the technical metadata associated with the SIP, including:

- **Quarantine**: The date, time and process used should be recorded, including the name and version of antivirus tool, together with the date or version number of the antivirus definitions used. The need to record additional information about quarantine failures has already been discussed above.
- **Characterization**: Metadata will certainly be created through characterization. As a minimum, this should include identification of file formats, but it may extend much more widely to the extraction of technical and descriptive metadata from within the digital objects. Again the timing and characterization tools used should also be noted.
- **Validation**: The date and processes used for validation should be recorded, with details of any tools used. Any failures and corrective actions taken should also be described.
- **Ingest**: The date on which ingest was successfully completed is a key event to document.

Descriptive metadata may also be manually added by human editors during accession. For example, a librarian or archivist may be required to create descriptive catalogue records, as well as quality-assuring (and possibly enhancing), the existing metadata. Descriptive metadata enhancement does not have to happen as part of accession; some repositories may choose to undertake detailed description and arrangement only once accession is complete.

6.8 Ingest: generating and storing an AIP

The final stage of the accession process will be to actually ingest the objects into the repository. This requires the files to be moved into a permanent storage location within repository control, and for the metadata to be incorporated into whatever metadata management regime is in use.

If using repository software, this will be an automated process; in other cases, it may entail manually moving the content files to a different location, using checksums to verify the move, and either moving metadata files to a final location or updating the content of a metadata database accordingly.

The successful completion of the accessioning process should be formally recorded as a part of the custodial history of the digital object, preferably as an event record in the object's metadata. It will normally also be necessary to provide a receipt to the original depositor, to confirm the transfer of custody, and serve notice that it is now safe for them to destroy any copies they retain.

Once the SIP has been successfully ingested, and is under the formal control of the repository, it is considered to have become an AIP. Depending on repository practice, this may or may not entail any physical transformation of the package – for example, it might involve a repackaging of the objects, or a transformation of the metadata to an internal format; on the other hand, it may be a purely conceptual change. Either way, the SIP exists purely for the purposes of ingest; it is the AIP which the repository preserves, and serves as the source for subsequent access through the generation of DIPs.

6.9 Normalization and other transformations

Some accession workflows may include additional steps to transform the content of the SIP in some way. The most common scenarios are *normalization* of data to preferred archival formats, or *format migration* to generate access copies. More subtle transformations may also be required. For example, it may be necessary to decompress or decrypt files, where such features have been discovered in the course of characterization (see above). Transformation processes are more properly considered a preservation activity, and are therefore described in detail in Chapter 8, 'Preserving digital objects'. Where they occur as part of accession, they will typically form the penultimate step, before ingest.

6.10 Automating accession

The processes of accession can be performed manually or as an automated workflow. The practicalities of automation will depend on the capabilities of any digital repository platform you may be using, and the level of access you have to the necessary IT expertise. Dedicated repository software usually includes some degree of automation for accession and ingest, and many platforms incorporate sophisticated workflow tools, which can be configured to automate almost every aspect. However, even within the simplest repository environment, individual ingest tools such as CINCH (Capture, INgest, & CHecksum), Curator's Workbench, Digital Preservation Software Platform and Prometheus can be used to automate the major tasks. A very wide and growing range of tools is available to support and automate the ingest process – for example, a 2007 survey by the Cairo project in the UK identified 54 separate tools, in 16 categories.[3] Examples of such tools, which may be especially useful for small organizations, are listed in Appendix 3.

6.11 First aid for digital accessions

The scenario that every digital archivist dreads is the package of unlabelled, undocumented and possibly unsolicited disks received in the post, or discovered on an office shelf. The dilemma this creates is that it may be difficult, if not impossible, to determine whether the content justifies the effort of recovering it, without first going through that very recovery process. Ultimately, this may well come down to a judgement call, but that decision can at least be supported and justified by adopting a systematic approach.

This 'first aid' scenario could logically be considered to form part of the selection process (a selection decision needs to be made if the data can be read) but is discussed here because it shares many tools and processes with accession and ingest.

The approach a digital archivist might take in such a first aid situation can be defined using a decision tree such as shown in Figure 6.6.

Each of these steps is discussed in the following sections.

Identifying the storage medium

The storage medium self-evidently needs to be identified before its content can be retrieved. Although in most cases accessions will be provided on familiar, modern media, older material might arrive on a bewildering array of storage devices; in particular, a plethora of magnetic disk and tape formats have seen service in the past. If the medium in question is not immediately identifiable some investigation may be required. Examine the item closely for any clues, such as manufacturers' names or product codes. The internet is an invaluable research tool in this regard. Websites such as the Centre for

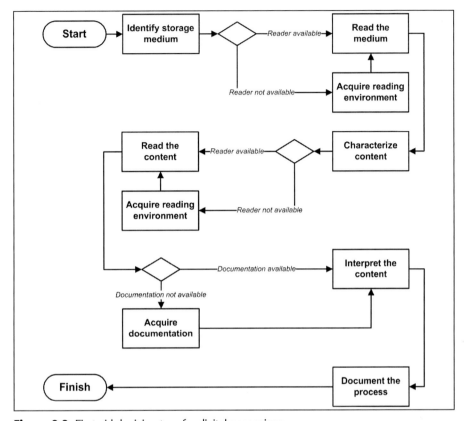

Figure 6.6 First aid decision tree for digital accessions

Computing History,[4] the Computer History Museum,[5] the National Museum of Computing,[6] the Virtual Museum of Computing[7] and Wikipedia[8] can be very helpful, while innumerable specialist sites can easily be found relating to specific storage devices – it is a fair bet that someone somewhere on the web has written about every storage medium ever manufactured. You also need to identify the file system used to format the device, such as NTFS, FAT32 or ext3, using the same methods.

Reading the medium

Having identified the medium and, by extension, the technology required to read it, the next stage is obviously to locate a means to do so. Obsolete drives are frequently available for sale through online auction sites, such as eBay,[9] and reconditioned units may also be sold by specialist suppliers. Such items are usually available very cheaply, although the main costs may actually lie in the time and expertise required to get them up and running in a modern environment.

If it is not possible or desirable to obtain the relevant hardware, it may well be that someone else already has it, and is willing to lend their services. Other digital repositories may well have faced the same problem before, and have the wherewithal to help. It is therefore well worth putting out an appeal through relevant discussion lists, such as the JISCMail Digital Preservation Listserv[10] or Padiforum-l.[11]

If the necessary hardware cannot be sourced, it may be possible to use a commercial data recovery service to read the medium. A number of specialist companies offer highly sophisticated services, which can give very impressive results. Such companies can potentially recover data from damaged or obsolete storage media, and convert data from outdated formats, but this can be an expensive option, and may be unviable for anything other than the most exceptional cases. It would certainly be hard to recommend such an approach unless the value of the data to be recovered is already well established, or at least highly probable, and considered to justify the expenditure.

The final option, which is almost certainly not viable other than for national bodies, and even then only in exceptional circumstances, would be to build a suitable hardware environment from scratch, either replicating the original lost hardware, or providing a modern equivalent.

The relative cost and technical expertise likely to be involved in each option is illustrated in Table 6.1.

Table 6.1	The relative costs and technical knowledge for the different options for reading digital storage media		
		Cost	
		Low	High
Technical knowledge	Low	Other digital repository	Commercial data recovery service
	High	Source hardware	Re-create hardware

Once the medium can be read, its contents can be copied to a modern storage environment.

Identifying the content

If the medium can be read, and the files stored on it physically recovered, then tools such as DROID can be used to determine the formats in which those files are stored. This essential step not only guides the archivist towards the software required to access the files now, but also allows a determination to be made as to the longer-term prospects for preservation; for example, if the files are all identified as being in obsolete formats, this suggests that the preservation process will be complex and potentially expensive.

Reading the content

With firm identification of the content, you next need to ascertain and possibly procure the software required to access it. Format registries such as PRONOM are invaluable here, either for identifying current access tools, or migration pathways for converting obsolete formats to accessible ones.

Identifying the format of a file does not of itself demonstrate that the file is readable; it may have become corrupted, or lack essential external resources, such as installed fonts, which are required to render it. Such issues are only likely to become apparent when you actually attempt to read each file. Again, the web can be an invaluable source in case of problems.

Making sense of the content

Being able to render a file successfully is not the same as being able to understand or interpret its meaning correctly, although it is certainly a prerequisite. For example, a statistical data file might be viewable, but without documentation to describe the interpretation and derivation of each column, it is simply a meaningless set of characters. If the data has already been adequately documented, it may be straightforward to interpret; otherwise, a certain amount of detective work may be necessary.

If available, the depositor should always be the first port of call; failing this, it will be necessary to rely on a combination of any existing documentation, research, common sense and inspired guesswork.

Documenting the content

Having successfully recovered the content into a form capable of preservation, it is essential to document the content and the process used to recover it adequately.

6.12 Case studies

Case study 1 Two UK local authority archives

This case study compares and contrasts the approaches taken to accession and ingest by two local authority archives in the UK – Gloucestershire Archives and West Yorkshire Archive Service.

Gloucestershire Archives is the local government archive service of Gloucestershire County Council, and began a programme of research and development in digital preservation in 2007.[12] In doing so, it faced two significant, but typical constraints: first, its IT support is outsourced, and limited to the standard desktop and office applications; and second, it has no funding for digital preservation activities. Consequently, these have to operate at no cost, or a low cost, on Gloucestershire Archives' standard IT infrastructure, and be accessible to all professional archivists.

The programme set out to develop a digital curation workbench – a set of tools for archivists to support the management of archival digital objects throughout their lifecycle. After initial internally supported development in 2008, it secured funding from CyMAL: Museums, Archives and Libraries, Wales, with support from the National Library of Wales, and the Society of Archivists, in 2009–10 to help further develop the main software tools. The result is SCAT (a recursive acronym for 'SCAT is Curation and Trust'), a suite of tools for creating and managing AIPs. SCAT (Figure 6.7) provides a simple graphical user interface allowing access to a set of custom-developed and third-party tools to support the ingest of digital objects. At the heart of the system is the 'gaip' file, Gloucestershire Archives's implementation of an AIP. This uses the common 'tar' file format, which, like Zip and RAR, allows multiple files to be packaged into a single container. The gaip file contains the data files themselves, separate metadata files describing each data file, and a single manifest file that lists the gaip content, with checksum values for every file. The gaip format allows complex digital objects, such as hierarchies of folders, websites or the contents of a CD, to be stored within the package, and complies with the Library of Congress' BagIt specification (see Chapter 7, 'Describing digital objects'), which is rapidly emerging as a standard for archival ingest packages.

Archivists wishing to ingest new content can access a range of existing curation tools through SCAT, including characterization utilities such as DROID, JHOVE, ExifTool, the NLNZ Metadata Extractor, FITS and the Xena normalization software. The custom-developed GAip utility (the Gloucestershire Archives Ingest Packager) can then be used to package

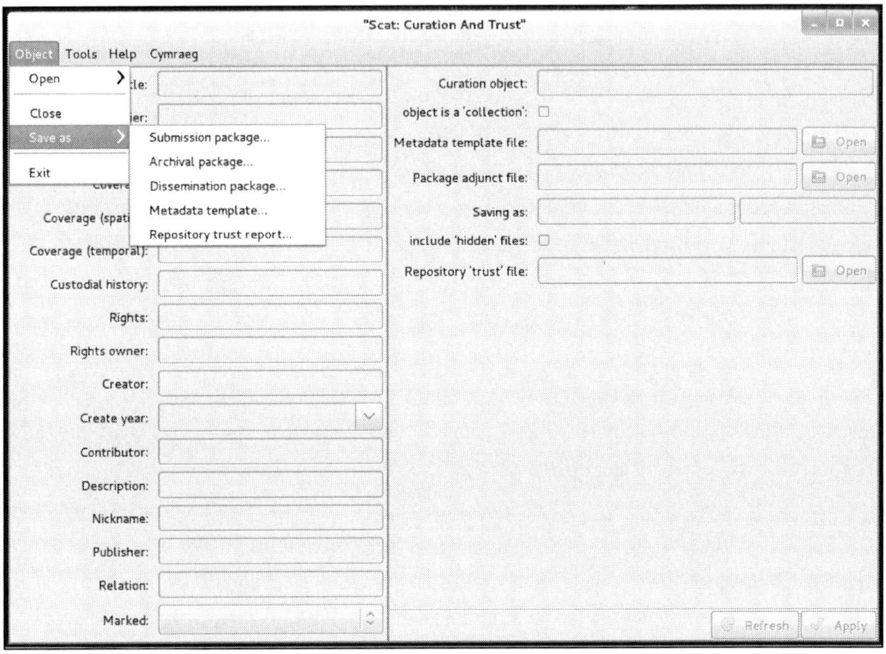

Figure 6.7 SCAT (Viv Cothey and Gloucestershire County Council)

content into a gaip file, and also provides templates for archivists to add additional metadata. SCAT supports arbitrary metadata, so existing standards such as METS and PREMIS (see Chapter 7) can easily be accommodated. The resultant gaip files can then be validated using BagIt, and finally uploaded to an archival storage location. SCAT is technology neutral with regard to storage, which might equally be a local network drive or remote cloud storage. SCAT also supports the SWORD (Simple Web-service Offering Repository Deposit) protocol (see Chapter 7), a web-based standard for depositing content with repositories.

SCAT has been developed to run on the Linux operating system, which may be relatively uncommon within small organizations, but is also available as an Oracle VirtualBox appliance,[13] a virtualization technology which allows it to be run on a wide variety of other operating systems including recent versions of Microsoft Windows.

Although SCAT focuses on ingest, as being the activity of most immediate concern to most archivists, it supports preservation management and access too, including fixity checking, which is an essential element of bitstream preservation (see Chapter 8, 'Preserving digital objects') and metadata harvesting (see Chapter 7, 'Describing digital objects'). It is freely available as open-source software, which is likely to be of interest to many other smaller institutions (see Appendix 3).[14]

Gloucestershire Archives has combined best-of-breed existing tools with targeted in-house software development to support and automate its ingest processes. Although many smaller archives lack the in-house technical resources to undertake software development on this scale, they can nonetheless use the wealth of existing tools, combined with common sense application of established curatorial techniques, to achieve significant results. This is exemplified by the work of another local authority archive in the UK, the West Yorkshire Archive Service (WYAS), which is the joint archive service for the five metropolitan councils in the county.[15]

The winding up in 2009 of MLA Yorkshire, the regional strategic development agency for the museums, libraries and archives sector, offered a timely and apposite testbed for WYAS's developing digital preservation programme: alongside the transfer of paper records, such as management board minutes and annual reports, the opportunity was also taken to investigate MLA Yorkshire's digital records, which comprised the contents of its server, together with its website and a set of e-mail bulletins. This amounted to in excess of 80 GB of data in total, created between 2002 and 2008.

WYAS was fortunate in being able to work closely with MLA Yorkshire staff, and particularly their IT team, during the winding up process, and this facilitated their initial appraisal of material and enabled them to influence the way in which it was prepared for transfer; for example, files held on removable media could be transferred to the central server, ephemeral data such as personal e-mails destroyed, and detailed directory listings prepared.

The physical transfer was performed using a portable hard drive purchased for the purpose. WYAS staff copied the data from the server using a free version of a digital forensics tool (FTK Imager Lite) to create a disk image. This image was then used to re-create the server's structure and content exactly on a standalone workstation at WYAS. This was deliberately isolated from the WYAS network to provide a quarantine facility, with virus checks being performed immediately, and again after a month's delay. High-level information about the whole transfer, such as technical details about the server and desktop environment, was documented manually on standard forms, with detailed technical metadata captured automatically using tools such as DROID. The forensic software was used to create spreadsheets listing every file, with its pathname and a range of technical details, including creation date, file size, and checksum value. The software was also able to identify duplicate items within the transfer.

For the MLA Yorkshire website, WYAS decided to capture a snapshot using the Archive-It web archiving service, while the e-mail bulletins, hosted by a commercial online marketing company, were exported as PDF/A documents. Although this resulted in the loss of some formatting and functionality, it did preserve important contextual metadata, such as when the bulletin was originally sent out, and to how many people.

WYAS was able to negotiate the provision of dedicated network storage space from its IT department, in return for allowing space in a WYAS outstore to be used to host a mirror of the corporate network. This provided benefits on both sides: improved resilience and business continuity for corporate IT, and fully supported, backed-up storage for WYAS.

Case study 2 The Wellcome Library

The Wellcome Library's digital library programme was introduced in a case study in Chapter 4, 'Models for implementing a digital preservation service'. It acquires content from internal and external sources. Internally, the main provider is its ambitious programme to digitize substantial proportions of its analogue collections, but it also collects digitized and born-digital material from external depositors, including the direct commissioning of digitization of collections acquired or catalogued by other UK institutions with support from the Trust's Research Resources in Medical History funding scheme.

At the heart of managing this complex programme of acquisition and ingest lies a major piece of the Wellcome's digital library jigsaw: a workflow tracking system, which manages and tracks the production of digital assets. The 2010 feasibility study described in Chapter 4[16] developed a set of requirements for such a system, and after a procurement exercise in 2011 the Library selected a commercially supported open-source tool called Goobi.[17] The chosen supplier, Intranda GmBH, then extended Goobi to meet the specific needs of the Library. Goobi went into production in March 2012.

Goobi enables staff working on digitization projects, and other forms of digital ingest, to manage these processes from beginning to end. It tracks digitization projects from initiation, through image capture, QA and post-processing, to conversion to a standard archival format (JPEG 2000), metadata capture and enrichment, and ingest into the SDB repository. It can also manage content acquired from external sources, such as other digitization projects or born-digital material. Goobi then generates METS metadata files describing the digital object, which are used by the digital delivery system (see the case study in Chapter 9, 'Providing access to users'). Staff users interact with Goobi via a personalized 'dashboard', which can display the status and progress of tasks, and generate statistics and management reports. Goobi can call other systems from within its workflows, and initiate processes in those systems, such as ingest into SDB and image conversion from TIFF to JPEG2000. The actual image format conversion is accomplished using a specialist tool, LuraWave.[18]

Case study 3 The case of the disappearing dissertation

This case study illustrates a first aid scenario involving the recovery of the author's undergraduate dissertation from obsolete hardware and software, undertaken in 1999.

The dissertation comprised 17 files, created in 1990 on an Amstrad computer of unknown type, using a scientific word-processing package called ChiWriter, which is now long-obsolete, being neither available nor supported since 1996.[19] The data files were all stored on a double-sided, double-density 5.25" floppy disk, also long-obsolete. The challenges faced in recovering the dissertation can therefore be summarized as to:

- extract the data from an obsolete physical storage medium, formatted for an obsolete operating system, onto a contemporary computing platform
- enable the information content of data files in an obsolete file format to be rendered in a contemporary computer environment.

Overcoming each of these obstacles required the use of a variety of preservation strategies, which are discussed in some detail in Chapter 8, 'Preserving digital objects'.

Reading the disk

The first problem was to actually copy the files from the floppy disk, and was dependent on two factors. First, an appropriate disk drive had to be found. Here, I was fortunate that, thanks to a conservative approach to hardware replacement, my then place of work retained a PC with a working 5.25" floppy disk drive. Had this not been the case, I would still have been able to source such a drive without too much difficulty: even in 2012 a quick web search reveals a number of second-hand and refurbished 5.25″ drives for sale through specialist sellers and sites such as eBay. Although installing such a drive in a modern PC requires some technical knowledge, there is guidance available online. This first challenge could therefore be overcome using the *computer museum* approach.

Second, the operating system, and therefore the disk filing system, used to create the disk had to be identified. It was assumed that an Amstrad PC of this vintage would use either MS-DOS or CP/M. In the event, it turned out to be the former, and the files were successfully copied onto the hard drive of a modern PC. However, a number of shareware utilities are also available that allow CP/M disks to be read under DOS.

Reading the data

Having physically recovered the data files onto the hard drive of a modern PC, there remained the challenge of reading the information within them. The preferred target format was Microsoft Word 97 .doc format, the desktop standard at the time. Although contemporary word processors offered facilities to import from a range of older formats, the ChiWriter format was too specialized to be supported, and I could find no means to convert directly from .chi to .doc format. It was therefore necessary to adopt a two-stage strategy: first, convert the data to a format which could be imported by Word, then save it in .doc format. Internet research quickly unearthed a freeware utility for converting ChiWriter files to WordPerfect 5.1 format, and all 17 files were converted in this way. The files were then opened in Word 97 (which could import WordPerfect 5.x format files), and copies saved as .doc files. For this step, I was therefore using a two-stage *migration* strategy.

Having completed the conversion, each file was printed from WordPerfect 5.1 and Word 97, and compared with the original hardcopy in order to assess the success of the migration process at each stage. None of the documents used much complex formatting, other than the use of endnotes, but some did incorporate special characters (specifically Þ, þ, Æ, æ, Ð, and ð). In both file formats the text, including special characters, migrated successfully. The only difference was in the base fonts: in the original documents some form of Courier was used. WordPerfect 5.1 interpreted this as Times New Roman 12 pt, whereas Word 97 converted it back to Courier New 10pt.

A few other differences were noted between versions. The original endnotes were converted to footnotes, which affected the pagination. In some sections, italicization was extended beyond the original words: this was due to incorrect termination of the formatting codes by the conversion utility. Double line spacing was also introduced in some sections of text, but the reason for this is unknown. The centring of text was no longer correct, but this appeared to be a result of leading spaces or tabs being used for centring in the originals. All of these problems were easily correctable, and most would have been obvious even without recourse to the original hardcopy. An attempt to migrate more complex documents, with no prior knowledge, might have presented greater problems. Nevertheless, this experiment demonstrated the relative ease with which an obsolete file format can be recovered. The dissertation had been recovered to a contemporary format, since when it has been a simple task to ensure that it remains in a current format (for example, migrating it to .docx format with the release of Word 2007).

6.13 Key points

- **Adopt a standard accession process**: Using a standard form of SIP and following a consistent accession workflow will make the process faster, simpler and less prone to error.
- **Always observe quarantine procedures**: Allowing malware into a digital repository would be potentially catastrophic – be rigorous in following virus-checking procedures.
- **Automate wherever possible**: There is a wealth of tools available to make ingest more efficient and effective – make full use of them.
- **Document everything**: The decisions you take, and interventions you make, during accession will affect that content for the remainder of its life. It is therefore essential to document your decisions rigorously, for the benefit of future users and curators.
- **Invest in accession and ingest**: Allocate the greatest proportion of your effort to developing and operating a robust, efficient accession and ingest process. This will ensure that your archived content is secure, well described and well managed, and repay you handsomely in terms of its future preservation and management.

6.14 Notes

1   For further examples of ingest procedures, illustrating how little thinking about the fundamental steps has changed over nine years, see Ruusalepp (2003) and

AIMS Work Group (2012).

2 Consultative Committee on Space Data Systems (2012, 1–12).

3 Thomas et al. (2007).

4 See www.computinghistory.org.uk/.

5 See www.computerhistory.org/.

6 See www.tnmoc.org/.

7 See http://museums.wikia.com/wiki/VMoC.

8 See http://en.wikipedia.org/wiki/Computer_data_storage.

9 See www.ebay.co.uk/.

10 See www.jiscmail.ac.uk/lists/digital-preservation.html.

11 See www.nla.gov.au/list-archives/padiforum-l/index.html.

12 See Cothey (2010) for further information.

13 See https://www.virtualbox.org/.

14 See www.gloucestershire.gov.uk/archives/article/103644/Digital-curation.

15 See Eveleigh (2010) for further information.

16 Henshaw, Savage-Jones and Thompson (2010).

17 See www.digiverso.com/en/products/goobi..

18 See https://www.luratech.com/products/imaging-solutions/lurawave-jp2-image-content-server.html.

19 See the ChiWriter FAQ at www.horstmann.com/ChiWriter/ for more information.

7

Describing digital objects

7.1 Introduction

It is impossible to manage any collection without some form of systematic description and documentation of its constituent parts. The catalogue has long been the fundamental tool of curators and information managers, and this remains ever more true in the world of digital collections, which have an even greater reliance on detailed, technical description, or metadata.

Metadata is often described as 'data about data'. While correct, this rather glib definition is not necessarily very helpful. A less succinct but perhaps more informative definition might be:

> The set of information required to enable content to be discovered, managed and used by both human agents and automated systems.

When developing a digital repository, you will need to consider metadata from two viewpoints:

- the *minimum mandatory* metadata that is always required to enable management of repository content
- the range of *allowable* metadata that you may wish to acquire if it is available.

You need to define a metadata standard that addresses both points, and determine how that standard will operate in practice.

Working with metadata is often perceived as a daunting challenge, a view undoubtedly reinforced by the bewildering plethora of standards available. This chapter provides guidance on choosing the metadata you need to support a digital preservation repository, how to acquire it, and how it can be stored and managed. It begins by discussing the role of metadata, and the different types of metadata you need to consider. It then provides an overview of the main metadata standards available, and how to choose among them. Next, it considers the various methods for creating and capturing metadata, and for managing it as part of a digital repository. It ends with three case studies, which exemplify this guidance.

7.2 The role of metadata

Metadata can serve a multitude of purposes. Certain types of metadata are always required, while others may only be necessary in particular scenarios. Broadly, a distinction can be drawn between *descriptive* metadata, which documents the content of the object of interest and supports its intellectual management, and *technical* metadata, which describes its technical characteristics and supports its preservation management.

Descriptive metadata concerns the conceptual information object, whether a publication, archival record or artwork. It tends to follow well established and domain-specific approaches to cataloguing and arranging collections, and these should apply equally in digital and analogue worlds; an archive or library catalogue describes information objects, and should be agnostic about their formats. In reality, the cataloguing standards developed by each curatorial discipline have evolved within a world of traditional formats, and embody certain implicit assumptions which reflect that. Nonetheless, they should be capable of application to digital content. Descriptive metadata may serve a number of purposes, including:

- **resource discovery**: supporting users to identify content of potential interest through techniques such as searching or browsing
- **interpretation**: enabling users to understand and use the content
- **provenance, context and structure**: allowing users to understand how the content was created and previously managed, and how it is arranged and relates to other objects; a good example is records management metadata, which supports recordkeeping by documenting the provenance, context and structure of digital records
- **access and rights**: defining the basis on which users can access and use content, and any restrictions thereon, such as copyright conditions.

Technical metadata may cover:

- **technical properties**: describing the technical characteristics of an object, in support of its preservation and use (see Chapter 8, 'Preserving digital objects').
- **preservation management**: This may include documentation of individual events associated with the preservation process, such as integrity checking or format migration. This metadata must also take into account the issue of dependencies between digital objects. This is of particular importance, given that digital resources are often compound objects composed of many inter-related files. It is essential to understand the nature of these dependencies in order to predict the full impact of a preservation action, which may require a complex set of format conversion processes, emendation processes, and management of the associations between objects. All actions undertaken as part of preservation must therefore be fully documented in the preservation metadata associated with each record, to provide an audit trail.
- **packaging and transmission**: describing the means of organizing and formatting content and metadata for transfer from one environment to another; this applies in all cases where interoperability with other systems is required.

Metadata can also be intended for a wide variety of applications; some is designed for direct human consumption (e.g. much descriptive metadata), other types for purely automated use (such as checksum values, or system identifiers), and some may serve both purposes (for example an access status field, which is meaningful to a human user, but might also be used programmatically to determine whether or not certain content is displayed in a presentation system).

The next section provides a guide to some of the most useful and relevant standards, explaining how to choose and apply them.

7.3 Metadata standards

The plethora of metadata standards in existence can seem overwhelming, the relationships between them confusing, and their applicability unclear. While it is beyond the scope of this book to offer definitive guidance on this subject, it is relevant to consider the most commonly encountered standards, and how they can potentially be applied. A non-exhaustive list of important metadata standards is considered in more detail below. Descriptive metadata is covered first, beginning with generic standards before considering the main discipline-specific schemes. This is followed by a look at technical and packaging metadata standards.

Descriptive standards
Dublin Core

The Dublin Core (DC) Metadata Element Set is the most widely used standard for resource discovery metadata.[1] Named after Dublin, Ohio, where the 1995 workshop was held from which the standard originated, it is maintained by the DC Metadata Initiative (DCMI). The core metadata set comprises 15 elements, each being optional and repeatable, which are designed to be sufficiently generic to apply to describing a wide variety of resources. The full set of elements is sufficiently brief and widespread to be worth listing in full here:

- title
- description
- date
- identifier
- relation

- creator
- publisher
- type
- source
- coverage

- subject
- contributor
- format
- language
- rights.

The DC standard supports two levels of application: 'simple' DC comprises the 15 elements above, while 'qualified' DC incorporates a number of extensions and refinements. Both levels are widely used.

On the basis that one size does not fit all when it comes to metadata, DC allows the specification of 'application profiles', which define a means of tailoring DC metadata to the needs of a specific community. A huge range of application profiles has been developed, for domains as diverse as libraries, government, education and agriculture.

DC metadata is most frequently expressed as HTML or XHTML, XML or RDF, and the DCMI has made recommendations for implementation in each case.[2] The current version is 1.1. DC had been ratified as an international standard (ISO 15836: 2009).

CIDOC Conceptual Reference Model

The CIDOC Conceptual Reference Model (CRM) provides an international standard for the controlled exchange of information describing cultural heritage collections between institutions. It achieves this through an extensible ontology for concepts and information, which allows them to be mapped between the specific descriptive standards used within particular institutions or knowledge domains.[3]

The CRM doesn't define what information cultural institutions should document, or the terminology they should use; rather, it provides a logical framework which explains what they do document, thereby enabling interoperability at a semantic level. It is founded on two forms of information: *classes*, which are categories of item sharing common traits, and *properties*, which express relationships between classes. Examples of CRM classes range from 'person' and 'document' to 'beginning of existence', 'spatial coordinates', and 'transformation'. Properties include 'has timespan', 'is composed of' and 'depicts'.

By providing a framework which embraces the very concrete and the truly abstract, the CRM offers an exceptionally powerful and flexible semantic 'meta-model'; capable of expressing more domain-specific approaches to description, such as ISAD(G) or AACR2 (see below), it also enables concepts to be mapped between them – it acts as a form of universal interpreter between documentation standards.

The CRM is implementation-neutral, but can be readily expressed in machine-interpretable forms, such as XML, RDF and OWL. It has been formally ratified as ISO 21127: 2006.

A recent initiative, FRBRoo, is working to harmonize CRM with FRBR (see below), to 'provide a formal ontology intended to capture and represent the underlying semantics of bibliographic information and to facilitate the integration, mediation, and interchange of bibliographic and museum information'.[4] Version 1.0 of the FRBRoo model was published by IFLA in 2009.

Library descriptive standards
AACR2

Anglo-American Cataloguing Rules, second edition (AACR2), is the predominant library cataloguing standard in North America and the UK, being published jointly by the American Library Association, Canadian Library Association and Chartered Institute of Library and Information Professionals (CILIP).[5] Although itself implementation-neutral, it is most frequently expressed in machine-readable form using one of the MARC formats (see below).[6]

MARC

Machine-Readable Cataloging (MARC) standards are a family of formats for expressing bibliographic information in machine-readable form, based on ISO 2709.[7] They are maintained by the Network Development and MARC Standards Office at the Library of Congress, in co-operation with the Standards, Intellectual Management Office at Library and Archives Canada and the National Bibliographic Service at the British Library, and are probably the most widely adopted means of encoding library catalogue data internationally. The current version is referred to as MARC 21, and includes formats for bibliographic, authority, holdings, community and classification data. MARC data can be encoded in a variety of character encoding schemes, as well as XML (MARCXML).

FRBR

Functional Requirements for Bibliographic Records (FRBR) defines a conceptual data model for describing objects of interest to users of bibliographic data.[8] Because this model embraces both the logical and the physical, in a very flexible manner, it lends itself well to describing digital objects. At the top level, this model comprises four entities:

- **Work**: This is a distinct intellectual or artistic creation. It is an abstract entity, realized in the form of one or more *expressions*.
- **Expression**: This is an intellectual or artistic realization of a *work*, which may take a variety of forms, including text, sound, musical notation, images, objects, physical movements, or a combination thereof.
- **Manifestation**: This is the physical embodiment of an *expression* of a *work*. It is normally associated with a particular medium, such as a printed volume, photographic print or film reel.
- **Item**: This is a single exemplar of a *manifestation*, in other words a concrete, physical instance.

The relationships between these items are illustrated in Figure 7.1.
    The model is perhaps best illustrated through example:

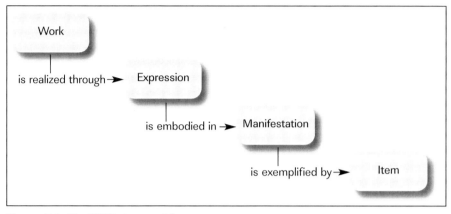

Figure 7.1 The FRBR data model

- **Work 1**: Tchaikovsky's *Swan Lake*
  - ☐ **Expression 1**: the ballet performance, premiere production, Bolshoi Theatre, 1877
  - ☐ **Expression 2**: the ballet performance, Matthew Bourne's production, Sadler's Wells Theatre, 1995
  - ☐ **Expression 3**: the musical work, conducted by Herbert von Karajan, and performed by the Vienna Philharmonic Orchestra, recorded in 1965
    - ▪ **Manifestation 1**: recording released on LP record in 1965, by Decca
    - ▪ **Manifestation 2**: recording rereleased on CD in 1999, by Decca
      - ○ **Item 1**: copy owned by the author.

FRBR then defines a series of attributes to describe each entity, although only at an abstract level. XML schemas have been developed for expressing FRBR data, and mappings to both AACR2 and MARC 21 have also been created.

MODS

The Metadata Object Description Schema (MODS) is a metadata standard for bibliographic descriptions, developed in 2002 by the Library of Congress.[9] It was designed to offer a comparatively simple means of encoding and exchanging the most commonly used elements of the MARC 21 standard, without the overhead of the latter's complexity, while also supporting the creation of new bibliographic records expressed directly in MODS.

MODS includes only key MARC 21 data elements, rather than the complete set, and also contains elements which are not compatible with MARC. Therefore MODS cannot completely represent every MARC record, and there is some loss in translating between the two. For libraries, it offers a descriptive metadata scheme which is richer and more expressive than Dublin Core, but simpler and more user-friendly than MARC.

MODS is used for a variety of purposes, including representing and exchanging simplified MARC records in XML, creating original descriptive records, and as a source for metadata harvesting. MODS XML may also be used to supply descriptive metadata for packaging with digital objects. In particular, it can be used as a means of extending METS (see below). The current version in 2012 was 3.4.

Archives and records management descriptive standards
ISAD(G)

ISAD(G) – the General International Standard Archival Description – is a standard for describing archival collections, developed and maintained by the International Council on Archives.[10] It provides general guidance for archival description, comprising a set of rules and 26 metadata elements, organized into seven categories:

- identity
- context
- content and structure
- conditions of access and use
- allied materials
- notes
- description control.

These metadata elements are combined to define 'units of description' – the archival entities being documented. ISAD(G) supports multi-level description; in accordance with archival practice, units of description can be defined at multiple levels within the hierarchy of an archival *fonds*. It is intended to be used in conjunction with a separate International Council on Archives (ICA) standard for authority records, ISAAR(CPF).[11]

ISAD(G) is designed to be format-neutral, and is therefore applicable to the description of electronic records. Indeed, its hierarchical nature, allied to the archival tradition's natural emphasis on context and provenance, is well suited to the task. Although the ISAD(G) standard does not itself specify any particular means of implementation, it is most commonly expressed in XML, using the Encoded Archival Description standard (see below).

EAD

Encoded Archival Description (EAD) is a standard for encoding archival finding aids in XML. It contains 146 elements and, like ISAD(G), supports multi-level description. The current version (2002) is expressed as both an XML schema and DTD, and documented in a published tag library.[12] EAD is fully compatible with ISAD(G), and is the most widely used means of exchanging ISAD(G) descriptions in machine-readable form. Examples of the application of EAD to cataloguing digital private papers, including e-mails and websites, are provided in Thomas et al. (2007, 175–98).

MoReq2010

Modular Requirements for Records Systems (MoReq2010) was developed by the European Commission as a standard set of requirements for EDRMSs.[13] It is the successor to the original MoReq, which had become a *de facto* standard across Europe and beyond, and to MoReq2.[14] It is intended to be consistent with ISO 15489 and ISO 23081 (see below); indeed, it effectively forms a subset of the latter. While MoReq and MoReq2 adhered to the traditional model of a single, centralized records management system, MoReq2010 also caters for the emergence of more heterogeneous architectures, which encompass 'in place' records management (where records are managed *in situ* within their creating systems), and 'in app' records management (where records management functionality itself devolves to the creating business applications). It specifies a set of core services, which every implementation must comply with, and additional modules which individual suppliers and customers may pick and choose between.

The MoReq2010 metadata set has been reduced to 107 elements (from the previous 345), and the standard includes an XML schema, for interoperability between compliant systems. There is an accompanying testing and certification scheme which as of 2013 was still being trialled, and it is too early to tell how widely it will be adopted by users or vendors.

DoD 5015.02-STD

The US Department of Defence's Electronic Records Management Software Applications Design Criteria Standard, known as DoD 5015.02-STD, defines requirements for electronic records management within the DoD, but has also become more widely accepted as a *de facto* standard within the USA. It defines a substantial set of recordkeeping metadata, but does not specify any encoding standard to facilitate interoperability. Many commercial EDRMS solutions support DoD 5015.02. The third and most recent version was issued in 2007.[15]

ISO 15489, 16175 and 23081

ISO 15489: 2001 is the international standard for records management, and establishes a framework for managing the authenticity of electronic records, through the preservation of the essential characteristics of reliability, usability and integrity. A conceptual framework for creating, managing and using metadata within the context of ISO 15489 is provided by ISO 23081, the international standard for records management metadata, which is in three parts, published between 2006 and 2011. This identifies six categories of metadata, about:

- the record itself
- the business rules or policies and mandates
- agents
- business activities or processes
- records management processes
- the metadata record.

It assesses a number of existing metadata standards, including Dublin Core, ISAD(G), EAD and ISAAR against itself and ISO 15489, and provides guidance on conducting a self-assessment of records metadata in relation to the creation, capture and control of records. It does not define a detailed metadata standard itself.

In 2008 the ICA published a set of principles and functional requirements for records in electronic office environments (ICA-Req), in three parts. Module 1 provides an overview and statement of principles, Module 2 gives a set of guidelines and functional requirements for EDRMS, and Module 3 sets out guidelines and functional requirements for managing records in business systems. It is consistent with ISO 15489, and uses ISO 23081 as a reference metadata standard. It preceded MoReq2010 in addressing alternative models for electronic records management systems, including the concept of 'in place' records management, and it remains to be seen which, if either, standard gains widespread adoption. ICA-Req has been ratified as ISO 16175: 2010.

Museum and gallery descriptive standards
SPECTRUM

SPECTRUM is the UK standard for museum documentation, maintained by the Collections Trust.[16] This effectively defines a metadata standard, comprising units of information arranged into groups. The majority of museum management software is compliant with the SPECTRUM standard. An XML DTD for the exchange of SPECTRUM metadata was developed, although its current status is unclear.

VRA Core

VRA Core is a data standard for describing works of visual culture, maintained by the Visual Resources Association (VRA).[17] It defines a set of metadata elements which can be used to describe three kinds of record: *works*, which are unique artworks; *images*, which are visual surrogates of a work; and *collections*, which are aggregations of works. It supports a range of authority standards used by the visual arts community, including the Thesaurus for Graphic Materials (TGM),[18] Art & Architecture Thesaurus (AAT),[19] Union List of Artist Names (ULAN)[20] and the Thesaurus of Geographic Names (TGN).[21] The latest version, published in 2007, is 4.0. It can be expressed through a set of XML schemas.

CDWA

Categories for the Description of Works of Art (CDWA) was developed by the Art Information Task Force (AITF), with funding from the J. Paul Getty Trust, National Endowment for the Humanities (NEH) and the College Art Association (CAA), and is maintained by the Getty Research Institute.[22] It provides a conceptual framework for describing works of art, architecture and other forms of material culture, and includes more than 500 elements, of which 36 are defined as being core. CDWA is closely aligned to the Cataloging Cultural Objects (CCO) standard (see below), which provides more detailed cataloguing rules for a subset of CDWA information, and also maps to MARC, Dublin Core, EAD and METS. The current version (2.0) was published in 2000, and most recently revised in 2009.

Alongside the full standard, the Getty Research Institute has developed CDWA Lite, a simplified version, which is encoded as XML and designed for harvesting via the OAI-PMH protocol (see later in this chapter). The current version (1.1) was published in 2006.

CCO

Cataloging Cultural Objects (CCO)[23] is a data content standard for the cultural heritage community. Sponsored by the Visual Resources Association Foundation, CCO is intended to promote cataloguing best practices for the museum, image collection, library and archival communities. Its primary focus is art and architecture, including painting, sculpture, prints, manuscripts, photographs, art installations and other visual media, but it can also be applied to many other types of cultural works, such as archaeological sites, and material culture artefacts. CCO does not specify a metadata element set *per se*. Rather, it defines concepts which can be mapped to a number of metadata element sets, including VRA Core, CDWA and CDWA Lite, as well as, by extension, MARC, Dublin Core and others. CCO addresses controlled vocabularies, suggested mandatory information, and rules for formatting and displaying data.

Other museum standards

The Canadian Heritage Information Network (CHIN) has published an excellent guide to museum metadata standards, including specific standards for particular types of collection.[24]

Technical metadata

The picture for technical metadata standards is, fortunately, rather simpler. The PREMIS (Preservation Metadata: Implementation Strategies) Working Group was established in 2003 under the joint sponsorship of OCLC and the RLG, with a remit 'to develop a core set of implementable preservation metadata, broadly applicable across a wide range of digital preservation contexts and supported by guidelines and recommendations for creation, management, and use'.[25] It published the first version of its data dictionary in 2005, and regular revisions have followed, with the current version (2.2) being published in 2012.[26] Maintenance of the standard is now sponsored by the Library of Congress.

Since its publication, PREMIS has gained widespread adoption, becoming the *de facto* international standard for preservation metadata. The importance of this achievement was recognized when the PREMIS standard was awarded the 2005 Digital Preservation Award in the UK, as well as the 2006 Society of American Archivists Preservation Publication Award.

PREMIS builds on, and is consistent with, the OAIS model, although it occasionally differs in its use of terminology. Given its importance, it is worth devoting some space to describing the standard, and its practical use by digital repositories.

The PREMIS data model

The standard defines a set of metadata elements, or 'semantic units'. It is underpinned by a data model, which organizes these units into five entities, illustrated in Figure 7.2.

These entities are defined as follows:

- **intellectual entity**: a logical set of content which is considered as a discrete unit for the purposes of management and description, such as a book, photograph, plan or website. Intellectual entities can be recursive, containing other intellectual entities; thus, an e-mail system might comprise individual e-mail messages, some of which might in turn include attached documents. An intellectual entity is represented by one or more objects

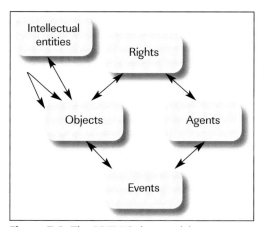

Figure 7.2 The PREMIS data model

- **object (or digital object)**: a technical instantiation of a discrete unit of information in digital form. Objects may either be *files*, *bitstreams* or *representations*:
  - ☐ *file*: a sequence of bytes, which is managed as a discrete unit by a computer file system (essentially the commonly understood IT sense of the word)
  - ☐ *bitstream*: a sequence of data within a file, which it is meaningful to describe separately for preservation purposes, such as an embedded image within a word processed document
  - ☐ *representation*: a set of one or more files that comprise an instantiation of an intellectual entity; for example, a representation of a website might comprise a set of HTML, CSS, PDF and GIF files. The separation between logical and physical entities for preservation is discussed in more detail in Chapter 8, 'Preserving digital objects'
- **event**: an action which relates to one or more objects or agents
- **agent**: a person, organization or system associated with events or rights which apply to an object
- **rights**: rights or permissions which apply to an object or agent.

It is informative to contrast this with the FRBR data model above. Both make a clear distinction between the logical object and its instantiations. FRBR works and expressions can both be viewed as types of PREMIS intellectual entity, while manifestations are essentially equivalent to representations.

The PREMIS Data Dictionary

The PREMIS Data Dictionary defines semantic units which are each associated with one of the entities in the data model. The set of semantic units associated with an entity defines its characteristics. The one exception is the intellectual entity – this is considered out of scope because of the existence of so many well established and domain-specific descriptive metadata standards.

Some semantic units can act as containers for other units, enabling closely related units to be grouped together. Each unit is defined in detail, with definitions and examples of use.

Encoding PREMIS

PREMIS is designed to be implementation-agnostic – the metadata could equally well be stored in a relational database, as XML documents, or by any other means a repository chooses. The standard defines a 'conformance statement' – a set of principles for a conformant implementation of the standard. It is also accompanied by an XML schema to support implementation by repositories.

Further information about the PREMIS standard, including resources to support implementation, is available from the PREMIS Maintenance Activity website.[27]

Type-specific technical metadata

Different types of digital object require varied technical metadata to support their management and use: a digital image has characteristics that differ from a word processed document or a website.

Many repositories therefore adopt the concept of type-specific extensions to their core metadata scheme. In other words, define a core set of metadata which applies to everything, and enhance it as required with metadata specific to a given type of object. PREMIS provides a mechanism for including such type-specific metadata through its <objectCharacteristicsExtension> element. This book cannot hope to offer anything approaching a definitive guide to the range of type-specific metadata standards, but a few examples should illustrate the point.

Still images

The principal metadata standard for describing digital still images is provided by ANSI/NISO Z39.87 – 2006. It provides a comprehensive set of technical and administrative metadata describing the image's characteristics, the means by which it was captured, and any subsequent processing. The Library of Congress and NISO have jointly developed an XML schema for encoding Z39.87 metadata, called MIX (Metadata for Images in XML). The version current in 2012 was 2.0.[28]

Still image metadata may be automatically generated by devices such as digital cameras and scanners, in a variety of formats, including EXIF,[29] IPTC[30] and XMP,[31] but Z39.87 is the standard of choice, and a variety of tools is available for extracting Z39.87 metadata from these other formats.

Moving images and audio

The Material eXchange Format (MXF) is emerging as an industry standard container format for professional audio and video content, and is being developed under the auspices of the Society of Motion Picture and Television Engineers (SMPTE). It includes standards for descriptive and technical metadata.[32]

The Library of Congress has developed two metadata schemas and data dictionaries for audio and video, called AudioMD and VideoMD respectively.[33] These allow for the encoding of technical metadata for these two content types. Both can be expressed as XML, and are commonly implemented as METS extensions (within the administrative metadata section), or within PREMIS. They can also be embedded within other formats, including MXF.

The Broadcast Wave Format (BWF) is an extension of the common WAVE audio format, developed by the European Broadcasting Union in 1997, and widely used as an archival format for audio content.[34] It differs from standard WAVE principally through the inclusion of a new Broadcast Audio Extension, or <bext>, chunk containing a standard set of descriptive and technical metadata. It also permits the inclusion of any valid XML metadata, within an <axml> chunk. BWF can be used on its own, or within an MXF container.

Datasets

The Data Documentation Initiative (DDI) is a metadata standard for describing datasets from the social, behavioural and economic sciences.[35] It is a *de facto* standard, although the DDI Alliance has a stated goal to formalize it as an ISO standard. It can be expressed in XML, for which an XML schema is available.

Metadata container formats

A number of standards have also been developed for packaging metadata (and, in some cases, objects) for transfer between systems, and storage within repositories.

BagIt

BagIt is a file packaging format designed to support the reliable storage and transfer of arbitrary digital content. Originally developed by the Library of Congress and the California Digital Library, and now published as an Internet Engineering Task Force draft,[36] it has been specifically designed to meet the needs of digital curators.

The specification defines a 'bag', which is a container comprising a 'payload' – the digital content – and 'tags' – metadata files documenting the storage and transfer of the bag. The payload can comprise a hierarchical structure of files and directories, and supports cross-platform naming conventions. A bag can also specify its payload as a list of URLs to be fetched across a network at the point of transfer – the ability to fetch multiple URLs in parallel allows large bags to be transferred very quickly. The tag files must include a manifest listing the payload content, together with checksums. BagIt is designed for transfer via physical media, such as removable hard drives, or across networks. BagIt does not specify any particular metadata standard: metadata can be included as part of a payload, in whichever formats suit the requirements of a particular repository.

BagIt is increasingly widely used as an ingest package format (a SIP), a means of transferring content between repositories (a form of DIP), and also as a convenient format for storage within the repository (an AIP). A number of tools have been developed to support the creation, validation and manipulation of bags; some of these are described in more detail in Appendix 3.

MPEG-21

MPEG-21 is a complex and sophisticated container format intended for audiovisual resources but, by virtue of its flexibility, capable of being applied to a wider range of object types.[37] Developed by the Motion Picture Experts Group, it is published as a set of ISO standards: ISO/IEC 21000 Parts 1–19.

MPEG-21 provides a wrapper for digital objects (usually some form of multimedia content) and a wide array of associated metadata. Objects can be complex, comprising multiple files; metadata can incorporate other standards, such as Dublin Core or METS, and the format allows specific metadata components to be related to particular parts of the digital object, such as a discrete segment of a video file. MPEG-21 also provides a sophisticated framework for describing how users can interact with digital content. This allows content to be tailored according to a user's technological capabilities, such as streaming it at a speed to suit the bandwidth of a particular user's internet connection. MPEG-21 also defines a machine-readable Rights Expression Language (REL).

Although currently used primarily in the audiovisual domain, there appears no reason why MPEG-21 could not be adopted as a generic container format, or to hold preservation-specific metadata.

METS

The Metadata Encoding and Transmission Standard (METS) is a metadata standard developed and maintained by the Library of Congress for encoding descriptive, administrative and structural metadata.[38] It is very flexible, and has become one of the most widely adopted generic metadata schemes, often being used by digital repositories to fulfil the role of an OAIS SIP, AIP or DIP.

METS is expressed as an XML document, with a standard structure comprising the following sections:

- **METS header**: contains basic information about the METS document itself
- **descriptive metadata**: can follow any appropriate standard, and may be embedded or linked to an external source
- **administrative metadata**: includes information on IPR, provenance, transformations and editorial relationships between digital objects
- **file section**: lists the digital files which make up the digital object; for digital objects that can be decomposed into smaller units, it is possible to group files accordingly
- **structural map**: defines the structure of the digital object, and links elements of that structure to associated content files and metadata
- **structural links**: enables a METS file to record links between elements of the structural map, which may be useful, for example, when describing archived web content
- **behavioural**: enables actions to be associated with content; every such action or 'behaviour' must be related to some form of executable code which implements it.

The METS file can either include embedded descriptive and administrative metadata, or link to such metadata stored externally. It can also include multiple instances of both kinds of metadata.

METS allows the development of 'profiles', describing how the standard can be applied in practice to a particular class of digital object, or by a particular community. Examples of current METS profiles include:

- print material
- musical scores and manuscripts
- audiovisual material
- bibliographic records
- photographs
- physical digital artefacts such as CDs.

Examples of using METS as a packaging format for digital private papers are provided in Thomas et al. (2007, 117–41).

Repository eXchange Package

Cornell University Library, New York University Library and the Florida Center for Library Automation have developed a Repository eXchange Package (RXP) format for exchanging AIPs between repositories, based on METS, PREMIS and BagIt.[39]

Web Archive Format

The Web Archive (WARC) format is a container format for packaging digital objects collected through web archiving. Based on the Internet Archive's ARC format, it is developed and maintained by the International Internet Preservation Consortium, and has recently been published as an international standard: ISO 28500: 2009. It is the most widely used format for storing and exchanging archived web content.[40]

7.4 Deciding on metadata standards

You will need to determine the metadata standards to apply to your digital repository. These must define the range of metadata which is acceptable, and the minimum metadata required. In making these decisions, you should always start from existing standards, and from the familiar.

The well established traditions for describing and documenting collections, such as AACR2 for libraries or ISAD(G) for archives, should form the starting point for thinking about metadata for digital objects.[41] In particular, they should prove sufficient for meeting descriptive metadata requirements, and indeed there is a growing body of experience in employing them for describing digital material. This requires some careful thought; for example, concepts such as 'format' or 'medium', which are inseparable from the logical object for traditional collections, apply only to the technical representation of a digital object, not its logical source. When using traditional descriptive standards for digital resources, it therefore becomes vital to ensure that the focus of description is the logical object, not a technical representation thereof.

Technical metadata will certainly be required, for which PREMIS provides a *de facto* standard. Consideration should be given to extending this with type-specific metadata, as required. For example, a repository with substantial image collections might well wish to use ANSI/NISO Z39.87 alongside PREMIS.

Most organizations wish to define a standard information package for their repository, which may be dictated by the choice of repository, but may well use an open packaging format such as METS or BagIt.

In thinking about metadata requirements, it is essential to bear constantly in mind the implicit costs and benefits. All metadata has to come from somewhere, whether automatically captured or extracted, or manually created, and the process of acquisition always has a cost attached. That cost needs to be recognized, and weighed against the perceived benefit of storing the metadata. Acquisitiveness is a common inclination among curators, and easily and naturally extends to metadata; there is a widespread tendency to keep metadata simply 'because it's there'. Indeed, it may be difficult to determine the future value of some metadata, which can argue for its retention, but the equation of cost versus value needs to be considered in each case, and the presumption to keep should always be questioned.

Precedence should be given to metadata that could not be derived at some future point. For example, it will be possible to extract technical metadata embedded within a digital object for as long into the future as the tools exist to do so, and the object remains in its current format – therefore, why extract it now, unless a specific use for it has been identified today? On the other hand, metadata stored in an obsolete system which is about to be decommissioned, will only be available within a small window of opportunity, and hence should be acquired at the earliest opportunity.

Furthermore, not all metadata needs to be stored in an easily manipulated form. Managing metadata in a highly structured form, such as a relational database, makes it simple to analyse and manipulate in myriad ways, but the costs of doing so include the overheads of maintaining the database system, and of processing the metadata into relational form. This is only necessary where there is a clear need to analyse and manipulate that metadata. A similar case applies to indexing metadata for searching – it should be self-evident that this should only be contemplated for metadata that requires fast searching.

Finally, metadata choices must be pragmatic: there is no point defining a minimum standard that is completely unrealistic to achieve. This is especially pertinent in situations where the repository has little control over data creation, and may be acquiring content from many diverse sources. For example, a regional archive may receive many one-off deposits from local groups and businesses, often with little or no forewarning; pragmatically, such cases are more about dealing with the material as is, with no real opportunity to influence its creation. Depositors may also be unwilling or unable to provide detailed technical documentation. The reason for specifying a minimum metadata specification is to ensure that content is always accompanied by sufficient information to enable its management and use, but specifying an onerous metadata requirement is likely to be counterproductive, and will generally result either in it being ignored, or in desired content not being acquired. The golden rule should therefore be:

> Be expansive in what metadata you allow, but parsimonious in what you require.

To summarize, in choosing metadata the following questions should be considered for each potential metadata element, or scheme:

- Do you need this metadata at all? If so, for what purpose? Does the benefit outweigh the cost?
- Can it be extracted automatically, or will it require manual creation?
- Could you derive it in future, if you don't do so today?
- If you do need to keep it, how do you expect to use it? Do you just need to be able to view it, do other systems need to be able to use it programmatically, do you need to be able to manipulate or search it?
- Is the minimum standard realistic and achievable?

A generic minimum metadata standard should include:

- **Descriptive metadata** documenting each information object. This should conform to existing local cataloguing standards.
- **Technical metadata** describing each data object. As an absolute minimum, for each file you should record:
  - □ name, including any extension
  - □ size, in bytes
  - □ format; this should be as specific as possible, and might take the form of a PRONOM PID, or a MIME type
  - □ last modified date
  - □ checksum value and type.

You also need to record any directory structure within which the files are stored. This can be done by recording the full pathname of each file. All this file level metadata can be easily and automatically generated using freely available characterization tools.

If at all possible, you should also collect additional technical metadata about the collection as a whole, such as the software used to create or manage it, and any available documentation.

Finally, your technical metadata needs to include structural metadata, describing the relationships between the data and information objects.

7.5 Sources of metadata

Having determined the range of metadata required, the next question to consider is how this metadata will be acquired. All metadata required for long-term preservation must either be created manually or generated automatically. The latter is clearly much preferred, provided it is of sufficient quality. Possible sources for acquiring metadata include:

- **The original authoring or management system**: The systems that were previously used to create or manage the content can be rich sources of metadata, e.g. content management systems, EDRMSs or casework management systems.
- **The object itself**: Digital objects can contain a variety of embedded metadata, placed there by the authoring application or human intervention. The extent and nature of this tends to vary between types of content and individual file formats.
- **An existing descriptive record**, such as in a catalogue.

- **Other documentation**: This might include system documentation, manuals, data dictionaries etc., and could be in paper form. In the latter case, it may be possible to extract metadata using scanning followed by optical character recognition (OCR) to generate a machine-processable version of the text.
- **Oral history**: Depositors, original users or end-users may all be invaluable sources of information about digital records, which has never been formally documented. In many cases, there will be a narrow window of opportunity to glean such information.

Metadata can either be explicitly extracted from a source as literal values, or derived through some form of calculation or logical inference. For example, a PDF document does not explicitly store a value representing the number of pages but, since each page is stored within the file as a separate 'content stream', a page count can be calculated by totalling the number of page content streams within the document. Likewise, the covering dates of a compound object might be calculated by identifying the earliest and most recent creation dates of the constituent files.

There is a range of tools and techniques available for automatically generating metadata from digital objects. These vary in sophistication from the extraction of literal metadata values from the object to deriving new metadata through analysis and interpretation of the content. Metadata extraction tools are discussed in more detail in Chapter 6, 'Accessioning and ingesting digital objects', and Appendix 3.

However sophisticated a battery of automatic metadata generation tools is deployed, it is likely that at least some metadata will need to be created manually. The key is to limit this to a minimum, and at least to a level that is supportable given the staff available for this task. Manual creation should only ever prove necessary for descriptive metadata – technical metadata should always be generated automatically; pragmatically, technical metadata that cannot be derived automatically will simply never be created.

In most scenarios it will prove difficult to avoid some manual creation at the highest levels of description; for example, it is hard to envisage automated creation of the detailed administrative and biographical histories which archivists create at fonds level. Nonetheless, lower levels of description should often be automatable from sources such as those described above.

7.6 Storing and managing metadata

Having identified metadata of interest, the next major decision to make is how to store and manage that metadata. Fundamentally, metadata is very simple to store: every piece of metadata consists of a value, which may be a string of text, a number, or any other meaningful information, with some form of label associated with it which defines what that value signifies. The value and its label together form a metadata *element*. There may be some kind of additional structure, for example to group related elements together. Metadata elements may be expressed in a number of ways, such as *name–value pairs* (e.g. <format> = <TIFF>), or *subject–object–predicate triples* (e.g. <file> <is of format> <TIFF>), but they are all equivalent.

There are many ways in which metadata elements can be encoded: as some form of text file, in a database, in an RDF triple store etc. For descriptive metadata, most repositories use existing collections management systems, or specialized descriptive tools such as ICA-AtoM,[42] ArchiveSpace[43] or Archivists' Toolkit.[44] Their principal concern is how to integrate these with their digital repository systems, and how to manage the additional technical metadata required to support them. The next section considers the main scenarios possible.

Embedded metadata

Metadata can be embedded within the digital objects which it describes. Many authoring applications insert metadata into the files they create as a matter of course; examples include the EXIF metadata that most digital cameras add into image files, recording everything from the date and time on which the photograph was taken to the shutter speed used, and the document properties stored in a Microsoft Word document. The extent to which objects can store embedded metadata is determined by the limitations of the format; most can store a predetermined range of metadata, although a few, such as PDF, use extensible metadata schemes to allow arbitrary metadata to be recorded. This approach has a number of other major limitations:

- It only allows metadata to be associated with individual digital files – this is fine for technical metadata relating to the file, but less satisfactory for metadata associated with the logical digital object, such as descriptive metadata, and provides no solution for metadata describing compound objects which may include many files.

- It is also unlikely that the full range of metadata required for preservation will be capable of being embedded; conversely, there is also a risk of storing superfluous information – not all the embedded metadata may be worth preserving.
- The embedded metadata is vulnerable to loss as a result of preservation actions such as format migration – such metadata is normally lost during the conversion process, and there is unlikely to be a comprehensive mapping between the metadata supported by the formats before and after migration.

Embedded metadata alone is therefore insufficient, and essential metadata required by the digital repository may need to be extracted. Certainly, any metadata of value must be extracted before a file is migrated to a new format, but it may be useful to retain existing embedded metadata, especially if it is not explicitly required in a more useful form.

External metadata

Metadata is usually stored externally to the objects it describes. Separating the means of representing metadata from the limitations of the file format of the object being described provides a much more flexible range of options. It also makes it easier to manage and maintain the metadata independently of any changes to the object. Finally, it allows the expression of metadata which relates to something other than a single digital file. A number of options are possible:

- **Store as an independent object**: This might take the form of a text file, spreadsheet, or XML document.
- **Store in a container format**: Metadata can be stored as a file within a larger package, typically also containing the digital objects themselves. This might be a generic type of container, such as a Zip file, or a purpose-designed one, such as provided by the BagIt format.
- **Store in a managed system**: Metadata can also be stored separately, within some kind of managed environment, such as a relational database system or XML repository. Nowadays, technologies such as the semantic web are frequently being used to manage metadata in more flexible, less rigidly defined ways.

Fundamentally the choice lies between whether to separate the metadata from the means of analysing and manipulating it, or to keep it together. The latter may offer better performance and a wider range of functionality, but at the cost of complexity and, in some cases, opacity. Some repositories choose to keep content and metadata together in a serialized form in the storage environment, on the basis that this insulates it from catastrophic failure of the repository software. Such an approach allows the repository software to be designed for availability, while the storage infrastructure is designed for resilience – requirements which can be in conflict. On the other hand, this must be weighed against the likelihood of such a failure, and the overhead of storing metadata twice, or in a less flexible form.

The most important requirements are that:

- the repository is capable of managing all required metadata
- it is possible to export all required metadata from the repository in a reusable format.

Given these assurances, the constraints of the repository platform can be allowed to dictate the choice of solution.

The maturity model introduced in Chapter 4, 'Models for implementing a digital preservation service', provides a perspective on the different levels of metadata management which you may consider, from a basic capability in which metadata is stored in a variety of different formats and places, depending on how it is produced, and managed primarily using text documents and spreadsheets, to very sophisticated systems that manage metadata holistically, and in very structured ways. Table 7.1 provides some example maturity levels.

Table 7.1 Metadata management maturity levels

3 Basic process	• documented minimum metadata requirement exists • consistent approach to organization of data and metadata implemented • metadata stored in a variety of forms using spreadsheets, text files or simple databases • capability exists to maintain persistent links between data and metadata • persistent unique identifiers assigned and maintained for all digital objects
4 Managed process	• metadata managed in a consistent form using spreadsheets, text files or simple databases
5 Optimized process	• metadata managed in complex, reusable forms, such as XML, Linked Open Data, or sophisticated databases

The CAMS database described in the case study on English Heritage in Chapter 4 might be considered an example of a Level 4 managed process, while the approaches described in the three case studies later in this chapter are perhaps closer to Level 5 optimized processes.

7.7 Associating metadata and data

The other fundamental requirement of metadata management is to maintain a link between the metadata and the data it describes; if this link were to be broken, it would render data and metadata meaningless. The association needs to be maintained in both directions; in other words, it must be possible to locate the appropriate metadata from the object, and the object from the metadata. In principle, this association can be achieved in one of two ways:

- **Physically joining data and metadata**: This requires data and metadata to be physically stored in close association. This might entail maintaining both within a consistent directory structure, or packaging both into some form of container, such as a Zip file, or an XML document containing the actual objects in serialized form. For an atomic digital object, it might also be accomplished by embedding the metadata within the object.
- **Creating a persistent link between the two**: This is usually achieved by assigning persistent identifiers to the objects, in accordance with some well documented scheme, and recording those identifiers within the associated metadata.

The latter approach is more flexible, but relies on the persistence of the identifier, as well as it being possible to match that identifier to the entirety of the relevant metadata record. A persistent identifier is simply another piece of metadata – usually a sequence of alphanumeric characters – which is uniquely assigned to a specific object, and by virtue of being generated in accordance with a scheme that is not specific to any particular repository technology can continue to be used as that technology changes. Examples include local catalogue references, or international schemes such as ISBNs or Digital Object Identifiers (DOIs). Persistent identifiers are considered in more detail in Chapter 9, 'Providing access to users'.

7.8 Interoperability

For as long as metadata is required only within a single repository system, it can reasonably be managed by any means which meets the requirements of that system. However, it is often necessary to exchange or move metadata between systems. This might be required when migrating a repository from one technology platform to another, or when sharing or exchanging digital objects with another organization. Interoperability is therefore something that every repository needs to consider: even if no exchange of content is foreseen, it will certainly greatly facilitate the sustainability of the repository system itself.

Interoperability requires only that the source and target repositories be able to export and import metadata respectively in a common format, or have some means to transform it between their respective local formats. There are a number of mechanisms that can facilitate such exchange, some of which are discussed below.

OAI-PMH

The Open Archives Initiative Protocol for Metadata Harvesting (OAI-PMH) is a web-based mechanism that allows digital repositories to share metadata.[45] It enables repositories to act as *data providers*, exposing structured metadata, which *service providers* can then harvest. A great virtue of OAI-PMH, which doubtless lies behind its widespread adoption, is that it uses the standard web communication protocol (HTTP) and comprises only six commands, or 'verbs', to perform actions such as requesting a list of available metadata, or an individual metadata record. OAI-PMH not only allows one repository to acquire metadata from another, it also provides a simple mechanism for harvesting and aggregating metadata from multiple sources. It also has a very low barrier to entry: it is comparatively simple to become either a data provider or a service provider, with many open-source tools available. OAI-PMH is also widely supported among digital repository platforms. It requires the data provider to expose simple Dublin Core metadata, but it also supports arbitrary additional metadata. Thus, for example, many repositories share MARC or EAD metadata via OAI-PMH.

OAI-ORE

The Open Archives Initiative Object Reuse and Exchange (OAI-ORE) standard provides a mechanism for describing and exchanging aggregations of web resources.[46] We often need to be able to describe aggregated web content, but existing web technologies offer no standard way of doing so. For example, we use the URL of a website's home page to cite the entire website. In another common scenario, a web page may contain a description of a document, with links to the actual document in several formats, such as PDF and HTML. OAI-ORE defines a protocol for describing such *aggregations* (conceptual entities composed of a set of web resources) and *resource maps* (machine-readable representations of aggregations, which describe their structure and constituent parts). These resource maps can be expressed in a variety of formats, including Atom XML and RDF XML. Any digital repository that makes its content available via the web is actually working with aggregations of web content. OAI-ORE therefore provides a mechanism whereby repositories can exchange digital objects, and complements the metadata exchange capabilities provided by OAI-PMH.[47]

SWORD

The Simple Web-service Offering Repository Deposit (SWORD) protocol is a standard for remotely depositing content with digital repositories, developed in 2007 with JISC funding.[48] It enables SWORD clients to deposit data with SWORD-enabled repositories. Many of the common repository platforms, including DSpace, EPrints and Fedora, now support the SWORD protocol.

7.9 Case studies

Case study 1 Defining metadata standards at the UK Parliamentary Archives

It is always easier to think about metadata standards using real-world examples. The Parliamentary Archives therefore began by identifying the types of information object that would be ingested into the digital repository from the outset, then collected actual examples of these objects and used them as a basis for defining and assessing metadata requirements. The types identified were:

- surrogates of analogue records created by digitization programmes, comprising image files in various formats
- snapshots of the parliamentary web estate captured as ARC files

- electronic records (primarily word processed documents, spreadsheets and e-mails) exported from Parliament's Electronic Records Management System (SPIRE)
- *ad hoc* digital objects, typified by a set of CAD drawings of the Palace of Westminster.

The Archives also used a combination of existing standards and pragmatic assessments of the metadata that would realistically either be already available, or could be created, as a starting point for defining standards.

The Parliamentary Archives had an existing cataloguing standard, based on ISAD(G), which offered a solid basis for defining descriptive metadata requirements for digital records. Workshops involving cataloguing staff were used to brainstorm how the example record types might be described using ISAD(G). These looked at how the catalogue record would be structured, in terms of archival levels of description, which metadata elements would be mandatory, optional or not relevant at each level, and how each element would be used.

For example, for archived websites it was proposed that a sub-fonds record be created for the web archive as a whole, with series records for each website, and file level records for each dated snapshot thereof (see Figure 7.3). Decisions about the particular usage of elements such as 'extent' in this context were also debated.

After testing and refining the approach against each record type, it was realized that the Archives' descriptive metadata requirements could entirely be accommodated within an ISAD(G) approach, and managed using the existing catalogue management system (CALM) – all that was required was to update the cataloguing standard to reflect the agreed usage for digital records.

The second, and in reality most involved, step was to identify the source for populating each metadata element, in the case of each record type. For example, the EDRMS export provided a very substantial XML metadata file, which could be mapped to the mandatory and desirable catalogue metadata elements. In some cases, such as a document title, this was a simple mapping; in others, such as creator name, a degree of data processing was required, to look up a system identifier and replace it with the equivalent person's name; in others still, some form of calculation was required, such as translating a closure period, expressed in years, into an opening date, expressed as a calendar date.

For other record types, such as digitized images, the principal metadata

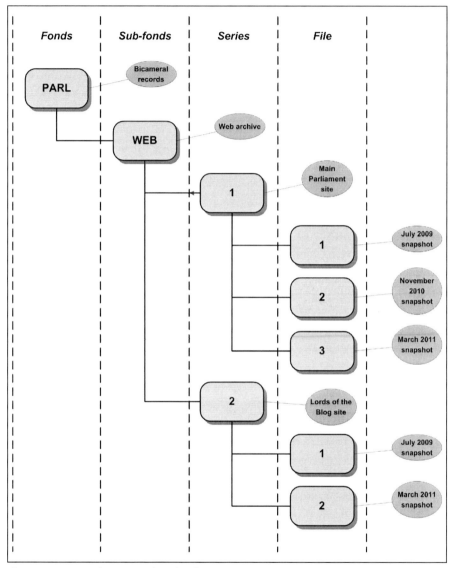

Figure 7.3 Describing an archived website

sources were the technical metadata embedded in the image files by the digital cameras and, for descriptive metadata, the catalogue record for the original document. A folder structure and file naming convention was devised, which allowed the repository to automatically associate each image file with the relevant catalogue record, and also to extract additional metadata about the composition of the document. Each image file is stored in a folder structure, which reflects the hierarchical catalogue structure of the original records being digitized, while the file names incorporate both a 'component name' – which describes the nature of the document, and can be used to distinguish between the component parts of a multi-document record – and also a sequence number for multi-page documents. Both pieces of information are automatically extracted as metadata, and used by the access system when displaying the document.

It has been found that the extent of manual descriptive metadata creation required varies according to the type of content: for digitized images, that metadata already exists; for EDRMS records, it is necessary to manually create the relevant series level record, if required, but the repository is then able to automatically create the file and item level records in CALM without human input; for archived websites and *ad hoc* content, the archivist must manually create the catalogue record in advance of ingest, although there is scope to automate elements of this in future.

For technical metadata, a decision was taken at an early stage in the requirements-gathering process to follow PREMIS. The repository system selected (SDB) was therefore chosen for being compatible with, and capable of importing and exporting, PREMIS metadata. As this was an existing feature of the software, no further consideration of technical metadata standards was required, other than to test compliance.

It was also recognized that some record types might be accompanied by metadata above and beyond that required by the standards. For example, the EDRMS export generated a wide range of recordkeeping and system metadata not explicitly required for descriptive, technical or administrative purposes. In some cases, such as internal system identifiers which had no wider meaning, it was decided that the metadata was genuinely extraneous, and therefore would not be preserved in the repository. In others, it was considered that the metadata might be of interest to future researchers, and that the small overhead of retaining it was justified by its potential future value. Rather than seek to explicitly accommodate it within the metadata scheme, provision was instead made for the retention of arbitrary metadata 'chunks' – the repository would do no more with them than to store them and make their content available via the repository search engine, and the only prerequisite was that they must be in XML format, and conform to a defined XML schema.

The packaging format for SIPs was determined by the choice of repository:

SDB uses a proprietary XML format (XIP) for metadata. This points to, rather than physically contains, the digital objects, and provides for the inclusion of arbitrary metadata in accordance with any schema.

The ultimate proof of success for the Parliamentary Archives' metadata scheme will not become apparent for some years, and the decisions taken today can only be validated by a substantial period of real-world operation, by the Archives staff and end-users. Undoubtedly, some of those decisions will need to be refined and revisited over time, but the early signs are optimistic: the level of manual metadata creation required is minimal and achievable, and the system is able to obtain all metadata necessary for current management and access purposes.

Case study 2 Defining metadata standards for the LSE Digital Library

The LSE Digital Library has already been described in some detail in a case study in Chapter 4, 'Models for implementing a digital preservation service', but it is instructive to consider the flexible approach to metadata which it has developed in more detail here. The Library has defined a preservation object model in which each digital object has a common set of the core metadata, with format specific extensions. For each object, metadata is required at both the logical and physical (or manifestation) level. The logical object metadata comprises:

- **identifier metadata**, including the internal repository Persistent Unique Identifier (PID) and any applicable external identifiers, such as catalogue references or ISBNs
- **descriptive metadata**, using Dublin Core and MODS
- **relationship metadata**, using the Fedora-specific RELS-EXT RDF scheme.

The physical object metadata comprises:

- **preservation metadata and rights metadata**, both using the PREMIS standard
- **technical metadata**, which is format specific.

The Library has defined three types of manifestation:

- **Preservation master**: This is mandatory, and may be a normalized or enhanced version of the object as deposited.
- **Original**: This comprises the object as submitted for ingest, and is optional, except where authenticity and provenance are critical. Thus it will always be retained for born-digital archives, but may be discarded for digitization projects.
- **Access**: This is also optional, and is regarded as disposable, having been generated from the preservation master.

The metadata is stored in the repository in RDF and XML format, conceptually but not physically packaged with the actual bitstreams. It was a fundamental requirement that all data and metadata should be stored in serialized form, rather than within databases; this gives independence from the repository software and would, for example, allow it to be accessed in the event of a catastrophic software failure.

Like the Parliamentary Archives, the LSE Library has used existing standards, such as PREMIS, and has worked with the metadata functionality of its chosen repository technology. This example also illustrates the importance of defining a coherent and consistent model for organizing that metadata, which distinguishes between the logical and physical object (this is considered in more detail in the next chapter).

Case study 3 Implementing metadata at the Wellcome Library

The Wellcome Library's digital library has also been described in previous case studies (see Chapter 4, 'Models for implementing a digital preservation service', and Chapter 6, 'Accessioning and ingesting digital objects'). It uses METS as a metadata container. The METS files are generated by the Goobi workflow tracking system, and aggregate a range of metadata, including selected descriptive metadata from the catalogues, administrative metadata exported from SDB, and metadata describing access permissions. The Library catalogue (Sierra) remains the authoritative source for descriptive metadata, but the METS files provide a convenient means for packaging and sharing that metadata between systems. The Library uses the standard METS profile developed by the Library of Congress. Descriptive metadata is stored according to the MODS schema, while technical image metadata uses the MIX standard. For digitized material which has been OCRed, the Library also uses an extension of METS, called METS-ALTO, which records the structure and position of the extracted text within a digitized image.

7.10 Key points

- **Build on domain-specific cataloguing approaches**: For descriptive metadata, use the existing approach relevant to your particular domain.
- **Follow existing metadata standards**: Don't reinvent the wheel – there are existing standards for almost every eventuality.
- **Define a realistic minimum metadata standard**: Ensure that this will provide vital metadata, but not act as a barrier to deposit.
- **Think carefully about what metadata you need, and why you need it**: Don't just acquire it because it exists; consider first whether you can see a practical need today, or expect it to have value in the future.
- **Identify how to acquire it in practice**: If there is no practical means to acquire a particular piece of metadata, there is no point specifying it as a requirement. Identify a realistic method for creating or acquiring every metadata element, and use this to sanity-check your metadata requirements.
- **Don't do more with your metadata than you need**: Don't invest in making all your metadata searchable, or extracting it into complex relational databases, unless you have specific reason for doing so.
- **Think about interoperability**: As a minimum, ensure that metadata can be exported from the repository in a reusable format.

7.11 Notes

1 See http://dublincore.org/.
2 See Section 2 of http://dublincore.org/documents/usageguide/.
3 See www.cidoc-crm.org/.
4 See www.cidoc-crm.org/frbr_inro.html and www.cidoc-crm.org/frbr_drafts.html.
5 Joint Steering Committee for Revision of AACR (2005).
6 See www.aacr2.org/.
7 See www.loc.gov/marc/.
8 IFLA Study Group on the Functional Requirements for Bibliographic Records (2009).
9 See www.loc.gov/standards/mods/.
10 International Council on Archives (2000).
11 International Council on Archives (2004).

12 See www.loc.gov/ead/.

13 DLM Forum Foundation (2011).

14 European Commission (2008).

15 See http://jitc.fhu.disa.mil/cgi/rma/standards.aspx.

16 Collections Trust (2009).

17 See www.loc.gov/standards/vracore/.

18 See www.loc.gov/pictures/collection/tgm/.

19 See www.getty.edu/research/tools/vocabularies/aat/index.html.

20 See www.getty.edu/research/tools/vocabularies/ulan/index.html.

21 See www.getty.edu/research/tools/vocabularies/tgn/index.html.

22 See www.getty.edu/research/publications/electronic_publications/cdwa/index.html.

23 See http://cco.vrafoundation.org/index.php/.

24 See the CHIN Guide to Museum Standards at www.pro.rcip-chin.gc.ca/normes-standards/guide_normes_musees-museum_standards_guide/metadonnees-metadata-eng.jsp.

25 PREMIS Editorial Committee (2012, 1).

26 Ibid.

27 See www.loc.gov/standards/premis/.

28 See www.loc.gov/standards/mix/.

29 See www.cipa.jp/english/hyoujunka/kikaku/pdf/DC-008-2010_E.pdf.

30 See www.iptc.org/IPTC4XMP/.

31 See www.adobe.com/products/xmp/.

32 See www.pro-mpeg.org/pages/main.php?page=0002.

33 See www.loc.gov/standards/amdvmd/.

34 See https://tech.ebu.ch/docs/tech/tech3285.pdf.

35 DDI Alliance (2009).

36 Boyko et al. (2012).

37 See www.multimedia-metadata.info/.

38 See www.loc.gov/standards/mets/.

39 See http://wiki.fcla.edu:8000/TIPR/1.

40 See http://archive-access.sourceforge.net/warc/WARC_ISO_28500_final_draft%20v018%20Zentveld%20080618.doc.

41 See, for example, AIMS Work Group (2012, 29–41) for a discussion of applying archival approaches to describing digital records.

42 See https://www.ica-atom.org/.

43 See www.archivesspace.org/.

44 See http://archiviststoolkit.org/.

45 See www.openarchives.org/pmh/.

46 See www.openarchives.org/ore/.

47 For an example of object exchange between Fedora and EPrints repositories, see Tarrant et al. (2009).

48 See http://swordapp.org/.

8

Preserving digital objects

8.1 Introduction

This chapter addresses the very heart of digital preservation – the strategies and techniques required to ensure that digital information remains accessible and usable over the long term. It is a complex issue, which remains the subject of wide-ranging international research, and this chapter focuses on practical, cost-effective approaches suitable for smaller organizations.

It begins by examining the goals of preservation, and the nature of digital information, before considering the main threats which it seeks to overcome. It then summarizes the key concepts and approaches, before a detailed consideration of preservation techniques and their practical application.

8.2 The goals of preservation

Before considering the process of digital preservation in detail, it is worth taking a moment to reconsider the fundamental objective of preservation, in the physical or digital world. This can be very simply stated as follows:

> To maintain the object of preservation for as long as required, in a form which is authentic, and accessible to users.

It is for the object's custodian to determine how far into the future that requirement extends; in many cases it will be in perpetuity. Similarly, they are the final arbiter of what constitutes an authentic and accessible form. Authenticity and accessibility must be determined with reference to the constraints of the object's creators, and the needs of its current and future users.

The concept of authenticity must be the informing principle behind any approach to preservation. Authenticity is the assurance that a thing is what it purports to be: if we are unable to demonstrate this for the digital objects in our care then our preservation activities are, frankly, entirely worthless. While different disciplines may require proof of authenticity with varying degrees of rigour – such as the demands of legal admissibility or scientific discovery – all require supporting evidence. This must be accumulated and managed through time, alongside the objects to which it attests, to provide confidence that those objects remain as amenable to investigation, analysis and interpretation as on the day they were created.

While the concept of authenticity described in this book is firmly rooted in archival approaches, it is equally applicable to the preservation of every kind of digital object, and every curatorial tradition.

The authenticity of a digital object derives from three essential characteristics:[1]

- **Reliability**: The object must be a full and accurate representation of the cultural or business activity to which it attests. This requires the establishment of trust in the curatorial processes used to manage the object throughout its lifecycle, and the continued ability to place the object within its original context. Within a repository, reliability is ensured through the operation of transparent and fully documented preservation strategies, and the provision of the metadata required to describe the content, context and provenance of the object.
- **Integrity**: The object must be protected against unauthorized or accidental alteration. In the repository, integrity is ensured through the process of bitstream preservation (see later in this chapter), and the provision of metadata to describe all authorized actions undertaken in the course of preservation.
- **Usability**: The object must be capable of being accessed by authorized users, across time and changing technical environments. This requires that it is locatable and retrievable by users, capable of representation in a current technical environment, and that it supports interpretation by users. Usability is ensured through the logical preservation function (see later in this chapter), and the provision of metadata sufficient to allow the record to be located, retrieved and interpreted.

We have many centuries of experience in the preservation of material artefacts, be they paintings, printed books, sculptures or parchment manuscripts. So why is digital preservation so often seen as being fundamentally more challenging than traditional preservation? The answer lies in the nature of digital information. If we put a book on a shelf, or a paper file in a box, and store it in even fairly rudimentary conditions without any further conservation, we can be pretty confident that in 50 years time it will remain usable. Store a CD or portable hard drive on a shelf for 50 years, and the story will be very different: even if the data survives intact, the technology required to read the storage medium will be long gone. Digital data requires continuous, active intervention to preserve it. It is therefore necessary to begin by considering the nature of digital objects, and how this shapes our approaches to digital preservation.

8.3 The nature of digital information

The nature of a physical artefact is indivisible from its material properties. It would be nonsensical to think of the Domesday Book or Michelangelo's 'David' purely in the abstract – their artistic, historical and cultural properties are ineluctably bound to a unique physical entity. The message and the medium are inextricable. In the digital realm, on the other hand, precisely the opposite is true.

The separation of message and medium

When we talk about a digital object, what do we really mean? In a physical sense, it is a sequence of binary digits (or bits) – 1s and 0s – encoded onto a storage medium such as a hard disk or a DVD. But that *bitstream* is not inherently human-readable, and indeed has no intrinsic meaning: information can only be extracted from it through the correct interpretation of that bitstream in accordance with some pre-existing knowledge. Thus, a digital image in TIFF format can only be rendered as an image using software that has been designed to interpret the bitstream in accordance with the TIFF format specification. The OAIS standard formalizes this distinction: the bitstream is a *data object*, while its realization as meaningful information is termed an *information object*.

The process of turning a data object into an information object is fairly complex, requiring the mediation of many layers of technology. First, some combination of hardware (such as a hard disk drive or DVD drive) and software is needed to gain physical access to the bitstream. Further software is then required to interpret that bitstream; that software will itself require a particular operating system, hardware platform and possibly other software in order to run. The information object may not rely purely on technology either – for example, documentation or even tacit knowledge may be required before a user can successfully understand it. OAIS refers to the various information and technology layers required to interpret a data object as *representation information*; understanding the representation information required to support information objects is therefore a fundamental digital preservation activity.[2]

The OAIS standard corresponds closely with a model developed by the National Archives of Australia, wherein a performance (information object) is produced through the interpretation of a source (data object) by a process (representation information).[3] This is usually explained through the analogy of a moving image film reel. The source data object is encoded as a series of photographic images on a filmstrip, wound around a reel, but the object cannot be accessed directly in this form – it needs to be run through a film projector first. What we actually experience is the resultant moving image as projected onto a screen. This 'performance' of the film therefore requires both the source object (the film reel) and the appropriate rendering technology (a film projector). In the same way, a digital performance requires the combination of data object (the bitstream) and the correct combination of representation information. It is this information object, or performance, which we must preserve – we can change the sources and processes used to render it, provided that the essential performance can be replicated over time.

The separation of message (information object) from medium (data object) (see Figure 8.1) gives rise to a second unique property of digital information: it is possible for the same information object to be represented by more than one data object. Imagine a digital photograph, created using a digital camera, and stored in TIFF format. For access purposes, a second version of that image is produced by converting it to JPEG format. The image, and hence the underlying conceptual information object, remains unchanged, but the format of its technical representation has changed. To put it another way, the 1s and 0s by which the two images are encoded are utterly different, but the array of coloured pixels on a computer screen which those 1s and 0s represent remains unchanged. Thus, the TIFF and JPEG versions of the image are different data objects, both of which can be used to generate the same information object. These alternative data objects are referred to as *manifestations* or representations of the same information object. The concept of manifestations is discussed in more detail later in this chapter.

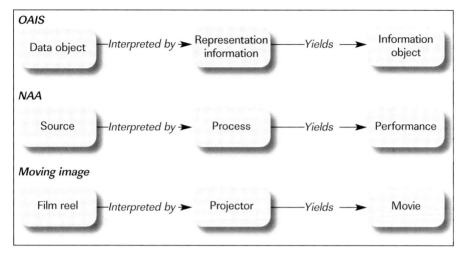

Figure 8.1 Separating medium and message

Preservation actions, which rely on some form of transformation, inevitably lose some of the properties of the original, but this is not necessarily an issue. First, we can have our cake and eat it, retaining the original with all of its evidential potential, alongside a transformed and more accessible alternative. Second, the properties we lose may be ephemeral, and not required to preserve the performance.

Significant properties of digital objects

The fundamental object of preservation is the information object: data objects and their representation networks are simply the building blocks that allow a given information object to be realized at any point in time. It is therefore essential to understand the properties of an object which relate to its informational nature – its conceptual form as an information object. These are frequently referred to as 'significant properties'. Although the term was first coined by the Cedars project in 2002,[4] the underlying concept had previously been developing in several quarters: Clifford Lynch discussed the notion of digital data having a 'canonical form' in 1999,[5] while the National Archives of Australia was developing perhaps the most fully realized description of the idea of 'essence' of a digital record in its previously described performance model.

The concept is intended to highlight that the properties of the information object, which should endure through technology change, and hence between different technological manifestations of an object, are more fundamental and of greater lasting importance than the technical properties of a data object; the latter may have great short-term value in determining how we approach preservation at a given point in time, but are transitory.

This can be illustrated by returning to the example of a digital image. Most digital images are made up of a two dimensional array of pixels, where each pixel can vary in colour. This is a fundamental property of an image, just as the concept of linear marks on a differently coloured background is a fundamental property of handwritten text. Every possible representation of a given image, in any file format, will share that property. Such properties are therefore 'significant' in the context of digital preservation, being intrinsic to the underlying information object. Extrinsic properties, on the other hand, pertain only to a particular physical manifestation of that format. Thus, the width and height of an image counted in pixels, and the colour of each pixel, are all significant properties of the image; the file size, which will vary by format, is not.

Indeed, one can define the act of preservation as being concerned purely with preserving the significant properties – the quintessence – of an object. The continued survival of these properties is fundamental to its authenticity. Unfortunately, and unsurprisingly, significant properties are also much harder to define and measure than technical properties. Some commentators have cited these difficulties to cast doubt on the practical value of thinking about significant properties. While the complexities of this task should certainly not be underestimated, they should by no means provide a reason to avoid them: without a rigorous, scientific means of defining the objectives of digital preservation, we cannot test, compare, or demonstrate the efficacy of any preservation technique. Put simply, significant properties provide a means to define what success look like for digital archivists.

They therefore continue to be the subject of much continuing research and debate, with projects such as InSPECT[6] and Planets[7] substantially advancing our understanding of how to model significant properties for many different kinds of digital information. On a very practical level, the 2012 study 'Rendering Matters' by Archives New Zealand examined how well different preservation strategies maintained the significant properties of a variety of office documents.[8] In the context of practical digital preservation techniques, it is useful to be aware of the concept, and some practical tools to support digital archivists in applying these ideas are now emerging, most notably validation tools such as DIFFER and the Planets XCDL validator, and repository platforms such as SDB (see Appendix 3). Nonetheless, much remains to be done to enable the theory to be put into widespread practice.

Originality in the digital world

Digital information also requires us to rethink our notions of originality. Consider the example of an analogue record, such as a handwritten paper manuscript, where the message and the medium are inextricably linked in a single and unique physical artefact – the 'original'. While one can make copies of this artefact, of varying levels of fidelity, they can never be equivalent to the original. The reason for this is that no copy of a physical artefact can replicate all the qualities – the significant properties – of the original. True, there are many ways to copy the gross visual properties of the manuscript – scanning, photocopying, photography – but any copy produced by such methods loses much of the original's evidential value. A significant part of this evidential value is potential value – the ability to answer future questions, perhaps using techniques we cannot yet envisage. One might wish to examine the physical and chemical properties of the paper: is it wood pulp or rag, wove or laid? How acidic is it? Does it have watermarks? One might analyse the ink – iron gall or carbon? Even the relative pressure applied in different parts of the pen stroke might be apparent to close investigation. Yet none of these questions can be answered using a copy.

And this is only considering the evidential value; even if we were to envisage a *Star Trek*-style replicator, capable of manufacturing copies of physical objects accurate down to the sub-atomic level, many people would instinctively and fundamentally resist the notion that such copies could replace the original. This reaction arises from our attitudes to concepts such as cultural value, and the connection that an artefact has through time with all those who come into contact with it.

Digital objects are different – we do have a *Star Trek* replicator for them, which we use every day without conscious thought. Each time we copy a digital file, e-mail it to someone, or back it up, we are spawning new copies which are literally indistinguishable from the original. Indeed the very notion of an original requires redefinition. No longer can we apply it to a physical artefact; rather, we must think only of versions or manifestations as having the quality of originality. Thus, while there is no value in distinguishing between the originality of multiple copies of the same image bitstream – one on the camera's memory card, one on the hard drive of the PC it was first downloaded to, another on a server it was copied to – it is meaningful to distinguish between the RAW format version of the image, as originally produced by the camera, compared with TIFF, JPEG or PNG manifestations created subsequently.

This is a wonderful advantage of digital objects: their longevity is no longer tied to the uncertain survival of a single artefact, in one location. Now, we can broadcast sow identical copies far and wide, effectively rendering them physically immortal. Furthermore, there are simple and efficient techniques (checksums) to confirm whether or not these copies are precisely identical. However, while the innate reproducibility of digital data offers an obvious preservation advantage over the analogue world, the mechanisms of digital decay are conversely much more aggressive.

Digital decay

Physical objects tend to decay gradually, and in that process their information content is slowly eroded, being lost by degrees. It is rare, except in the case of catastrophic disasters such as fire, for physical artefacts to be completely destroyed in a single moment. On the other hand, instantaneous and complete loss is the norm for digital data. Its decay profile is generally 'binary', having only two possible states: 'readable' and 'unreadable'. Although the physical medium on which the data is stored may decay gradually, there will typically be a single point along that graph of physical degradation at which the information content will flip from being completely readable to utterly lost.

There are exceptions: for example, data recovery experts may be able to retrieve some intact data from a damaged hard disk, while an image file that is repeatedly compressed will remain viewable, but visibly degraded in quality. Also, just as in the material world, loss can occur through alteration: in the same way that a painting can be damaged by vandalism, or a document through a careless reader spilling ink, so digital objects can be falsified or edited to remove information. However, whereas approaches to physical preservation tend to therefore focus on minimizing the factors that cause decay where possible, and repairing or retarding the effects of that decay when it does occur, for digital preservation, the emphasis must be almost entirely on prevention: heroic digital archaeology can only be regarded as the last resort, if it is even possible.

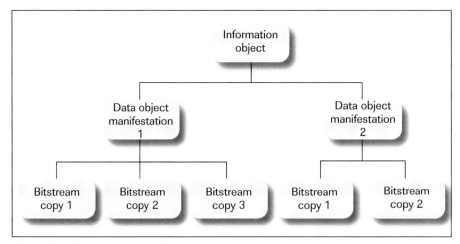

Figure 8.2 The digital object hierarchy

The objectives of digital preservation

To summarize then, digital objects differ fundamentally in nature to their physical counterparts. While material artefacts are atomic, corporeal entities, their digital equivalents inhabit a number of distinct levels of existence, as illustrated in Figure 8.2.

Each conceptual information object can be manifested through one or more different data objects, which can in turn exist in multiple identical copies. Digital information objects are unique in that:

- The message (information object) is separate from the medium (data object).
- The information object can only be derived from the data object using the appropriate representation information, such as hardware and software.
- The information object can exist in multiple manifestations of data objects.
- Manifestations can exist in multiple physical copies.
- Originality resides in the information object and its manifestations, not the physical copies.
- Digital decay tends to be sudden and catastrophic.

Bearing in mind these unique properties of digital information, and the demands of authenticity, we can restate the objectives of digital preservation more precisely:

- to maintain the usability of the information object, by ensuring that we always have some combination of data object and representation network which can be accessed using available technologies and knowledge
- to maintain the integrity of each data object, by ensuring that it is protected from alteration or loss
- to maintain the reliability of the information object, through appropriate documentation and curatorial processes.

8.4 The challenge: threats to preservation

Digital objects are fragile: our ability to access them – to render them into meaningful information – is under constant threat from many directions. The risks range from the physical to the conceptual, the trivial to the profound. This section discusses the main challenges, as a precursor to considering possible mitigations. Fundamentally, there are two threats to preserving authentic, accessible digital information over time:

- **Loss of the data object**: Physical loss of the 1s and 0s that encode that information. By definition, we must always have at least one fully intact physical copy of the bitstream available.
- **Loss of the information object**: Losing the means to correctly interpret those 1s and 0s as meaningful, authentic information. This will occur if one or more elements of the representation network required by the underlying data objects cease to be available.

These two threats can arise as a result of a whole host of more specific risks. There are many ways of categorizing them,[9] but it may be most helpful to consider how they threaten the authenticity of the object.

Generic threats

There are two overarching threats, which can affect more than one aspect of authenticity:

- **Technology obsolescence**: Information technology is a rapidly advancing field, with new and improved technologies regularly being developed. As new products are brought to market, existing products cease to be supported. The currency of a given technology is typically very short –

perhaps five to ten years. Obsolete products become increasingly difficult to obtain, and may cease to interoperate correctly with other technologies. Obsolescence applies to hardware and software. A principal challenge of digital preservation therefore lies in maintaining the means of access to digital objects in the face of rapid technological obsolescence. This risk can apply to the integrity and usability of information, and is discussed in both contexts below.

- **Inadequate skills and resources:** Digital preservation remains a new and developing discipline, requiring skills from a wide range of curatorial and technical backgrounds, and sufficient resources. If data creators or repository staff lack the necessary skills and resources, this may lead to reduced efficiency, poor decision making, mistakes, and information loss.

It is also important to note that threats may not manifest in isolation – they can combine to create chain reactions, which may be much more difficult to predict, prevent or recover from.

Threats to reliability

The reliability of a digital object is dependent on external information about it, and is therefore at risk from loss or damage to that information. The context and provenance of digital information may be recorded in metadata or other forms of digital or physical documentation. We can consider such documentation as an information object in its own right; thus, its reliability may itself be asserted recursively through further documentation, while its integrity and usability will be subject to the same set of risks as described below.

Reliability also arises from the trust which users place in the repository itself (as discussed in Chapter 4, 'Models for implementing a digital preservation service'). The factors that engender and maintain trust are elusive, and trust can be considered an emergent property of the technologies, processes, standards and organizational characteristics of the repository. If, for whatever reason, that trust begins to fail, it will have an impact on the perceived reliability of digital objects it manages. While loss of trust may arise from operational failures within the repository, it is also susceptible to risks arising from how its parent organization works. Organizations may change their missions, reducing or removing altogether the organizational will to conduct digital preservation activities. In a worst case scenario, organizations may cease to exist at all, whether through financial failure or some other circumstance, in which case their archival collections will be at severe risk of loss unless some form of succession plan is in place.

Threats to integrity

The principal threats to the integrity of a data object include:

- **Accident**: Digital data can easily be changed or deleted unintentionally, through human error.
- **Malicious activity**: People may attempt to alter data for malicious reasons. This might be targeted, such as an unauthorized intruder into a system, or incidental, for example as a result of a widespread virus infection.
- **Media decay**: Storage media are subject to physical decay, and may naturally degrade to the point at which the data is no longer recoverable. For example, chemical reactions within the media may cause it to become unusable, such as 'sticky shed syndrome' in magnetic tape.
- **Media damage**: A specific event may cause sufficient damage to the medium to prevent data recovery. Examples might include exposure of a magnetic disk to a strong magnetic field, or mechanical damage, such as scratching a DVD.
- **Bit rot**: This is a form of accidental damage to stored data, arising from a variety of causes, including natural phenomena such as cosmic rays striking the medium and causing alteration. Bit rot is manifested through one or more bits within a stored bitstream being changed – either 'flipped', so that a '0' becomes a '1' or vice versa, or losing their value altogether, for example through demagnetization. The impact of bit rot can be severe – the change of even a single bit may cause the entire bitstream to be rendered unintelligible.
- **Media loss**: Total loss of the storage medium may come as a result of major damage. This might include a range of disaster scenarios, such as fire, flood or earthquake.
- **Hardware failure**: Other forms of hardware – such as servers, drives and network components – are also susceptible to failure. At best this may cause a temporary interruption or degradation of operational capability; at worst it may cause temporary or permanent data loss. For example,

terminal failure of the last operational example of a particular form of tape drive may prevent any future recovery of data stored on tapes that rely on that drive. Failures may also arise because the technical infrastructure is insufficient to meet the requirements of the repository.

- **Network and service failure**: The networks we use to communicate – whether internal networks or the internet – are a key source of risk. They may introduce errors during the transmission of data, or suffer failures. External network services we rely on, such as format registries or resolution services, may suffer temporary outages or vanish completely.
- **Software failure**: Software is subject to accidental and deliberate errors arising from human fallibility or malicious intent – bugs and viruses may cause data loss.
- **Replication failure**: Systems to generate multiple copies of the data object, whether conventional back-ups or LOCKSS-style networks, may fail. Equally, they may propagate errors originating in one copy to the replicas.
- **Technology obsolescence**: If the storage medium or the technology required to access it becomes obsolete, it may cease to be possible to read the content. The inevitability of this process makes it one of the greatest threats to integrity over the longer term.
- **Lack of audit**: Failure to keep a complete audit trail documenting significant events in the management of the digital object can compromise its integrity, by laying it open to question.
- **Disasters**: The natural world can pose risks of varying magnitudes; these may range from major disasters, such a fire, flood or earthquake, to more minor events which may still have significant consequences, such as rodent damage to cabling. Events of manmade origin, such as war or terrorist attack, can have similar impacts. In most cases, these factors pose a threat to the fundamental physical infrastructure on which digital preservation systems depend, including data centres, office buildings, and communication and power networks. They may threaten the continued operation of the systems required to manage digital repositories or, most significantly, the systems on which repository content is stored.

Threats to usability

Usability is primarily at risk from:

- **Technology obsolescence**: If the hardware and software platforms required to interpret data objects as information become obsolete, this may render the object unusable. Format obsolescence has long been cited as one of the principal threats to preservation. While this has certainly been true in the past, there is some doubt as to how major a concern it is today. Commentators such as David Rosenthal argue that the availability of multiple open-source implementations of renderers for most modern formats makes format obsolescence unlikely in the foreseeable future.[10] Nonetheless, it undoubtedly remains an issue for extant older formats and special cases, and will remain a challenge over sufficiently long timescales. Furthermore, while obsolescence itself may be a declining problem, changing user expectations remain a constant challenge: most repositories migrate files today not because they are obsolete, but because their users wish to consume them in alternative formats.
- **Loss of representation information**: Aside from the technology components, other forms of representation information required to access a data object may be lost. For example, if the data dictionary for a dataset is lost, it may prove impossible to interpret the rows and columns, even though the necessary rendering software remains available.
- **Cultural obsolescence**: In the longer term, cultural changes will inevitably threaten usability. In the same way that medieval languages and manuscript hands are inaccessible to many modern users, so the languages and writing systems of today will, in time, become archaic. Even over much shorter timescales, subtle shifts in fashion, idiom and cultural reference can impede our ability to interpret information correctly. This is not just a theoretical concern: the designers of nuclear waste facilities, in considering how to propagate knowledge of the hazards across millennia, have had to apply great care – and a not inconsiderable degree of lateral thinking – to the communication methods and iconography they choose. Thus, for example, the 1984 Human Interference Task Force proposed everything from the development of an 'atomic priesthood' to the breeding of cats that would change skin colour on exposure to radiation.[11]

Legal issues for preservation

Most legal considerations for digital repositories relate to accession and access, and these are considered in Chapters 5 and 9 respectively, but they can have some impact on preservation itself, most notably with regard to the rights required by the repository to perform preservation actions on digital objects.

These will certainly include the creation of bit-perfect copies of the objects, but may also require them to be transformed in some way, for example by migration to a new format. Copyright laws are typically formulated with traditional forms of content and notions of originality in mind. As discussed earlier in this chapter, these concepts are essentially obsolete for works which are 'born-digital', and the application of copyright legislation in such cases can therefore be ambiguous.

Copyright law often provides dispensations for memory institutions to carry out certain activities for the purposes of preservation. For example, in the UK, the Copyright, Designs and Patents Act 1988, as amended by the Copyright (Librarians and Archivists) (Copying of Copyright Material) Regulations 1989, makes provision for prescribed libraries and archives to make copies of material for preservation purposes. However, while this may well cover the needs of bitstream preservation, it seems likely that procedures such as migration would be considered to be an adaptation, for which no exception is available.

Digital objects may also be protected by rights protection mechanisms – technologies designed to prevent unauthorized copying or use – which are discussed in detail in Chapter 9, 'Providing access to users'. These mechanisms are proprietary, and tend to change very rapidly as part of the technological arms race against piracy. They are therefore very likely to become obsolete over time, and preservation may require the circumvention of such mechanisms in order to maintain access to the content. This would be an infringement of copyright under the World International Property Organization's 1996 Copyright Treaty, and its subsequent enactment in national legislation. While it may be hoped that future changes to copyright law will address these problems, for the time being, at least, it remains an area of ambiguity. A very detailed examination of the implications of IPR legislation for digital preservation is provided by Charlesworth (2012) which, while focused on UK law, is likely to be of wider interest.

Understanding risk

It is one thing to identify potential threats, but quite another to understand the probability that they will affect your collection, the likely impact if they do, and the imminence of the risk. It is easy to fall into the trap of making assumptions about threats, without real evidence to back this up. Such evidence is now starting to be gathered, as in a 2012 study by the British Library, which analysed a corpus of more than 2.5 billion archived web resources, in order to examine the changing usage of digital formats over time, and the extent to which format obsolescence could be detected in reality.[12] Similarly, the previously mentioned 'Rendering Matters' report undertook a systematic analysis of the quantifiable impact of different preservation strategies on digital objects.[13]

A rigorous approach to preservation planning is therefore vital. Tools and techniques for this are discussed as part of logical preservation, later in this chapter.

8.5 Preservation strategies

The potential strategies for mitigating these risks can best be explained with reference to the performance model introduced earlier in this chapter. Logically, any performance can be preserved in one of three ways:

- Maintain the original source object (e.g. the film reel or data object) and process (e.g. the projector or representation network). The digital equivalent of this approach is the 'computer museum'.
- Transform the source object to a new form capable of being rendered by a contemporary process. Thus, if film projectors are replaced by DVD players and LCD projectors as the preferred technology, we could convert the film to DVD, and still maintain the original performance. For digital objects, this strategy is known as 'migration'.
- Develop a new process capable of rendering the original source object. In this case, we might build a new kind of projector, capable of projecting obsolete film reels. When applied to digital objects, this is referred to as 'emulation'.

These strategies have been described in detail in many sources,[14] but are summarized in the following sections.

Computer museums

Maintaining both the data object and the original environment required to access it has the obvious advantage of preserving the object in a form closest to its original usage; the equally obvious disadvantage is that there is no practical way to preserve operational technology over long time periods. The spare parts and technical skills required to keep the hardware physically running, together with the software on it, will rapidly become almost impossible to source. Thus, while this may be viable as an interim approach, it cannot be used as a long-term strategy.

There is, however, a quite separate and vital need for computer museums to preserve the history of information technology itself. A number have emerged, of varying scales, from the UK's National Museum of Computing at Bletchley Park[15] to the American Computer Museum in Montana.[16] There are also a number of online museums, such as the Virtual Museum of Computing[17] and the Living Computer Museum.[18] Such museums can be invaluable sources of obsolete hardware and software, as well as expertise – this can be especially vital in supporting the development of emulators, or when digital archaeology or first aid is required.

Migration

The second option is to transform the original object to a form that is no longer reliant on obsolete technology, but can instead be accessed using whatever is standard at the time. The third case study in Chapter 6, 'Accessioning and ingesting digital objects', illustrates the use of migration to convert documents created with an obsolete word processor into a format accessible using modern office software. Migration requires the use of software tools capable of transforming data objects from one file format to another. While the theory appears simple, and many such tools are available, there are a number of practical challenges.

Any process of transformation admits the potential for information loss which, in the case of migration, can arise from two main sources:

- The target format may not support the full range of significant properties required to preserve the performance of the original. For example, converting a Word document to plain text will lose much of the formatting.
- The migration process may not be capable of transforming all the properties of the original. As an example, the MS Word 97 filter for converting WordStar documents did not correctly interpret how

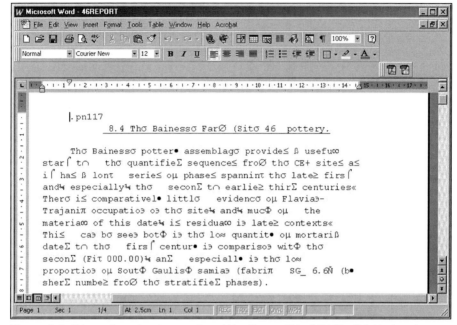

Figure 8.3 Errors after migrating text from WordStar to Word 97 (English Heritage)

WordStar used the 8th bit of each ASCII character, resulting in the insertion of incorrect typographical characters, as illustrated in the screenshot in Figure 8.3.

This means that it is critical to choose appropriate formats to migrate to – which must not only offer a significant improvement in usability, but also be capable of retaining the significant properties of the source format – and suitable migration tools. The combination of source format, migration process and target format is commonly known as a *migration pathway*. Direct migration between the source and target format may not always be possible, and hence a pathway may entail multiple migration processes through intermediate formats. The validation of migration pathways, to ensure that they give the requisite quality of conversion, can be very labour-intensive and complex. It requires the test migration of representative sample files, and comparison of the result with the original. While this comparison can be automated in some cases, for many types of migration pathway a visual inspection remains the only option. Cochrane (2012) illustrates some of the approaches and complexities involved in testing and validating strategies such as migration.

File to file migration (e.g. converting a GIF image to PNG) is only the simplest case; as we shall see later in this chapter, preservation actions may need to be applied to complex objects, made up of many files, and may involve not only format migration, but also associated emendation of other files. This is explored in more detail in the discussion of multiple manifestations later in this chapter.

Three forms of migration are most frequently discussed: normalization, migration on obsolescence, and migration on access:

- **Normalization**, which is sometimes known as migration on ingest, aims to minimize the number of formats to be preserved in the repository, by proactively migrating to a small number of preferred formats from the outset. This approach invests resources up-front, with the intention of minimizing the complexity of future preservation, but it incurs the risk of nugatory effort.
- **Migration on obsolescence**, conversely, leaves migration until the last possible moment, on the basis that this is the point at which effort is justified, and allows economies of scale through mass migration. It also potentially benefits from more sophisticated future migration techniques. On the other hand, it can result in a more complex collection to manage, and runs the risk that migration may, in fact, be left too late.
- **Migration on access** takes a middle way, by investing effort only when an object is actually required to be accessed. Once migrated, the repository may choose to retain the new manifestation to avoid the inefficiency of repeated migration. This is, potentially, a very efficient strategy, and one that most easily allows migration to be tailored to current user needs. On the other hand, usage does not equate to value, and by linking migration to the former, it runs the risk that low-use content may be lost because there is no extant migration pathway by the time it is accessed. Migration on access would therefore need to operate in tandem with a migration on obsolescence strategy in reserve.

The timing of preservation strategies is discussed further in 'Deciding when to execute preservation actions' in Chapter 8.

There are a wide variety of migration tools available, for many different formats (Appendix 3 provides some examples), and new tools are relatively easy to develop. Migration is also very amenable to automation, and batch migration of very large collections is eminently possible. It also has the benefit of always providing access in formats with which contemporary users are familiar. On the other hand, migration can be especially prone to information loss, and it can be difficult to quality assure the results with a high degree of confidence. Migration is also unsuited to the preservation of software, or other digital objects which display complex behaviours.

Because of the issues, any repository practicing migration must always retain the original manifestation of the data object, alongside any migrated manifestations; this ensures that alternative future preservation strategies will always remain viable.

Emulation

The final option is to maintain the object in its original form, and instead develop ways to access it within the current technology environment. Typically, this involves the use of emulators – software that recreates the functionality of an obsolete technology environment on a modern platform. Emulation can be carried out at several levels: you can emulate a specific piece of software, the operating system required to run the software, or the hardware platform required to support the software and operating system. As an example, in the Chapter 6 case study, rather than migrate the data object from ChiWriter format to a modern one, an emulator of the original Amstrad PC platform would have allowed a copy of the ChiWriter software to be run, and the documents to be viewed in their original form.

The most widespread use of emulation to date has been in the preservation of games, and very early computer systems. Games that ran on obsolete arcade systems, consoles or home computers are being made accessible once again, through the creation of emulation software for those specific environments. Thus, for example, the BeebEm software emulates the long-defunct BBC Microcomputer on a range of modern operating systems, including various versions of Microsoft Windows, Linux and Apple OS X, and therefore allows any software written for the BBC micro to be run on these platforms.[19] Similarly, emulators have been developed for a huge range of historic computer systems, through initiatives such as the Computer History Simulation Project.[20]

Emulators can be extremely complex and expensive to create, and may necessitate access to original hardware and software to develop and use.

They also require the user to have detailed knowledge of how to operate obsolete technologies – this may not be a problem with computer games, but is likely to become a huge obstacle for future users of emulated operating systems or productivity software – how many users in 2013 would know the variety of keystroke combinations required to perform basic tasks in WordStar, for example? Emulators are also susceptible to the same dangers of information loss as migration, as a result of errors in the fidelity of their emulation, and must therefore be subjected to equally rigorous testing and validation; however, unlike migration, these losses do not affect the underlying data object.

Nonetheless, emulation is potentially of huge interest as a preservation strategy. Where emulators do exist, they can be used to provide access to unlimited numbers of digital objects. This contrasts with migration, which must be performed on a per-object basis. Emulation also provides the best current means to preserve objects with complex behaviours, such as games or interactive multimedia content.

Much research into the development of emulation as a practical preservation tool has therefore been undertaken in recent years, most notably at the Koninklijke Bibliotheek (the National Library of the Netherlands), the Dutch Nationaal Archief and the University of Freiburg. As a result, systems such as Dioscuri, a modular emulator specifically designed for digital preservation,[21] are now beginning to emerge, while active research continues through projects such as KEEP and TIMBUS (see Chapter 10, 'Future trends'), as well as the bwFLA project at the University of Freiburg.[22] Further information about emulation tools is provided in Appendix 3.

Preservation strategies in context

No single preservation strategy offers a panacea for maintaining authentic digital objects: all have advantages and disadvantages. These continue to be the subject of much debate within the preservation community, with the arguments sometimes appearing quite doctrinal. The acid test of any preservation method is whether it materially contributes to the objectives described earlier in this chapter; we should be dispassionate in rejecting those that do not, however widely cited or cherished they may be.

The computer museum is not a viable long-term strategy, but can be immensely useful in the development of other strategies, and for rescue scenarios; migration can appear quick and simple to implement in many cases, but contains hidden dangers for authenticity, and should only be employed when the end result is clearly understood and justified; emulation is complex and expensive to develop, but potentially very cheap to apply, and is the only proven strategy for certain types of material.

Any repository should therefore expect to implement different strategies over time, and for different types of digital resource. The process of identifying the correct strategy for a given situation is known as preservation planning, and is discussed later in this chapter.

Finally, the argument is occasionally advanced that migration, or presumably any other form of logical preservation, is an unnecessary level of intervention, going beyond anything that would be contemplated for analogue collections. A false analogy is sometimes drawn with historical documents, which may be written in languages such as Latin or Middle High German, or in manuscript hands such as chancery hand, which are inaccessible to the majority of users; why, so the logic goes, should we migrate a Lotus 1-2-3 spreadsheet to a modern format, if we would not contemplate translating or transliterating a Pompeian papyrus for non-expert users? In fact, preservation is primarily concerned with maintaining the *potential* for user access, and hence more analogous to a conservator stabilizing the papyri, in order to ensure that its content remains legible for future generations. It is just as essential to preserve the tacit knowledge required to translate historic language and letter forms, even if its application is not a widespread skill. The same logic applies to preserving the representation information required to access digital objects, as illustrated by the example of documenting nuclear waste facilities earlier in this chapter. There is plenty of scope for debating how simple we make it for users, but we cannot avoid the responsibility to maintain a genuine means of access.

8.6 Managing change: the concept of multiple manifestations

Digital preservation requires the management of objects over time, using techniques that may result in frequent and profound changes to the technical representation of that object. Any approach to preservation must therefore be underpinned by a rigorous logical framework that supports the concept of multiple technical representations of an object, and the processes of change through which they arise. This may be achieved through the concept that an information object may exist in 'multiple manifestations'.

Such manifestations can range from the simple, such as the example of TIFF and JPEG manifestations of an image given above, to the much more complex. Take the case of a compound information object, such as an archive snapshot of a website. This comprises a series of sub-objects – the individual web pages – each of which may be constructed from a variety of components: text, images, interactive forms and so on. Suppose that an archive decides to convert all of the JPEG images within the archived website to PNG format. At the level of the individual image, the PNG version forms a new manifestation of the JPEG image, as in the previous example, but it also has implications for the higher-level information objects of which it is a component. The original manifestation of a web page may comprise an HTML file, two JPEG images and a CSS stylesheet. The change of image format means that we must now consider there to be a new manifestation of the same page, comprising an HTML file (amended to link to the new image files), two PNG images and the CSS stylesheet.

It is critical to distinguish between manifestations, being technical representations of the same information object, and different editorial versions of an information object. For example, if a TIFF image were to be manipulated in some way before being converted to JPEG, such as cropping or rotating it, this would constitute a change to the underlying image, and should therefore be considered a new conceptual object – a different editorial version – rather than a new manifestation of the original image.

The origin of the concept of 'manifestations' in this context is unclear, but has almost certainly evolved independently within a number of different initiatives. Although it does not explicitly form part of the OAIS model, it was adopted by the Cedars project, in the development of an outline preservation metadata model based on OAIS.[23] The concept also appears in the National Library of Australia's 1999 preservation metadata scheme.[24] However, the approach described here originates in a development of the concept within English Heritage's Digital Archiving Strategy,[25] and its subsequent implementations in the CAMS preservation metadata management system,[26] and then the National Archives' digital repository (and hence SDB).

Some of the implications of the multiple manifestations approach can best be illustrated through example. Imagine an information object, A, which is a text document in five chapters. The original manifestation, A_1, is the word processed report in WordPerfect 5.1 format, comprising separate files for each chapter; the document also includes a logo in TIFF format. In the future a

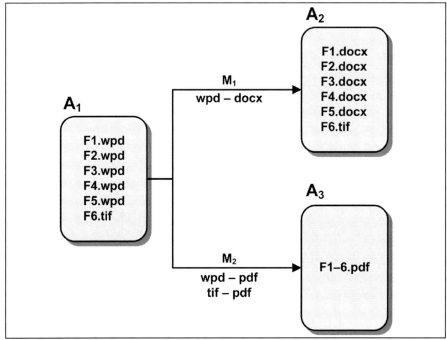

Figure 8.4 Migrating to new manifestations

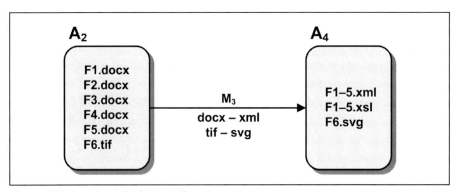

Figure 8.5 Creating a further manifestation

decision is taken to migrate certain formats stored within the repository. In the case of object A, it is decided that WordPerfect files are to be migrated to Microsoft Word 2007 format for preservation, and PDF for public access. In the latter case, the separate elements of the report will be amalgamated into a single document. Two new manifestations of A are therefore created as shown in Figure 8.4.

Subsequently, a new XML document format is adopted, which meets the needs of both preservation and public access. This format stores images separately in SVG format. As a result, the two previous manifestations of A are now superseded by a new single manifestation, as shown in Figure 8.5.

Although manifestation A_4 is derived only from A_2, it supersedes both previous manifestations (A_2 and A_3). This example only hints at the potential complexities involved in preservation actions, but should reinforce the need for a rigorous means for modelling them. Multiple manifestations must be managed through detailed technical metadata describing them, and the processes through which they are created.

Any preservation strategy is driven by the need to maintain at least one manifestation that is currently accessible. Over time, existing manifestations may be superseded by new ones. These obsolete manifestations may eventually be deleted, for reasons of space, although pragmatism necessitates the ability to roll back preservation decisions, such as migration, to at least the previous generation. However, the *relationships* between manifestations, as recorded in the technical metadata, must never be destroyed: the authenticity of a record requires the maintenance of an unbroken chain of provenance. It is therefore necessary to be able to define whether a given manifestation should be considered current or superseded, and its precise derivation.

The original manifestation of a record enjoys a uniquely privileged position within an archive, and must always be preserved. As the one manifestation for which it is possible to assert absolute authenticity, and as the source of all subsequent manifestations, it must be clearly differentiated from all other manifestations.

New manifestations are created via preservation actions such as migration or emulation. A migration process may entail three distinct types of action:

- **Transformation**: Files of a single format may be migrated to a new format using a defined migration pathway.
- **Emendation**: Files may need to be emended to reflect changes to other files with which they have a dependency, as in the website example at the start of this section.
- **Association**: Files associated with an existing manifestation may be additionally associated with the new manifestation without change. This is the case in the example of migration process M_1, where the TIFF file from manifestation A_1 is associated with manifestation A_2.

A single migration process may comprise multiple actions in each category.

There is an important corollary to this: there is no direct relationship between the files within two related manifestations, only between the manifestations themselves.

The case of emulation is different: although the original manifestation of an object will form the basis for emulation, differing emulation environments may be considered to give rise to different *experiential* manifestations. Although each aims for a complete and accurate emulation of the original system, in reality there may well be differences, and these are best understood as separate manifestations.

8.7 Bitstream preservation

The first requirement of digital preservation – to maintain an intact physical copy of the digital object – necessitates the use of techniques that are commonly referred to as 'bitstream preservation', because they focus on preserving the 1s and 0s, rather than the means to interpret them as useful information. The goal of bitstream preservation can be stated simply as follows:

> To maintain the integrity of every bitstream ingested into the repository, by ensuring that a demonstrably bit-perfect copy can be retrieved on demand, for as long as required.

The integrity of a digital object arises from the assurance that it has not been altered in any unauthorized manner, with total loss of the bitstream being simply the most extreme possible case of integrity loss. The principal threats to that integrity have been discussed earlier in this chapter. Protecting against these threats requires us to do three things:

- Maintain at least one available copy of each bitstream at all times.
- Ensure the integrity of the bitstream – that it cannot change in any way.
- Collect rigorous evidence to prove that we have achieved the first two points.

What this entails in practice is discussed in the following sections.

How many copies to keep

Digital data has a significant advantage over analogue material, which can be exploited in the cause of preservation, namely the ability to create bit-perfect copies on demand. Logic suggests that the more copies we have the more likely it is that at least one will survive any disaster, while the law of diminishing returns dictates that beyond a certain number of copies the cost of creating and maintaining additional copies outweighs the benefit. So how many copies is enough?

There is no standard answer to this: ultimately, it is a matter of risk management. However many copies are kept, there is some residual risk of total loss, and a repository needs to weigh the costs of keeping a certain number of copies against the level of risk that it is prepared to tolerate.

The absolute minimum number of copies you should keep is three, which enables recovery from the loss of a single copy, with a degree of redundancy. Many repositories, especially those not using distributed storage systems, keep three or four copies, but higher numbers are common – for example, the minimum number of copies recommended in a LOCKSS system is seven.[27] Assuming the copies are appropriately isolated from one another (see the next section), there is unlikely to be any great advantage to going significantly beyond this level.

The number of copies is also determined by practical considerations, such as cost and performance. Each copy being managed has an associated cost, and an attendant impact on the performance of the system, for example, the time taken to perform an ingest or an integrity check. You should therefore take three copies as your starting point, then assess whether it is practical or desirable to keep more.

Many organizations choose to create at least one copy through traditional back-up procedures. While this is a perfectly reasonable approach, it is important to recognize that the nature of back-up technology does create an additional dependency – the back-up copy can only be accessed using the appropriate back-up software, and is often only suitable for recovering data to the same type of storage system from which it was originally backed up. It is also unlikely that standard integrity checking procedures will work with back-ups, which tend to be stored in compressed form. It is therefore essential to test the viability of back-up copies periodically, including the ability to restore from them.

Where to keep copies

The value of keeping multiple copies is highly dependent on where they are kept – five copies stored in the same data centre offer much less redundancy (and hence safeguarding against loss) than if they are split between five different geographical locations. You should therefore keep at least one copy in a separate location from the others. This may be straightforward for organizations that occupy more than one site. In other cases, it may be possible to come to a reciprocal arrangement with another organization. For example, two regional archives might agree to store one another's off-site copies.

Ideally, the locations should be sufficiently separated to avoid both being affected by any likely disaster. Determining an appropriate disaster scenario is key here: while keeping copies on different continents might insure against anything short of the fall of human civilization, most organizations take a more pragmatic view of the risks that it is practical to mitigate. As a minimum, the separation should be sufficient to avoid being affected by the total loss of a single building; greater distance is highly desirable if practical.

What technologies to use to keep copies

Geographical separation is not the only consideration – you should also seek to create copies which are *technologically* isolated. In the same way that the former safeguards against physical disaster, so the latter protects against issues that may emerge with a particular technology. It is therefore preferable that at least one copy be stored on a different type of media. For example, you might have two copies on hard disk, with a third on tape or DVD.

How to protect them from loss or change

While the maintenance of multiple isolated copies reduces the impact of damage or loss to any single copy, or the likelihood of it being propagated to other copies, further steps are required to prevent it happening in the first place. You therefore need to consider security measures to control physical and virtual access, and procedures to protect your storage systems from physical degradation or technological obsolescence.

Security controls

IT systems must be protected from intrusions and malicious damage, either by external attackers and other unauthorized users, or from malicious code and other forms of software attack. Countermeasures to consider may include the use of password controls, firewalls, air gaps and antivirus software.

You also need to control the access rights that users and other systems have to the repository and its content; systems for authenticating and authorizing user and system access are required. This may be as simple as using existing network logins, and appropriately set permissions to certain network folders. Most repository platforms include some form of access control mechanism as standard.

The repository must never allow digital objects to be altered, under any circumstances: changes should only be permitted to copies of the original, which effectively become new objects in their own right. Permissions to perform changes, whether it be editing metadata or migrating digital objects, should be strictly controlled. Deleting content is an exceptional event, and should be managed equally securely. When deletion is required, you must ensure that it is carried out correctly; it is one of the ironies of digital information management that, although data is notoriously fragile when required to be retained, it can prove surprisingly durable when deletion is necessary. The proliferation of copies can make it difficult to ensure that every one has been removed, while standard delete commands don't actually physically destroy the data – it can easily be recovered using forensic techniques. Secure deletion techniques are available, which may include the physical destruction of the storage medium, or overwriting multiple times with nonsense data. These should be used when robust deletion is required, such as for sensitive data.

Wherever possible, system security should be rigorously tested. For example, security consultants can conduct 'penetration testing' to assess how watertight your IT security really is. You should also consider what should happen if a security breach occurs – how will this be reported and managed? If your organization has an existing IT incident management system, you should use it. In the worst case scenario, the system may be required to support a forensic investigation. The international standard for information security is ISO 27001: 2005, which many organizations, including service providers, will already comply with.

It is just as vital to ensure that the physical infrastructure of the repository is protected from accidental or deliberate damage. A range of controls may be used, including physical access controls and intruder detection systems, fire detection and suppression systems, and back-up power supplies. In many cases, you should be able to rely on the existing security features of your organization's server room or data centre.

Managing your storage media

No computer storage medium can be considered archival, irrespective of its physical longevity – technological obsolescence is inevitable. In many cases, the technologies required to access a certain medium will become obsolete long before deterioration of the medium itself. The need to refresh electronic records onto new media periodically is inescapable for the foreseeable future. Nevertheless, through careful selection of appropriate media, you can maximize the periods between refreshment cycles, and simplify the refreshment process itself, in addition to providing the most secure storage environment possible. For an example of the criteria and methods that can be used for selecting appropriate storage media at any given point in time, see Brown (2008a).

The need to change media should be identified through a standard process of technology watch, risk assessment and mitigation planning. These techniques are described in more detail in the context of logical preservation, later in this chapter, but can be applied equally well to managing storage. When media change is inevitably required, this should be managed through the technique of media refreshment, which entails the periodic transfer of digital information from one storage medium to another, which may be of the same or a different type. Every media refreshment action must be verified at the bit level, using the integrity checking techniques detailed below, to ensure that the content has been copied without corruption or loss.

You can also reduce the threat of loss through the way you manage your storage systems. For example, storing data in compressed format, as many storage systems do to minimize space, will greatly amplify the effects of bit rot: changing one bit in an uncompressed image file may only cause the colour of a single pixel to change – in a compressed image it almost certainly renders the entire file unreadable. Similarly, while encryption may be essential in some cases during data transfer, it creates an undesirable additional technical dependency – an additional barrier to usability.

Compression and encryption should therefore be avoided in archival storage, without a very compelling counter-argument.

How to detect if loss or change occurs

While threats to the integrity of repository content should be controlled prophylactically through the various measures described in the previous sections, the effectiveness of this also needs to be monitored regularly; preservation of integrity is the fundamental goal of bitstream preservation, and integrity checking therefore provides the ultimate assurance that this function is being performed successfully. The speed with which any integrity failure is detected is critical to the success of any bit preservation system – the faster this can be done, the greater the likelihood of successful recovery. The usual method for detecting integrity failures is through the use of checksums (see Chapter 6, 'Accessioning and ingesting digital objects'). The process for detecting failures is simple enough and fully automatable. Each file is retrieved from storage, and a checksum calculated based on its content. This is then compared with the existing checksum for the same file, as calculated on ingest; if the two checksums differ, this implies an integrity error.

Most digital repository systems are capable of undertaking integrity checks at a defined frequency, using the common checksum algorithms. Otherwise, simple tools are available to accomplish this on any storage device (examples are suggested in Appendix 3). The main point at issue is not how to perform integrity checks, but how frequently to do so. While it may seem desirable to do this as often as possible, technology is likely to be the limiting factor. Integrity checking can make significant demands on the performance of a repository; the retrieval of files from storage is typically a bottleneck in any system and, while the process may be rapid for an individual file, the number of files stored in a repository is typically very high, ranging into the millions or billions of objects. It is therefore essential to ensure that the repository is actually capable of performing integrity checks at the required frequency, and to set that requirement at a realistic level. It may well be possible to improve the performance of a given system, for example by using faster hardware, or performing multiple checks in parallel, but this will inevitably incur higher costs, which will need to be balanced against the benefits.

Integrity checking needs to include all stored copies of each file, and this may be another consideration when determining how many copies to keep (see above).

While there can be no hard and fast rule for determining how frequently to perform integrity checks, the following questions should be taken into account:

- Is there a time limit affecting the potential to recover from the failure? For example, if it relies on a system back-up that is only retained for a month, files will need to be checked more frequently than this.
- What are the consequences for end-users of an integrity failure being undetected for a given period? A failure affecting a publicly accessible copy may have more immediate or far-reaching consequences than one affecting a copy in a deep archive.
- What is the maximum frequency the system can support in its current configuration, and is any increase to this possible or affordable?

How to repair loss or change if it is detected

Detecting an integrity failure has limited value if the damage cannot be repaired. Normally, such a repair is accomplished by simply replacing the damaged file with another copy. Again, this is fully automatable: the repository simply retrieves another stored copy of the file, verifies the integrity of that copy via the checksum, and replaces the damaged version with it.

There is a risk that the checksum value stored by the repository could itself be altered, either deliberately or accidentally, At best, this might result in a checksum that did not match any stored copies of the associated file; at worst, it might be deliberately altered to match a falsified copy of the file. It is therefore necessary also to have safeguards in place to protect the stored checksums. As a minimum, some form of back-up of the checksums should be regularly created, stored separately from the repository system, and subject to equally high or higher security. This can be used in the event of any suspected compromise of the checksums. A very sophisticated system may perform regular integrity checks on the stored checksums; while in principle such checks on checks could be repeated *ad infinitum*, in practice this should be sufficient.

The PrestoPRIME project has developed tools for modelling preservation storage environments, which can help to understand the cost and operational consequences of different choices.[28]

Other considerations

There are a number of other general issues to consider in developing a bitstream preservation facility:

- **Architecture**: No storage system remains in use unchanged for more than a few years. It is therefore essential to design systems in such a way that they can be modified easily, with minimal disruption to other parts of the repository. This is often referred to as using a *modular architecture*. The key to this is ensuring that the interfaces between the components of the repository – the lines of communication – use common standards, rather than proprietary methods. Thus, for example, using storage systems that use standard file system protocols such as CIFS/NFS should avoid becoming locked into any particular storage technology.
- **Data export**: Think about how data would be extracted from the storage system if and when you wish to move to a different solution. The storage system must be able to provide all stored content back in its original format at any time, and support the migration of all data to an alternative storage environment in a timely manner, without modification of the data in any way. You should test this.
- **Performance and availability**: The system needs to be able to read and write at an appropriate speed, and scale to the predicted volumes of data. Think about how fast you want or need to ingest data, and ensure that the storage can accommodate it. Similarly, consider how quickly you need to be able to retrieve content. In most cases, repository storage is not accessed by end-users directly, so does not need to provide rapid access. You should also take account of availability – how long can you afford the storage system to be unavailable, following system failures or routine maintenance? Deep storage can generally tolerate a lower level of availability than a front-end system such as a website. These factors in turn usually allow lower-cost storage to be used. Bulk ingest and export can be lengthy processes, measured in hours or even days. This means that it is important to ensure that a failure part way through a process can be recovered from without loss – this is known as being *transactionally secure*.
- **Disaster recovery**: Bitstream preservation requirements should be incorporated into any incident management framework or business continuity planning process used by the organization, to ensure the continued availability or restoration of archived resources in the event of

an incident or disaster. The relevant plans should be tested periodically through various types of disaster recovery exercise.

Many organizations are now starting to consider outsourcing their storage infrastructure, and especially the use of the Cloud. This raises some particular issues, which are considered in detail in the next section.

Thinking about storage in the Cloud

The term 'cloud computing' refers to the provision of IT resources as services across a network. The name symbolizes the fact that the underlying technologies used to provide those services are hidden from the user. It comes in many flavours, including:

- **Infrastructure-as-a-Service (IaaS)**: providing servers or storage space as a service, accessed via an internet connection
- **Platform-as-a-Service (PaaS)**: providing a computer platform, usually including an operating system and the underlying hardware and storage
- **Software-as-a-Service (SaaS)**: providing on-demand software, typically through a web browser.

Cloud services can range from public, open services such as Amazon Web Services[29] to private clouds operated within a single organization. Cloud computing has a number of attractions as a means for organizations to provide IT services, including:

- **Elasticity and agility**: Customers can quickly and easily adjust the services they use to match demand. Thus, you could temporarily increase the bandwidth on your internet connection, or the number of web servers, to meet an anticipated peak in demand for the launch of a new online service. It is also easy to procure additional kinds of service, without having to physically acquire, install and support them.
- **Costs**: Cloud services are generally priced on a pay-per-use basis, allowing very fine-grained cost control, and avoiding expenditure on underutilized systems.
- **Technology and location independence**: Customers don't need to worry about the underlying infrastructure used to provide the service, or where it is physically located.

- **Virtualization and multi-tenancy**: Physical infrastructure can be more easily shared, and more efficiently used, while costs can be reduced through economies of scale.

However, the Cloud raises a number of risks, which must be considered very carefully alongside the opportunities. Those particularly associated with archival storage are briefly summarized below:

- **Legal and regulatory compliance**: Cloud technology could compromise an organization's ability to meet its legal obligations, most notably with respect to privacy and freedom of information legislation. This may arise because the provider does not comply with domestic legislation, or is subject to foreign legislation. Cloud services can obfuscate legal jurisdiction – different jurisdictions may apply to the owner of the data, service provider, physical storage location and data subject. Liabilities and responsibilities may be subject to dispute, for example concerning statutory duties under privacy legislation. Jurisdictional issues can also create risks around data ownership and privacy – for example, data hosted in the USA or by US-headquartered companies is subject to the Patriot Act, and accessible by US law enforcement agencies. This may compromise information security for non-US organizations.
- **Authenticity**: The nature of the Cloud raises concerns that the evidential value or authenticity of archival records could be compromised, if there is a lack of auditable information about exactly how they have been managed, including the robustness of measures to safeguard their integrity and reliability.
- **Information management**: The Cloud poses new and increased risks that an organization's archives may be lost as a result of contractual disputes, bankruptcy or takeover of the service provider, operational failures within the provider, or incompatible technology changes introduced by them. Existing threats to data, such as loss or damage through disaster or malicious attack, may also be more difficult to mitigate in the Cloud. There is a separate risk that information may not be disposed of in accordance with legal or business requirements, because of the failure or inability of the service provider to delete all extant copies securely in accordance with a disposal instruction from the customer.
- **Open standards**: Cloud services can create a risk of supplier lock-in, from either technical or legal perspectives, which could compromise

access to repository content. This could occur during, or on termination of, the contract. It is essential that the storage layer must return archival content on demand in the same formats as originally stored, and must not modify it in any way.

- **Performance and availability**: Performance and availability may be concerns: although the performance requirements for the master digital repository storage in supporting user access are likely to be relatively low, it will probably need to be capable of ingesting and exporting substantial volumes of data (e.g. 10s of terabytes) in a timely fashion, which may be challenging across an internet connection. Owing to the reliance on internet infrastructure, there is also a greater risk of service disruption, leading to temporary loss of availability of content.
- **Contractual issues**: Many of the risks above relate to the contractual relationship with any cloud service provider. There are also risks around establishing liabilities and obligations, applicable jurisdictions, sub-contracting and changes in service provision. Absolute and contractually binding assurances will be required about the geographical location of data hosting and any data transfers.

More generally, customers will be wholly dependent on the supplier for this function; for institutions where preservation is a core business, this may be undesirable.

This is not to say that the Cloud should be avoided – far from it. It can be a very attractive proposition, especially for organizations that either have limited IT infrastructure, or a strategic goal to move towards cloud-based services. Indeed, in some cases it may be the only feasible or affordable option. However, if you do consider it, you should do so with a full understanding of the issues. The use of the Cloud for digital preservation has been considered in some detail in a number of recent studies, including Aitken et al. (2012) and Cloud Sweden (2011). Further studies and guidance can be expected to emerge in future. The use of the Cloud to provide PraaS is considered in Chapter 10, 'Future trends'.

8.8 Logical preservation

Logical preservation, sometimes known as 'active' preservation, is concerned with ensuring the continued accessibility of meaningful information content. It requires bitstream preservation – without the bits there can be no information – but goes far beyond it. If bitstream preservation is the essential foundation of any preservation management regime, logical preservation is its culmination.

As previously discussed, bitstreams can only be rendered into meaningful information through a combination of the correct technological environment, and sufficient additional information to allow it to be interpreted and understood. This gives rise to two key challenges: the complexity, variability and rapid evolution of those technologies, and the ease with which the tacit knowledge required to interpret information can be forgotten.

It is important to note that logical preservation is not just concerned with tackling technological and cultural change, although this tends to be the most commonly cited threat; it is also required to meet changing user expectations and needs. For example, a new access technology may emerge, which users then expect a repository to support. The existing access technologies may continue to be perfectly usable, but the repository might still need to migrate content into different formats to meet the new demand. Fortunately, the same approaches can be applied to both issues, and we can treat user expectations as another facet of the changing technology environment.

The goal of logical preservation is to overcome those challenges, and digital archivists today have access to a growing arsenal of techniques to do so. Tackling technology change requires us to do three basic things:

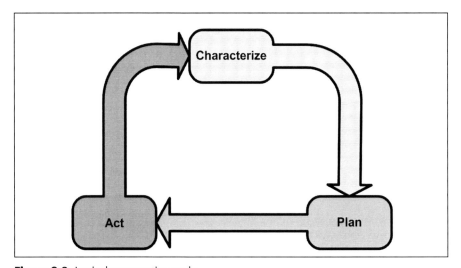

Figure 8.6 Logical preservation cycle

- Understand what the technological requirements and dependencies of the objects stored in our digital repository are.
- Identify how, why and when technology change is likely to compromise our ability to access those objects.
- Identify and execute appropriate plans of action to counter such changes.

In digital preservation parlance, these tasks are accomplished through the processes of characterization, preservation planning and preservation action, respectively, operating in a continuous cycle, as illustrated in Figure 8.6.

Characterization

Characterization covers the range of activities required to understand the nature of the digital objects stored in a repository, and from this their preservation requirements. It underpins all subsequent preservation activities: if the precise characteristics of a digital object are not sufficiently understood, it is almost impossible to preserve it in an accessible, authentic form. The basic characterization tasks – format identification, validation and metadata extraction – have already been discussed in some detail in Chapter 6, 'Accessioning and ingesting digital objects', as a key part of the ingest process. It makes sense to perform characterization at the earliest opportunity, during ingest. However, it is also an essential part of the ongoing preservation management of objects post-ingest. It will need to be repeated for two reasons. First, characterization tools are continually improving, and new tools being developed; this may, for example, enable us to identify formats where this was not previously possible, or extract an improved range of metadata. Periodic recharacterization of repository content, as tools are updated or added, is therefore an important maintenance task. Second, when preservation actions create new manifestations of digital objects, these need to be characterized in their own right. This is discussed in more detail later in this chapter.

A number of practical tools are available to support the characterization process; most are free to use, and many are at a mature stage of development, and therefore suitable for use in a production setting. Some of the most common have been discussed in Chapter 6, while a more comprehensive list is provided in Appendix 3.

It is important to understand not only the properties of individual objects, but also to develop and maintain a profile of the technical characteristics of your collection as a whole. For example, knowing the number or volume of files you have in a particular format, which use LZW compression, or which include password protection, could all influence the nature and priority of your preservation planning decisions. This too can be automated. For example, the DROID tool provides a variety of filters and reports to allow collection profiles to be created.

Preservation planning

Preservation planning forms the decision-making heart of the preservation process. Its function is to identify threats to the continued availability and accessibility of authentic digital objects and, if such threats are identified, to determine appropriate countermeasures. This requires an ongoing cycle of monitoring and assessing threats, and developing strategies to counter them, as shown in Figure 8.7.

Monitoring threats: technology watch

Since a key source of potential threats is changing technology, the monitoring of these changes – a process known as 'technology watch' – forms a vital element of preservation planning. This may seem a daunting process – how does any organization keep track of the constant, myriad evolutions of technology? The answer is that they don't need to; much of that change is irrelevant, relating to technologies with no bearing on their sphere of operations. For example, moving to a new e-mail management system has no impact unless existing e-mails are being preserved in the repository, and can no longer be read using the new system. What is really required is a technology watch that focuses on that particular repository and its users, rather than attempting to monitor technology in general. Furthermore, it only needs to consider the subset of that technology used to

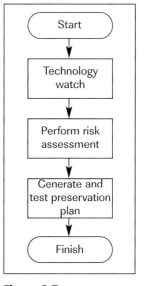

Figure 8.7
Preservation planning workflow

manage and access digital information requiring preservation. This becomes a much simpler proposition, although still a task of some complexity for larger organizations, or for complex collections with diverse users. You need to do three things:

- Understand the range of technologies required to manage and access your collection. This is achieved through characterization.
- Monitor support for those technologies within your organization and user community.
- Trigger an alert if a required technology is likely to cease either to be available to your repository, or to meet the needs of your users.

For example, if your collection includes a substantial number of Microsoft Outlook e-mail messages, and your organization decides to move to using Gmail as its e-mail solution, this should trigger a technology watch alert to assess the likely impact. The same might apply if you use MP3 as a standard access format for audio, but begin to receive substantial feedback from users that they would prefer BWF.

Ideally, you should seek to embed technology watch within existing organizational processes for implementing technology change. For example, many organizations have an existing change management process, whereby any modification to the IT infrastructure must be tested and approved before it is deployed. If this is unrealistic, you may need to develop your own process.

Risk assessment

Once a technology watch alert has been raised, you need to understand the severity of the potential threat, and the extent of its likely impact on your collection. This requires assessing the results of your technology watch in combination with information obtained from characterization. For example, technology watch may determine that tools to render a specific word processed format will soon be unavailable, but the urgency or necessity of corrective action will be determined by the number of files in that format present in your collection. You might also determine that an external event has caused the risk of future loss to increase, but not yet to an extent requiring immediate action. For example, a crucial tool may require a specific operating system to run; plans to move to a newer, incompatible operating system in 12 months' time would pose an increased risk, but might not require immediate mitigation.

You should base your risk assessment on evidence, not conjecture – this will ensure that you only commit to preservation actions when they are required, and that you identify the best possible mitigation. You can assess risks here using the method introduced in Chapter 2, 'Making the case for digital preservation', for creating a digital asset register, by calculating their probability, impact and proximity. Using a numerical scoring system will help you to prioritize them for action.

Preservation plan generation

The final stage of preservation planning is to determine the detailed preservation action required to mitigate an identified threat. This should be described in a *preservation plan*, which defines the precise steps required to perform the necessary preservation actions, and the criteria on which the successful execution of those actions can be judged.

A preservation plan should include the following information:

- a definition of the type of digital object to which it applies, e.g. TIFF 6.0 images or archived websites. Preservation plans often relate to a specific file format, but this need not be the case
- a description of the threat which the plan is intended to counter, e.g. cessation of availability of TIFF viewing tools
- a description of the intended outcome, e.g. migration of TIFF 6.0 images to JPEG2000 format, or emulation of dBASE IV software on a Windows 8 platform
- a detailed definition of the steps involved. This should include the precise name and version of each piece of software or hardware involved, together with any necessary configuration required, and the exact sequence and nature of steps; for example, it may be necessary to copy the source files to a specific folder, run the conversion tool with output settings configured in a particular way, then copy the resultant files from a different folder
- a description of the success criteria. This may be framed as the significant properties to be retained, e.g. the pixel dimensions and bit-depth of an image.

You also need to develop a rigorous process to test, approve and document potential preservation plans – never use a preservation plan in earnest until you have tested it thoroughly with dummy data, to ensure that it performs as you require.

Preservation planning in practice

Preservation planning does not require a high degree of automation – indeed, in most cases the amount of time dedicated to this task would not warrant investing in such automation – but a number of useful tools and services are available to assist.

Format registries such as PRONOM (Figure 8.8) and the Library of Congress' digital formats website[30] are invaluable sources of information to support technology watch, risk assessment and the generation of preservation plans. Indeed, PRONOM can, in principle, provide information about risks relating to formats, as well as possible migration pathways although, in practice, such information is only sparsely recorded at present.

Community wikis and discussion lists can also be great sources of up-to-date information, as well as excellent forums for discussing issues, and learning what others are thinking about or doing. For example, the Library of Congress' blog The Signal,[31] and the monthly online summary 'What's New in Digital Preservation' issued by the Digital Preservation Coalition and Digital Curation Centre,[32] are two excellent starting points for keeping abreast of new developments. The Open Planets Foundation's Knowledge Base wiki,[33] and especially its section 'Requirements and Solutions',[34] contains a wealth of information to assist with preservation planning, as well as a broader range of preservation topics, while the nascent Digital Preservation Stack Exchange website allows anyone to post questions about digital preservation topics, which are then answered by other community members.[35]

Perhaps the most sophisticated preservation planning tool currently available is PLATO,[36] an online service developed by the Planets project. This guides users through the entire process, from defining your goals, to evaluating alternative strategies and devising a preservation plan. As a community-based service, it also offers the potential to see how others have tackled similar problems, and learn from their experience. However, that sophistication comes at the price of complexity, and may be over-elaborate for many organizations. PLATO is now being developed further within the

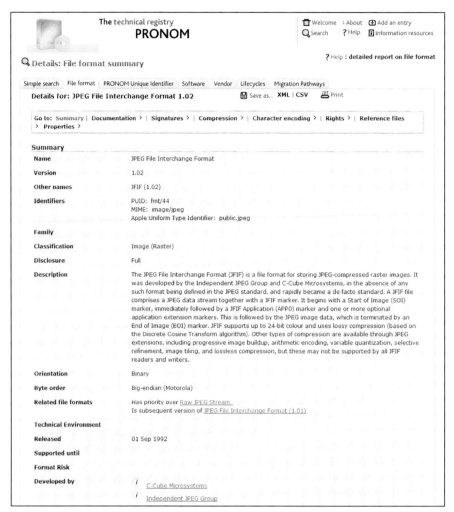

Figure 8.8 The PRONOM registry (The National Archives)

SCAPE project,[37] which should lead to improvements in functionality and scalability.

The Open Planets Foundation is developing a 'health check' methodology for conducting preservation risk assessments, which may lead to further practical tools and techniques.[38] Appendix 3 contains more information on tools and resources for preservation planning.

Preservation action

The final stage in the logical preservation cycle is to put the results of preservation planning into action. In principle, this should be a largely mechanistic process, the intellectual effort having already taken place in the previous stage. A number of repository platforms provide automated preservation action facilities, at least for format migration. Typically, they provide a framework within which individual third-party conversion tools can be executed automatically under the control of the repository. Such repositories only support a limited number of migration pathways out of the box, although adding more is a simple development task.

If such generic frameworks are not available, individual tools can still be used to automate preservation actions. For example, many image format conversion utilities support batch migration of multiple images. Where the tool itself does not support automation, it may still be possible to achieve the same result by writing simple command-line scripts. For example, a batch file (in Windows) or shell script (in Unix or Linux) can be used to automate tasks such as running programs or moving files, although writing such scripts requires a degree of technical knowledge.

For emulation-based preservation strategies, preservation actions take a rather different form, consisting simply of any steps required to make a given digital object available within the chosen emulation environment. The process varies considerably depending on the type of emulator used, but typically involves packaging the content in some way and moving it to a specific file system location.

It is not enough to simply enact a process as critical as a preservation plan; the results of that preservation activity must be validated, to ensure that it has had the desired effect. The final part of preservation action is therefore to compare the actual result with the desired one. The concept of significant properties again comes to the fore here, as a yardstick for measuring preservation success. If we have been able to previously measure the 'performance' of a digital object using characterization, we can compare this against a new measurement of the same, carried out post-preservation. Techniques for practical preservation action validation are still very immature, although some tools are available. For example, the DIFFER tool[39] can compare the properties of an image in different formats, and measure the degree of difference, while some repository systems such as SDB also support comparison for a limited range of object types and properties.

A migration-based preservation action results in the creation of a new manifestation of a digital object, and hence a new AIP to be ingested into the repository. The ingest process follows a simplified version of that discussed in Chapter 6, 'Accessioning and ingesting digital objects' – the new manifestation still needs to be characterized, validated and stored, and metadata created to record these actions, but virus checking and quarantine should not be required unless the object has left the controlled environment of the repository at any stage during processing, and cataloguing or arrangement tasks will be unnecessary.

The preservation action workflow is illustrated in Figure 8.9.

Organizations such as the Digital Curation Centre[40] and the Open Planets Foundation[41] maintain detailed catalogues of preservation tools and services. Examples of these are listed in Appendix 3.

Deciding when to execute preservation actions

Preservation plans are often time-critical, in that the threats they are designed to counter are likely to be imminent, and the window of opportunity for doing so limited. It is therefore important to enact them in a timely fashion. There are a number of schools of thought on the timing of preservation actions, which can broadly be divided into 'just in time' and 'just in case'. The 'just in time' camp advocates leaving preservation action to the last possible moment, only carrying it out reactively when it is actually required to prevent loss. Such an approach restricts effort and investment to the moment when it is necessary, and when the optimum action can best be judged, but restricts the ability of the repository to match available resources to preservation needs, and can result in a collection with a very complex and varied range of preservation needs.

Proponents of the 'just in case' argument prefer to intervene as early as possible, in order to minimize future preservation challenges. For example, some repositories choose to proactively 'normalize' all content to a minimal set of preferred formats at the point of ingest or shortly thereafter, on the basis that this reduces the range of formats to be preserved in future, and allows preservation

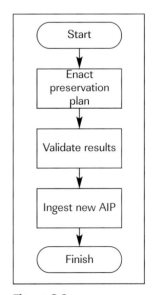

Figure 8.9
Preservation action workflow

activity to be scheduled according to the availability of resources. The risk it runs is that poor choices made today, whether over the formats chosen or migration pathways used, have lasting consequences across the whole collection, or that resources will be wasted on undertaking preservation actions which ultimately prove unnecessary.

In reality, we have insufficient experience of the long-term practice of digital preservation to pronounce unequivocally on this dilemma. Perhaps the best advice is that you should think very carefully about where to allocate your resources, and not embark on costly preservation actions without weighing up the pros and cons. In reality, the main driver for most preservation actions undertaken by repositories today is current access. For example, the Parliamentary Archives chooses to immediately create a second, PDF access copy of objects ingested in Microsoft Office formats, not because it is considered more 'archival', but because it suits the current access needs of the widest range of users. You should therefore not be afraid to carry out preservation actions where there is a clear requirement. Furthermore, if you follow minimum practice of always preserving the original format alongside any future manifestations, the worst you should suffer is wasted effort, rather than loss of content.

8.9 Conclusion: preservation in practice

Organizations are always constrained in their digital preservation activities by the resources available to them; it is very unlikely that any organization can undertake every digital preservation activity it wishes, as quickly as desired. Having probably had to fight hard for these resources, it is critical that you deploy them to maximum effect. It is therefore important to think very carefully about priorities, when putting digital preservation theory into practice.

So what is the practical minimum for a viable digital preservation service? At the most fundamental level, some form of bitstream preservation is essential – without the assurance that the bitstream can be preserved, more sophisticated forms of preservation are inconceivable. Allied to this, you require some form of metadata management to control the documentation required for preservation management, as discussed in the previous chapter.

In terms of logical preservation, characterization should be your first priority – you must understand your collection before you can preserve it. You should also consider at least a rudimentary preservation planning process, to understand what your users want, and monitor possible threats to accessibility. These initial building blocks will provide an excellent basis for preservation. Be wary of investing substantial resources in preservation actions until you have identified a clear need.

The concept of a maturity model, introduced in Chapter 4, 'Models for implementing a digital preservation service', provides a framework for considering this in more detail. Basic, managed and optimized processes for preservation can then be envisaged, as shown in Table 8.1.

Table 8.1 Preservation maturity levels	
F Bitstream preservation	
3 Basic process	• dedicated storage space on a network drive, workstation, or removable media • at least three copies maintained of each object, with back-up to removable media • basic integrity checking performed • virus checking performed • existing access controls and security processes applied
4 Managed process	• managed storage environment with automated replication and back-up • specialized repository platform used to manage content • automated integrity checking • automated virus checking • repository-specific security measures applied as required • reactive storage management, which identifies and manages threats to bitstream preservation as they arise
5 Optimized process	• hierarchical storage management or storage appliances, with dedicated storage management software • security and access controls proactively monitored and reviewed • proactive storage management to predict and mitigate threats to bitstream preservation before they occur, including automated repair of integrity failures
G Logical preservation	
3 Basic process	• basic characterization capability exists, allowing at least format identification • *ad hoc* preservation planning takes place • *ad hoc* preservation actions can be performed if required • ability to manage multiple manifestations of digital objects
4 Managed process	• advanced characterization capability exists, including automated metadata extraction • reactive logical preservation: the institution can identify and react to threats to the usability of stored objects, mitigating them in a timely fashion
5 Optimized process	• proactive logical preservation: the institution can identify and predict threats to the usability of stored objects before they arise, proactively identifying, testing and implementing appropriate mitigations before the threat materializes

Every organization with a need for digital preservation should aspire to at least the basic process; how far beyond this you wish or need to go depends on the scale of preservation required, its significance to the organization and the available resources.

You can also make scarce resources go further through collaboration, and maximizing your reuse of the work of others. While national bodies, or those with an explicit research remit, may well invest a proportion of their resources in more speculative research activities with no guarantee of immediate benefits, the majority of smaller organizations will have neither the resources nor desire to undertake pure research themselves. However, they can still participate in, and benefit from, research activities being led by others. As well as using the tools and services made available through them, there can be opportunities to act as partners in large, multi-institution projects, for example testing the project outputs.

Using the tools and techniques described in this chapter, as well as Appendix 3, digital preservation is an achievable, affordable prospect for all organizations.

8.10 Key points

- **Authenticity is key**: If you can't preserve authentic digital objects, you aren't preserving anything of value. You must therefore understand the properties on which authenticity depends if you are to demonstrate successful preservation.
- **Digital objects are different to physical objects**: The separation of medium and message in the digital world creates both unique problems and opportunities for preservation.
- **There are wide-ranging threats to digital preservation**: These arise from many different sources, and must be clearly understood if they are to be effectively mitigated.
- **There are many possible forms of preservation action**: There is no single strategy suited to every case – you will need to be flexible in identifying solutions.
- **Prioritize bitstream preservation**: If you do one thing, develop a robust bitstream preservation process. While this cannot, of itself, address all the threats, it will at least ensure the survival of your data until such time as it is possible to do so.
- **Avoid compressing or encrypting digital objects in storage**: These

technologies create additional and unnecessary obstacles to preservation.

- **Ensure that you manage multiple manifestations of digital objects correctly**: Always retain the original manifestation of each object, as well as one which is currently accessible, if different, and at least one generation of superseded manifestations. Also maintain a detailed metadata record of every manifestation created, and its derivation.
- **Prioritize characterization**: Of the logical preservation functions, focus first on characterization; if you don't understand what you hold you can't undertake proper preservation planning, and run the risk of making unnecessary or inappropriate preservation decisions.
- **Prioritize preservation planning**: Next, you should develop a basic means to understand and assess threats to accessibility, even if you cannot act on them immediately.
- **Don't invest in preservation actions unless or until you have a clear need**: Be aware that the need for such action may be driven as much by user needs as preservation threats.

8.11 Notes

1   Based on ISO 15489.
2   For an introduction to the concept of representation information, and approaches to its collection and management, see Brown (2008c).
3   Heslop, Davis and Wilson (2002).
4   Cedars Project (2002, section 13).
5   Lynch (1999).
6   See www.significantproperties.org.uk/.
7   Dappert and Farquhar (2009).
8   Cochrane (2012).
9   See, for example, Rosenthal et al. (2005) and Vermaaten, Lavoie and Caplan (2012).
10 See, for example, Rosenthal (2010).
11 See Human Interference Task Force (1984) and Posner (1984).
12 Jackson (2012).
13 Cochrane (2012).
14 See, for example, Brown (2006, 86–99) and Jones and Beagrie (2001, 102–10).
15 See www.tnmoc.org/.
16 See www.compustory.com/.

17 See http://museums.wikia.com/wiki/VMoC.

18 See www.pdpplanet.com/default.aspx.

19 See www.mkw.me.uk/beebem/.

20 See http://simh.trailing-edge.com/.

21 See http://dioscuri.sourceforge.net/.

22 See http://bw-fla.uni-freiburg.de/.

23 Russell et al. (2000).

24 National Library of Australia (1999).

25 Brown (2002a).

26 Described in Brown (2003).

27 Reich and Rosenthal (2009, 3).

28 See http://prestoprime.it-innovation.soton.ac.uk/.

29 See http://aws.amazon.com/.

30 See www.digitalpreservation.gov/formats/index.shtml.

31 See http://blogs.loc.gov/digitalpreservation/.

32 See www.dpconline.org/newsroom/whats-new.

33 See http://wiki.opf-labs.org/display/KB/Home.

34 See http://wiki.opf-labs.org/display/REQ/
   Digital+Preservation+and+Data+Curation+Requirements+and+Solutions.

35 See http://area51.stackexchange.com/proposals/39787/digital-preservation.

36 See www.ifs.tuwien.ac.at/dp/plato/intro.html.

37 See www.scape-project.eu/.

38 See www.openplanetsfoundation.org/projects/preservation-health-check.

39 See http://differ.nkp.cz/about.php.

40 See www.dcc.ac.uk/resources/tools-and-applications.

41 See http://wiki.opf-labs.org/display/TR/Home.

9

Providing access to users

9.1 Introduction

Access provides the very *raison d'être* for digital preservation: what we are seeking to preserve is a viable means of access to digital objects, now and into the future. Everything we do in this regard must therefore be informed by the needs of current and future users: their requirements should dictate how we go about the business of digital preservation. While the preceding chapters have considered how to maintain a digital object's *potential* for access, this chapter looks at the realities of actually providing access to users today. However, while approaches to providing access to digital objects should be driven by an understanding of what users need, they must inevitably be tempered by the constraints of practicality, legality and curatorial responsibility.

This chapter discusses some of the issues that you need to consider when presenting preserved digital records to users. These include the practical, technical and legal challenges involved in providing access online and within a search room environment.

9.2 What do we mean by access?

Access means many things to many people: for some it may simply entail the ability to view something onscreen, for another to download a file, for a third to extract the content in format suitable for reuse elsewhere. Some users expect extensive documentation and step-by-step guidance, others are happy with minimal information or assistance. It is essential for every repository to consider what forms of access it wishes to provide for its user community, taking account of the capabilities of the former, and the expectations of the latter.

Fundamentally, access requires users to be able to do three things:

- **Find things of interest**: Resource discovery encompasses a range of techniques for searching and browsing the content of the repository.
- **Understand the options for accessing a given digital object**: It is not necessary that every digital object be available to every user, nor for objects to be available through any particular mechanism – such as the web – but it is essential that a user be able to understand whether or not access is possible and, if so, how. Availability pertains to what is technically possible, and any conditions of use that apply either to the repository in general, or specific digital objects in particular. These may include restrictions relating to copyright, confidentiality or citation, for example.
- **Access the object**.

These are discussed in detail in the remainder of the chapter.

9.3 Finding digital objects

Users will expect to be able to search for specific content of interest, or to browse collections in various ways, and the principal means by which they will do so is through some form of catalogue. Many organizations choose to document digital collections within their established catalogues, thus providing a single point of access to their analogue and digital holdings. It also means that the existing resource discovery functions provided by the catalogue can be used. The cataloguing of digital material using established standards has been discussed in Chapter 7, 'Describing digital objects'. You should therefore certainly consider your existing collections management system as the starting point for enabling users to find digital content.

Digital collections also provide opportunities for new forms of resource discovery, some of which are discussed below.

Full-text searching and advanced search techniques

The content of text-based digital objects can potentially be searched as easily as any catalogue, and this clearly offers much richer possibilities for resource discovery. Many digital repositories either provide full-text searching directly, or allow a third-party search engine to be used. The chief complexity here is likely to lie in how this is integrated with existing catalogue search tools, and presenting the results in a user-friendly manner.

Faceted search is another technique for improving the users' experience of search. It allows users to refine their search by applying multiple filters, or 'facets'. For example, a library catalogue might allow the user to narrow their search to a particular subject or genre, language, or date range. Users may also wish to be able to bookmark search results for future reference, or to save regular searches. Many search engines and collections management systems now support faceted search and other advanced search techniques.

Advanced visualization

Much recent research has been devoted to the problem of visualizing archival metadata. In particular, this has focused on finding new ways to visualize complex, hierarchical finding aids, so that users can more easily navigate around them. A couple of examples from the UK National Archives (TNA) illustrate the possibilities:

- **Cabinet Papers Keywords**, which provides a visualization over time of concepts and figures automatically extracted from Cabinet Office papers[1]
- **Timelines of Government Departments**, a graphical representation of changing departmental responsibility for foreign affairs in UK government, linking through to the TNA catalogue, as shown in Figure 9.1.[2]

An overview of current visualization research is provided by Lemieux (2012).

Geospatial discovery

Much of the information in the analogue and digital collections of memory institutions has a geographical aspect. For example, archival records such as registers of births, marriages and deaths, published works, photographs and paintings, or archaeological artefacts may all describe, depict, originate from, or otherwise relate in some way to a physical place. Repositories are therefore increasingly experimenting with map-based approaches to resource discovery. Examples include:

- **Cheshire Tithe Maps Online**, which provides searchable access to digitized historic tithe maps and to their associated apportionments (documents describing detailed land ownership and use), linked to a modern base map (see Figure 9.2)[3]

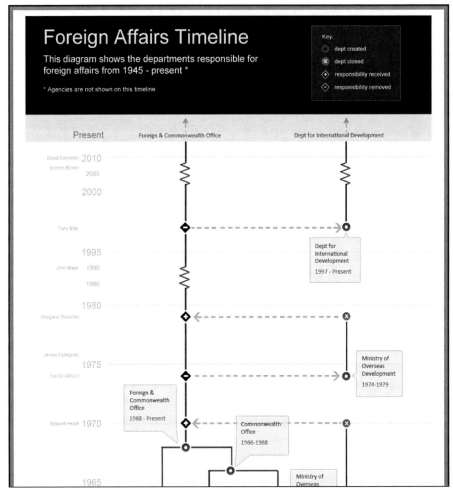

Figure 9.1 Timeline visualization (The National Archives)

- **Maps in Time**, part of the TNA Cabinet Papers 1915–1981 online collection, which uses a series of geo-political world maps over time to provide a context and access route into the underlying digitized documents[4]
- **Collections on a Map**, also from The National Archives, and providing map-based access to selected collections[5]
- **Digital Collections Map** at the **J. Willard Marriott Digital Library,** University of Utah, which offers map-based browsing of the digital library holdings.[6]

Many libraries and archives are building geospatial services using online tools such as Google Maps,[7] or existing services like HistoryPin,[8] to offer map-based access to parts of their collections.

Curated content and personalization

Repositories may also wish to proactively direct users towards certain content. For example, they may provide curated content, showcasing aspects of the collection, such as a 'document of the month', highlighting topical records, or supporting exhibitions. This can be a good way to expose less well known parts of the collection to users. More advanced access systems may include personalization features, analysing users' behaviour in order to suggest other content which might be of interest. Thus, a library catalogue might recommend books to a reader based on what they have previously viewed, and the reading habits of other users who viewed the same thing.

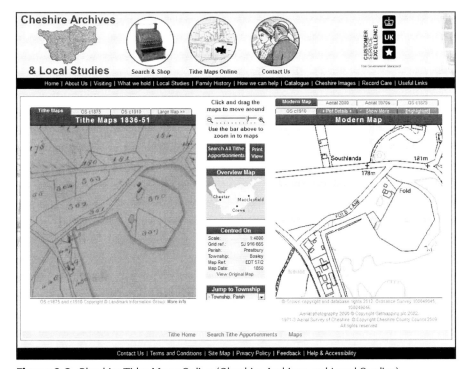

Figure 9.2 Cheshire Tithe Maps Online (Cheshire Archives and Local Studies)

9.4 Options for access: technical considerations

There are a number of models for how digital content can be made available from a digital repository. OAIS uses the concept of a DIP, which is a conceptual chunk of information provided to a user in response to a request for access. However, it is important to remember that DIPs are not necessarily packages in any physical sense; they simply provide a useful way to think about the set of information that a user needs to be given in order to answer an access request. This could be as simple as opening a web page or viewing a document in a book viewer.

Access to a digital object involves two steps:

- The user must be given access to the bitstream that encodes the content of interest.
- The bitstream must be rendered into meaningful information for the user, which may require a combination of technologies.

Every repository must by definition support at least the first of these, subject to appropriate access controls and conditions of use, but they have much greater latitude in how far they choose to support the latter. This choice is partly determined by technical restrictions. An obvious case in point is the format of the data: digital objects in formats that can be rendered directly within a standard web browser are technically very straightforward to access; those in obscure formats, not widely available within the user community, or unsuited to web delivery, are more challenging.

It is also influenced by the capabilities and expectations of your user community. At one end of the spectrum, one might assume a very basic technological user capability. This might either lead the repository to offer a similarly constrained set of access options, or to place a high degree of importance on providing viewing tools. At the other extreme, a very technically sophisticated user community might require no more than the ability to download a bitstream, to which it will then apply its own access and analysis tools.

A number of basic models can be considered here, providing increasing levels of support to the user:

- **Copy and forget**: The most basic form of access is simply to provide the user with a copy of the required bitstream, either via download or on removable media, and leave them to provide the necessary access environment.

- **Informed download**: A level up from this would be to additionally provide the user with information about the required access environment, perhaps including a suggested means for acquiring it. For example, a document might be provided in a standard word-processing format, but accompanied by technical metadata, which explains which format it is in, and gives examples of software capable of rendering it, perhaps with links to where this may be acquired.
- **Assume common viewer available**: The next step would be to provide access copies in formats for which access environments are easily available. For example, a policy decision might be taken to only use formats for which free viewers are available (e.g. PDF).
- **Provide viewer**: Beyond this, the repository can actually provide the necessary access environment to users. This might be accomplished online (for example, by providing a web-based video player embedded in a web page), or on-site, by providing workstations which have appropriate software installed. Viewers tend to be specialized to certain types of object, such as page turning software for viewing digitized books, or audio players.
- **Reuse tools**: The ultimate level of access would be to provide tools which go beyond simply rendering the information, to allow manipulation and reuse.

What constitutes an appropriate level of access will vary according to circumstances, and indeed individual repositories may offer different levels according to the type of object. These levels should also not necessarily be considered to occupy a sliding scale of desirability: while any repository should aspire to at least the second level, anything beyond this depends on the type of content and needs of users.

For example, two repositories might store digitized images in JPEG 2000 format – which is widely used but not directly supported by most web browsers – with each page of a document stored as a separate file. One repository might provide a document viewer on its website, which can render those individual files into a universally supported format, such as JPEG, and allow users to easily and seamlessly navigate between the pages of the document. The other might simply offer the JP2 files for download, leaving it to the user to supply a tool capable of viewing them, and to open each page as a separate file.

Neither choice is inherently right or wrong; in practice, repositories with any degree of variety in their holdings may incline to a hybrid approach. For example, one might provide enhanced access for the most popular or significant content, and more rudimentary access to the remainder.

9.5 Options for access: conditions of access

Most repositories wish to place certain conditions on access to their content, which may arise from a variety of legal or organizational considerations. For example, they may wish to prevent or limit copying of the data, ensure that any reuse is appropriately acknowledged and licensed, limit use to a specific time span, or prevent reuse or reworking of the content into derivative works. Some of the most common reasons are considered in the first part of this section. The second part then looks at options for applying such conditions in practice, ranging from advisory notices, to physical restrictions or simply prohibiting access.

Legal issues

The main legal issues that you will need to consider in the context of providing user access, including intellectual property, content liability, privacy and freedom of information, have already been discussed in Chapter 5, 'Selecting and acquiring digital objects'. It is worth looking in a little more detail at one aspect of the first of these – content licensing – which explicitly governs what users can and can't do with the content to which you provide access.

As discussed in Chapter 5, at the point of transfer you must ensure that you establish the nature of the IPR in the content, and either acquire all rights or at least a perpetual licence therein, which will allow you to manage the content in a way that respects the rights of rights holders and enables appropriate access for users. You then need to consider the terms under which you grant user access.

You might simply assert copyright, permitting no use beyond the standard 'fair use' exceptions contained within most copyright legislation, but the growing impetus for opening up access to different types of digital content is a consideration for many repositories when thinking about access conditions. Perhaps the most established of these 'open' movements is open access, which relates to scholarly publications and is therefore most relevant to libraries, institutional repositories in higher and further education, other research institutions and academic publishers. The open data movement originated in the scientific research community but, driven by broader moves towards transparency and openness in public administration,[9] has recently and notably expanded to embrace public sector data, with many national, regional and local governments now making a wide variety of datasets freely available, under licences that encourage reuse. Notable early examples include data.gov in the USA, data.gov.uk and data.govt.nz, and the most comprehensive and up-to-date list of open data catalogues around the world, maintained by datacatalogs.org,[10] contained over 250 such catalogues as of 2012. Open data is therefore likely to be significant for all archives containing data created or funded by the public sector.

Many content licensing regimes have been developed to facilitate sharing and reuse, of which the most well known and widely adopted is the range of Creative Commons (CC) licences.[11] These are based around four conditions, which can be applied in various permutations:

- **Attribution (BY)**: Licensees may copy, distribute, display and perform the work, and make derivative works based on it, but must credit the author or licensor in a specified manner.
- **Non-commercial (NC)**: Licensees may copy, distribute, display and perform the work, and make derivative works based on it, but only for non-commercial purposes.
- **No derivative works (ND)**: Licensees may only copy, distribute, display and perform copies of the original work, but not make or distribute derivative works.
- **Share-alike (SA)**: Licensees may distribute derivative works, but only under a licence identical to that governing the original work.

Licences are created using combinations of these conditions: of the 16 possible combinations, five contain mutually exclusive conditions, and five more have been retired following lack of demand, leaving six possible licences. These are typically referred to using their codes for shorthand. Thus, for example, the LSE Library licenses many of its digitized collections under the CC BY-NC-SA licence, so users can reuse and build on the content, but only for non-commercial purposes, crediting LSE Library and licensing any derivative works under identical terms.

Organizational issues

The law may not be the only reason for wishing to restrict access: the information management policies of either the creator or the repository may also dictate this. Organizations may wish to restrict access to certain information, for example by reason of commercial or political sensitivity, and may therefore choose to close it to public access, usually for a defined period. A more nuanced approach to restricting access may be achieved through the use of a protective marking scheme, defining gradated levels of sensitivity, such as 'Commercial – in confidence' or 'Top Secret'. The protective marking scheme in question determines who can access information with particular markings. Organizations may also wish to restrict access in order to protect revenue streams.

Protecting your content

A variety of technologies and practices may be used to protect your content. The simplest method for restricting access is closure – not making the content available to a particular user community at all. However, a range of more nuanced approaches are possible, which may be divided into advisory and enforceable methods – those that simply inform the user of the rights which apply, and any limitations on use, and those that enforce those limitations through some technological means.

Advisory techniques

The most fundamental approach is to provide a clear written statement of the terms and conditions of use. This can be made available, and signposted to potential users in a number of ways. First, it can be displayed on, or linked from, a web page which the user must visit before accessing the digital object itself. Going a step further, the access system can require the user to accept the terms and conditions explicitly, for example clicking a button on a form. The terms can also be incorporated into the actual digital object, as provided to the user. For example, if the objects are made available as a download or on removable media, they can be included as a text file; alternatively, they might be incorporated as a cover sheet at the start of a document-like digital object.

Rights information may also be described in metadata, either within the object or in a separate metadata file supplied with it. At the simplest level, this might be a simple copyright statement, but formal languages for defining rights have also been developed, such as the Creative Commons Rights Expression Language (CC REL),[12] which might be used in more IPR-conscious environments.

Rights information can also be applied to the object itself, using the technique of watermarking. Its simplest, most widely used form is a visible element superimposed onto an object, which serves two main purposes: first, it acts as an obvious reminder of the ownership and provenance of the object; second, it limits unauthorized reuse by effectively compromising its quality – parts of the object are obscured, and its illicit nature is very clearly indicated. By definition, such watermarks can only be applied to digital objects with a visual dimension, such as images or documents, and so do not provide a universal solution. They can be easily applied – many image editing software tools allow the automated insertion of standard watermarks into batches of images. On the other hand, depending on exactly how they are applied, and the nature of the image, they may be relatively simple to circumvent. For example, a watermark applied to an area of consistent colour in an image could be easily erased without obvious trace. However, despite their limitations, watermarks can provide a simple and effective means to protect a wide range of digital content, at least against all but the most determined abuser. Figure 9.3 shows a watermarked image.

More advanced digital water-marking techniques use a process known as steganography to hide information in any digital object, such that its presence is not apparent to the user. This allows illicit use to be tracked, and may be regarded as a digital equivalent of methods for secretly marking physical items as a theft deterrent, such as ultraviolet ink and smart water, but is not routinely used by many digital repositories.

Figure 9.3 Watermarked image

Enforceable techniques

A whole range of technological methods for restricting user access to digital objects has been developed, under the umbrella of digital rights management

(DRM). These can limit or prevent certain actions being performed by users, such as printing, copying, altering or indeed accessing the content. This type of protection relies on functionality specific to a certain format, publishing platform or access technology, such as an e-book reader, so it is not a universal solution. It can also be controversial, as when, in 2009, Amazon remotely deleted copies of two George Orwell novels from customers' Kindle e-readers.[13] Obviously, such an extreme form of copy protection needs to be clearly advertised to potential users in advance. Methods for circumventing particular DRM techniques also emerge regularly, but they may be useful in cases where very strict control is required.

9.6 Options for access: online versus on-site access

One of the most obvious and significant differences between user access to analogue and digital collections is the ability to provide concurrent access for multiple users in a variety of environments, which need not be tied to a specific physical location. Digital repositories may provide online access to their content, restrict it to users within a physical location such as a reading room, or a combination thereof.

It is easy to become focused on the issues of providing online access, to the detriment of considering on-site users, but to do so may represent a missed opportunity. For memory institutions with physical collections, on-site access has traditionally had primacy, and the decoupling of artefact from physical location which the digital world allows should not cause us to lose sight of the role that on-site access can continue to play.

There are a number of practical reasons which may dictate on-site access in some cases. These include:

- **Legal restrictions**: For example, libraries may be restricted to providing on-site access by virtue of copyright restrictions. A case in point is provided by the legal deposit legislation in the UK,[14] which permits the designated legal deposit libraries to provide access to digital publications within their search rooms, but not online.
- **Technical restrictions**: These may arise from the size or type of content. For example, it may be impractical, or impossible, to allow download of very large image files via a web browser. There are also limitations on the extent to which online access to unusual formats can be supported.

A reading room can provide visitors with a seamless experience of physical and digital collections, and may encourage use of the latter among users who might not otherwise naturally do so, for example because they do not have ready internet access, or lack the confidence to explore online resources. Not being tied to the limitations of delivery across the web, a physical reading room can allow more advanced forms of access: dedicated workstations can be provided, configured to offer sophisticated access tailored to the needs of the collection. Specialized software, which would not typically be available to the end-user, can be made available, which may be invaluable for proving rich access to more complex or esoteric types of digital content, such as CAD models or GISs.

Online access, by definition, is not wholly within the control of the repository, depending as it does on the user to provide part of the required technology, such as a web browser. Since you cannot wholly predict or control the nature of that technology, you will need to make certain assumptions, coupled with an understanding of the needs and expectations of your users.

9.7 Understanding user expectations

Having a clear, accurate understanding of the needs and expectations of users is a prerequisite for providing the best possible service to them. It is always best to base decisions about user services on as much empirical evidence as possible, rather than simply making assumptions; information managers and curators are rarely typical users, and may also simply be too close to the collection to be able to take an objective view.

Fortunately, there is a range of methods which can be used to gain a better understanding of your users, and what they want. Many of these have been developed in the context of improving the usability of websites, and can easily be extended to all aspects of the delivery of digital content. Some of the most common are discussed below.

Questionnaires

These are best used to ask general questions and elicit overall comments about a service. They can easily be implemented online, and a range of affordable services are available which allow these to be easily set up. There are variations in the range of services provided: some offer full analysis and reporting of the results, while others simply provide the raw answers. Online questionnaires tend to have very low hit rates – most people simply ignore them – but this can be counterbalanced by the sheer volume of visitors; even though the conversion rate may be very low, this can still yield a large number of responses.

Structured workshops

The most elaborate and detailed approach to understanding user requirements is through a formal, structured workshop. A representative sample of users can be asked to perform specific tasks, typical of those which they might undertake in the real world, and the approach they take subjected to the closest possible scrutiny. This method is widely used, for example, in analysing the usability of websites, and there are many specialist companies available to facilitate such workshops. The level of analysis possible can be very sophisticated, such as using cameras to track the movement of the user's eyes across the screen, and thereby determine the optimum layout for the page. This approach offers the most rigorous and detailed results, but is also likely to be the most costly in money and other resources.

Captive users

Any organization that has physical interaction with its users, such as within a search room environment, can easily tap into them as a source of feedback. For example, users can be asked to complete a questionnaire, fill in an online survey at a search room terminal, and be interviewed or even invited to participate in a workshop. Any such requests need to be made sensitively, and in accordance with privacy legislation, but this approach is likely to yield a higher conversion rate than an online survey, albeit from a much smaller sample.

Staff

An institution's staff are also users. Even though, as noted earlier, they may be atypical of the wider user population, they are uniquely accessible and offer a particular perspective. Therefore it makes sense to use them as a source of feedback. This could be carried out through structured workshops and/or questionnaires.

Other organizations

Much can be learned by looking at how analogous organizations support their users, and how those users regard that service. If you can find exemplars for your type of institution, they can be enormously helpful in suggesting what might work for your own user community.

9.8 Access and reuse

A distinction is sometimes made between access and reuse; in some respects this is not particularly helpful, and it can certainly be argued that all forms of access constitute reuse of a kind. Nonetheless, the intention behind it, which is to differentiate between the passive consumption of information and its active reinterpretation or reformulation into new kinds of information, is one that the designer of any repository access system must at least consider. It may be perfectly valid, after such consideration, to conclude that the distinction has no meaningful impact on the requirements of that system, but the question is still worth asking. The answer is determined by a combination of the types of information being made available, the requirements of the institution, and the profile of the end-user community.

Where passive consumption is key, the emphasis is on simplicity of access (including, for example, the use of widely supported formats, or viewing tools), and greatest fidelity to the characteristics of the original. Where active reuse is essential, that focus shifts to delivery methods and formats that offer the greatest flexibility and richness in accessing and manipulating the information content.

For example, users who simply wish to view images are probably content provided the relevant detail within the image is readable, and it is in a widely supported format; but users who wish to manipulate that image, or to publish or broadcast it, require the maximum possible resolution, and an uncompressed file format. With a word processed document, ease of viewing and maximum fidelity to the original layout may be best-served using PDF/A, whereas ease of editing dictates an 'office' format, such as DOCX or ODT.

In some cases (e.g. copyright material with a high commercial value), an institution may wish to actively discourage, or indeed prevent reuse, while in others (e.g. open access repositories of scientific data), the reverse may be true.

Future usage also influences the kinds of interpretative and contextual information that the repository may need to provide to accompany the content. For example, the information required to support a user viewing an e-book will be substantially different from that needed to interpret a dataset of scientific instrument readings from a space probe. For structured data, it may be necessary to offer tools that allow interoperability with differently structured data, or indeed transformation between those structures. The precise requirements for this tend to be rather domain-specific, and are beyond the scope of this book.

9.9 Access systems in practice

A repository access system is unlikely to be developed in isolation: it will need to coexist or even integrate with other systems such as catalogues and existing access systems. It may even be provided entirely through such systems. This section considers the scenarios for how an access system can be provided in practice.[15]

Using existing access systems

Copies of repository content may already be available through existing access systems, in which case it may be considered preferable to link to them rather than replace or replicate them. For example, the UK Parliamentary Archives has existing systems for providing online access to a number of its collections, including archived websites and some digitized documents. In these cases, the archival master of the content is stored in the repository, but the repository access system links to the existing external presentation systems, rather than providing direct access itself.

Another scenario might involve records stored in an EDRMS. Since EDRMSs do not themselves provide long-term preservation functionality, it might well be the case that records appraised as requiring permanent preservation are periodically exported to a separate digital repository. Many EDRMSs can maintain a metadata 'stub', including a link to data stored in an external system. This feature can be used, once a record is exported from the system, to maintain continuity of access for users of the EDRMS. Rather than needing to know that their document has moved, they can continue to access it in its original location, through the user interface with which they are familiar; the only noticeable change might be a slightly slower speed of access.

Presentation through the repository

Any repository has to provide some form of access mechanism. This might be intended purely for administrative and preservation management purposes, and not suited to end-users, but some repositories do offer end-user interfaces. The decision whether and how to use such an interface cannot be determined purely on the basis of the functionality available – security is also a fundamental consideration. In most scenarios, it is considered highly desirable or essential to prevent end-users from directly accessing the master repository. Keeping this system isolated provides a powerful prophylactic defence against malicious attacks, but even in this scenario, the user access functionality can be used, by establishing a mirror copy of the repository, which is accessible to end-users and kept in synchronization with the master system via some form of secure replication.

Presentation through a separate system

On the basis of using the technologies which are best suited to each task, it may be considered more appropriate to use a specialized delivery system, designed purely for that purpose. In this scenario, the repository is used to provision the delivery system with its content, and to update or replace that content as required, but is not directly linked to that system. Thus, the Parliamentary Archives uses an external host for providing public access to its web archive, because of its unique technical requirements.

Hybrid approaches

In many cases, a mixed economy of access methods may be appropriate. For example, the Parliamentary Archives' digital repository has a single access system, linked to the catalogue, but that common access system can use different delivery methods, depending on the nature of the content: records exported from the EDRMS continue to be made available to internal users through the EDRMS system; records already made available through other systems are linked to, as described above; and records with no existing presentation system are made available through the repository access system, either online or, if not suited to web delivery, on-site in the public search room, or via removable media.

The models are illustrated in Figure 9.4. Here, the user discovers content through a single catalogue, which then links to a variety of access systems as required.

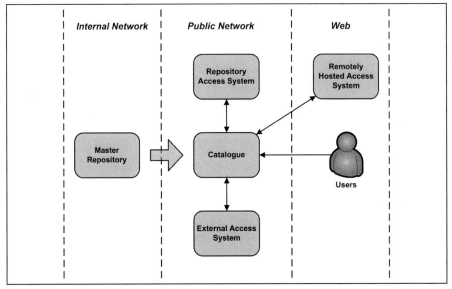

Figure 9.4 Possible access scenarios

9.10 Designing a front end

Successful web design is a skilled, specialized process, and if you are considering a web-based access system, you should certainly think about using a professional web design or user experience company. This will be essential if you don't have in-house expertise available, but is still worth considering even if you do. Your website will be the shop window for your digital collections, and getting its design right is therefore critical to ensuring that it works for your users.

Web design tends to be an iterative process. The designers will start by elucidating the requirements for the system. To support this, they may ask customers to put together 'mood boards', containing reference materials and examples of similar sites. They usually create wireframe models to develop the layout and functionality of each type of web page required, which will typically go through a number of revisions before agreement. These wireframes will then form the basis for the actual development. Further work will be required to finalize the style and branding of the pages.

A good example of this process is provided by the LSE Library's approach to building a web front end for its digital library (the overall development of which is described in a case study in Chapter 4). The Library began by defining technical and functional requirements, undertook a procurement process to select a supplier, then worked with the chosen supplier through the design, implementation, testing and release of the system.

The design process started with a workshop for stakeholders, leading to the development of an information architecture for how the site should work, and wireframe models describing the layout and function of each component page (as shown in Figure 9.5). After various iterations and reviews, these were approved and put into development.

In developing the design, the project team considered a number of *personae* – representative types of end-user: an undergraduate, researcher, lecturer, journalist and public policy adviser. For each, a number of questions were considered, such as how they would find the digital library, what features and functions they would want, what types of content they would be

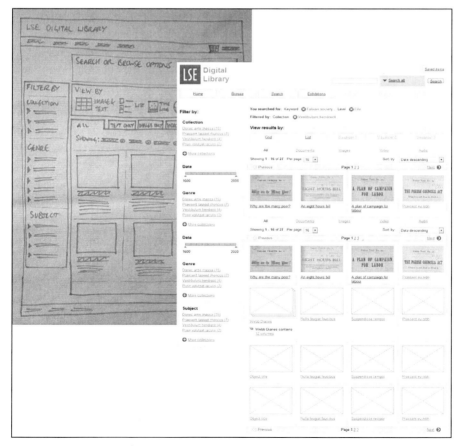

Figure 9.5 Wireframe designs for the LSE Digital Library (London School of Economics and Political Science)

interested in, and what messages the Library might want to convey to them.

The design was then developed using mood boards and wireframes. The finished system was tested extensively by the project team, internal stakeholders, students, library staff and external users.

However well designed and user-friendly the access system is, it is highly unlikely to be completely intuitive to everyone, especially for institutions with diverse user communities. You therefore certainly need to provide guidance and help for your users. This normally includes a series of help pages, explaining the various features of the system. If possible, the help should be contextual – available from, and relevant to, the part of the system the user is currently viewing. It is also common to include frequently asked questions, which should be updated as required to stay current with users' enquiries.

9.11 Citing digital records: persistent identifiers

A repository needs to provide a means for users to cite and otherwise reference its digital collections. This must support a number of different scenarios, from an academic researcher needing to formally cite an electronic record in a publication, to a family historian wishing to persistently bookmark a particular catalogue record in their browser. It requires that every digital object has a reference that refers to it uniquely, and can be relied on to remain meaningful (capable of being interpreted as referring to that object) for at least as long as the object itself exists. Such a reference is commonly known as a 'persistent identifier'.

Most curatorial traditions have established methods for providing persistent identifiers to collection objects: archives use catalogue references, museums and galleries assign accession numbers, while libraries use shelfmarks or accession numbers for individual items, and other forms of classification such as ISBN or Universal Decimal Classification (UDC) for works. Such schemes can, and indeed should, be applied equally well to digital objects, but in a world where digital resources are increasingly available via the web, they may not be sufficient in themselves to provide a means of citation suited to the online environment.

There is, in fact, a standard means of citing web resources, which is familiar to all: the Uniform Resource Locator, or URL. These are actually a form of Uniform Resource Identifier (URI) – URIs are strings of characters which identify a thing; URLs are simply URIs which also specify the means of locating that thing, using the web's HTTP protocol.

Although URLs certainly satisfy the requirement for uniqueness, they do not necessarily offer the same assurance of longevity. Many URLs contain elements that relate to the operation of an underlying content management system, or the technology used to generate the page. They tend to look something like this:

www.example.co.uk/index.php?c=214&br=177&x=11456

Such URLs have a number of disadvantages, particularly in circumstances where the information resources they relate to are expected to be persistent. First, they are so closely tied to the underlying technology (in this case PHP) that any change in that technology also requires a change in the URL. Second, they are fundamentally unintuitive and meaningless to human users.

Tim Berners-Lee, the inventor of the world wide web, defined the concept of 'cool URIs', to address this problem.[16] Essentially, a 'cool' URI is one that is simple, meaningful, independent of the underlying technology, and therefore more likely to be persistent. A cool version of the above URL might look something like this:

www.example.co.uk/publications/2012/report17

This is obvious to a user, and likely to remain valid for a long time, irrespective of the technology used at any given time to provide access to the resource.

It is possible to combine existing identifier schemes with the principles of constructing cool URIs to create persistent, citable web-based identifiers for your repository content. An example of such an approach is given in the case study of the Parliamentary Archives at the end of this chapter.

However, this may not be a suitable solution in all cases. For example, the existing identifier scheme may not lend itself to the restrictions of a URI, perhaps because it includes forbidden characters. In addition, this approach is only valid for as long as the organization (and hence its web domain name) remains in existence, and maintains those URIs. Some memory institutions and other very stable organizations (such as the British Parliament) may have justifiable confidence in this, but others may not.

A number of dedicated persistent identifier schemes for digital objects have therefore emerged. These include Persistent Uniform Rresource

Locators (PURLs),[17] Handles,[18] Digital Object Identifiers (DOIs)[19] and Archival Resource Keys (ARKs).[20] Each has advantages and disadvantages, which should be considered thoroughly before deciding whether or not to implement any of them. A thorough overview from the perspective of smaller organizations is provided in Thomas et al. (2007).

9.12 Case studies
Case study 1 Citing UK parliamentary records

The citation of parliamentary records can be complex. Consider the case of legislation. Various versions of the draft legislation, or Bill, are published as it proceeds through the different stages of parliamentary scrutiny and amendment. Having been signed into law, the archival copy of the Act is deposited in the Parliamentary Archives (printed onto parchment and distinguished by virtue of the handwritten formula of Royal Assent and signature of the Clerk of the Parliaments). The text of the Act is also a published work: printed copies are available for sale through TSO (the Stationery Office, which publishes printed legislation in the UK), and included in the relevant bound volume of all Acts passed in a given parliamentary session, typically purchased by major reference libraries. Finally, the electronic version is published on the Government's online publishing portal for legislation, www.legislation.gov.uk. This plethora of publications is matched by a multitude of identifiers: the archival version is assigned a catalogue reference by the Parliamentary Archives, the printed version has an ISBN, while the online version has a persistent URI; the Act itself can also be cited through its title, year of assent and chapter number (uniquely identifying it within the year).

It was a point of principle for the Archives that, just as born-digital records should be described in its catalogue alongside analogue records, so the same referencing scheme should apply universally. An example of how this is applied to cataloguing archived websites is described in Chapter 7, 'Describing digital objects', but the reference in itself is insufficient to meet the needs of persistent online access and citation. The Parliamentary Archives therefore decided to implement a URI scheme for its collections, which could be applied to a range of web resources, including:

- descriptions of archival records in its online catalogue, Portcullis
- analogue archival records in the physical repository

- digital surrogates of analogue records
- born-digital archival records in its digital repository.

The scheme also needed to be compatible with, and complementary to, any wider URI scheme for published parliamentary information, as well as other relevant URI schemes, such as that used by legislation.gov.uk.

It quickly became apparent that the scheme could be simplified to two forms of URI:

- **Catalogue descriptions**: Each catalogue description of a record should have a unique URI. Analogue records would use the same URI as their catalogue record, since this represents the record in the online world.
- **Digital records**: Born-digital records and digital surrogates should have their own URIs, since both exist as entities in the digital domain.

Fundamentally, a URI can be decomposed into a domain, and an identifier that is unique within that domain:

<uri> ::= <domain> "/" <identifier>

The Archives has a well established system of unique identifiers for its records, which take the form of an alphanumeric catalogue reference. In accordance with archival principles, this reference is hierarchical and derives from the provenance of the record. Thus, the reference for the Legal Deposit Libraries Act, 2003 is HL/PO/PU/1/2003/c28, which can be decomposed as follows:

- **HL**: Records of the House of Lords
- **PO/PU**: Records of the Public Bill Office
- **1**: Original Acts
- **2003**: Original Acts receiving Royal Assent in 2003.

These references are persistent and already provide the standard means of citation by users. It therefore made sense to use these to provide the <identifier> component of the URI.

The catalogue already sits within its own web sub-domain – portcullis.parliament.uk – so it made sense to create an additional sub-domain – archive.parliament.uk – and use it to distinguish the <domain> part of the URI.

Multiple manifestations may be available for a given archival record. At present, these are not assigned URIs – the URI applies only to the information object, and resolves to a 'landing page' providing details of how that object may be accessed, including available manifestations. However, a future extension of the scheme to incorporate manifestations would be possible.

The examples in Table 9.1 illustrate the URI scheme.

Table 9.1 Examples of the Parliamentary Archives URI scheme	
URI	Description
http://portcullis.parliament.uk/hl/po/pu/1/2003/c28	Catalogue description for record reference HL/PO/PU/1/2003/c28 (a file level description)
http://portcullis.parliament.uk/hl/po/pu/1	Catalogue description for record reference HL/PO/PU/1 (a series level description)
http://archive.parliament.uk/hl/po/pu/1/2003/c28	Landing page for digital surrogate of record reference HL/PO/PU/1/2003/c28 (an analogue original)
http://archive.parliament.uk/parl/web/1/1	Landing page for digital original of record reference PARL/WEB/1/1 (an archived website snapshot)

The Wellcome Library has developed a similar system of URIs for its digital content: a URI of the form library.wellcome.ac.uk/player/b123456 would take a user directly to the object with catalogue reference number b123456, in the Library's online delivery system. Their URI scheme is also intended to allow citation within a work; thus, a URI such as

library.wellcome.ac.uk/player/b123456#/35

would point to page 35 of that book. Indeed, they hope to go even further, enabling citation of, for example, a particular section of a page, which users could then share with one another.

Case study 2 Wellcome Library

The Wellcome Library's public access system is based on two key components: a new website, through which users will discover and view content, and a digital delivery system (DDS), which is responsible for actually extracting the relevant content from the digital repository, and passing it to the website in a form suitable for the user. Wellcome contracted a technology integration company, Digirati, to deliver these two components, as well as a separate user experience consultancy, Clearleft, which focused on the look-and-feel and usability of the website.

The building blocks for the presentation system were already in place, as a result of earlier projects to develop SDB (see Chapter 4, 'Models for implementing a digital preservation service') and the digitization workflow system, Goobi (see Chapter 6, 'Accessioning and ingesting digital objects'). In addition, the Library has well established traditional catalogues of its holdings: Sierra for its library collections, CALM for its archival collections, and Wellcome Images for its rich and diverse visual collections, and it intends to extend these to its digital collections. Metadata from these catalogues is harvested and made available via a single search interface, Encore. SDB stores every digital object, and assigns it a unique identifier. Each object also has a corresponding METS file, generated by Goobi, containing all the key metadata describing that object and its structure. The METS file references the SDB identifiers, providing the means to retrieve all the components of that object (such as the pages of a digitized book), and understand how to assemble them into the complete object. Other metadata files, such as METS-ALTO files describing the position of searchable text within a digitized image, may also exist for some types of content.

SDB does not necessarily store objects in a format suitable for providing to end-users. For example, it stores digitized images in JPEG2000 format; this format is not supported by web browsers, and the files may not be of an optimum size for online delivery. Nor is the METS metadata directly suited to consumption by users. The role of the DDS is to translate object and metadata into a form which the Library's website can deliver. The example of digitized images provides a good illustration of the steps which may be involved here.

The normal approach to the problem of delivering JPEG2000 images online is to break them up into smaller pieces, called *tiles*. Each tile is converted to a format suitable for viewing in a web browser (e.g. JPEG or PNG), and sufficiently small that the browser can render it very quickly. A given tile shows only the small portion of the image visible to the user in their browser window (known as the *viewport*), and at a given resolution: as the user moves around the image, or zooms in or out, the system delivers the corresponding tiles for display.

Google Earth[21] and Google Maps[22] are good examples of this approach. Although they allow a user to explore most of the Earth's surface at a very high level of detail, they don't require a web browser to download the entire map in one go; they simply provide a sequence of small image tiles for the portion of that map in the user's viewport at any given moment.

None of this behind the scenes processing is apparent to users, who interact with the Library through a web-based viewer application. Because of the diversity of digital content to which the Library provides access, which includes not only digitized images, but also audiovisual material and a wide variety of born-digital records, they have chosen to call this system a *player*, rather than simply a *viewer*. The design of this player was technically challenging, and critical to the success of the delivery system as a whole. It had to be simple and intuitive for users with widely varying technical skills, and capable of displaying a broad range of content. It must also be scalable in line with the Library's ambitions, ultimately serving up millions of objects to users around the world in a timely fashion. The player also uses the access control mechanisms embedded in the METS file to manage access to content. Finally, in order to enforce the Library's copyright controls, such as online user registration, the system is designed to prevent users from bypassing the player to access content directly. Figure 9.6 shows the Player displaying a digitized manuscript and a video, illustrating how it offers different options and controls depending on content type.

The Library is also making changes to its search system, Encore, to enable it to incorporate full-text searching and provide improved support for archival metadata.

The proposed system may appear complex, but it comprises a number of separate components, each serving a distinct purpose, and working in concert to provide user access. Some of these components are cutting edge, and required bespoke development – or at least customization – to meet the Library's needs, but many are standard, off-the-shelf technologies. It may be helpful to end by summarizing how these various components work together.

The user finds an item of interest through the Library's catalogues, using standard search and browse facilities. If that item is available digitally, the player is automatically launched for the user. The player sends the relevant library catalogue reference to the DDS (or cache), and receives in response a chunk of METS XML metadata containing all of the information required for the player to understand how to display that particular content. The player

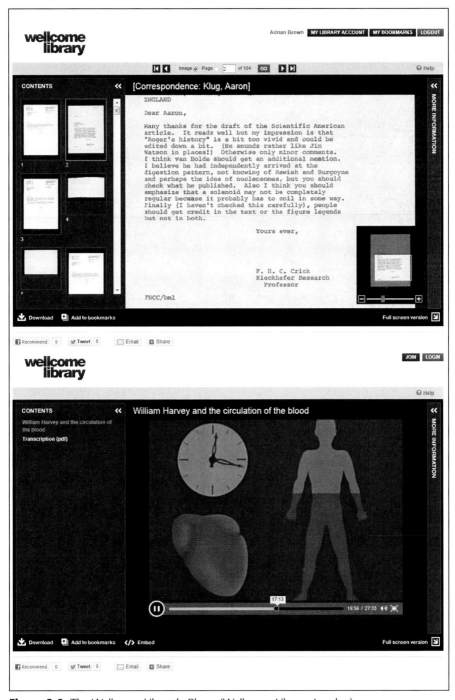

Figure 9.6 The Wellcome Library's Player (Wellcome Library, London)

then uses the references contained within this XML to request the actual content from the DDS. In the case of digitized images, those requests are met by an image server, which generates tiles for the player to display; for other types of content, additional back-end components are being developed which serve an equivalent function.[23]

Case study 3 LSE Library PhoneBooth

With the increasingly widespread use of mobile devices, such as tablets and phones, to access a huge range of information, the app is emerging as an important new channel for memory institutions to deliver content to their users. There can be a danger with any new technology trend that organizations leap to embrace it without necessarily understanding the costs and benefits of doing so. However, the LSE Library's project to develop a mobile app which will broaden access to one of its most striking collections, illustrates how new technologies can open up a whole range of new possibilities for access, when they are harnessed to a clearly defined business need.[24]

The Booth maps are a seminal example of social cartography. Created in the late nineteenth century by the social researcher Charles Booth as part of his research into working class life in London, the maps are colour coded street by street to illustrate relative levels of wealth and poverty across the city, and provide a unique resource for sociologists and historians. Booth's team of investigators accompanied policemen on their beats as they prepared the maps, recording vivid descriptions of the streets and their inhabitants in notebooks, which form an essential accompaniment to the maps themselves. The maps and notebooks have previously been digitized by the LSE Library, and are already accessible online via a conventional web-based interface,[25] but map-based resources naturally lend themselves to mobile use, and library staff realized the potential to develop an innovative access tool, which could link the Booth maps to modern mapping, and use the navigational abilities of mobile devices. Thus a user could stand on a modern London street and, through their mobile phone, automatically retrieve the Booth map for that street. They could overlay a modern street map, or link to the relevant notebook describing the Booth investigators' detailed observations about the street. The Booth maps are studied on LSE undergraduate courses and such an app therefore has the potential to support students in their academic studies, as well as being likely to be of widespread public interest, not least among Londoners.

Funded by JISC, and working in partnership with EDINA,[26] a UK academic data centre that develops and delivers online services for research and education, the LSE has been developing and testing a mobile app called PhoneBooth to realize this vision. Besides linking to a modern base map, the app also combines the historical mapping with the Index of Multiple Deprivation, a 2010 government dataset providing statistics about deprived areas within UK local authorities. A key part of the development has been extensive field testing by LSE students. The results from this have been encouraging,[27] and are helping the developers to fine tune the tool before a public release. The project has created an engaging and appealing focus for highlighting the wider aims of the digital library programme, while providing an opportunity for the digital library team to develop new skills in mobile and geospatial technologies, which can be applied to other parts of the collection in future.

Although still a work in progress, the PhoneBooth project shows the importance of thinking creatively about access, and looking for new opportunities to deliver it in different ways, to different audiences.

9.13 Key points

- **Base resource discovery around existing systems where possible**: Using any existing catalogue will not only provide a more seamless experience for users, but also enable you to draw on proven functionality.
- **Understand the needs and expectations of your users**: This will enable you to deliver an access system that meets their requirements.
- **Choose an appropriate access model**: This should balance technical considerations and user needs. Reuse existing access systems wherever possible.
- **Consider conditions of use**: Make sure that you have identified any constraints or conditions regarding use of your digital material, and defined an approach for managing them.
- **Define a scheme for persistent, citable identifiers.**

9.14 Notes

1 See http://labs.nationalarchives.gov.uk/wordpress/index.php/2011/01/cabinet-papers-keywords/.

2 See http://labs.nationalarchives.gov.uk/wordpress/index.php/2012/08/foreign-

affairs-timeline/.

3 See http://maps.cheshire.gov.uk/tithemaps/.

4 See www.nationalarchives.gov.uk/cabinetpapers/maps-in-time.htm.

5 See http://labs.nationalarchives.gov.uk/wordpress/index.php/2012/04/collections-on-a-map/.

6 See www.lib.utah.edu/collections/digital/map.php.

7 See https://developers.google.com/maps/.

8 See www.historypin.com/map/.

9 See, for example, Cabinet Office (2012).

10 See http://datacatalogs.org/.

11 See http://creativecommons.org/.

12 See http://wiki.creativecommons.org/Ccrel.

13 See www.nytimes.com/2009/07/18/technology/companies/18amazon.html?_r=1.

14 Legal Deposit Libraries Act 2003.

15 The AIMS project has published useful guidance on models for discovery and access, which may also be of interest, see AIMS Work Group (2012, 42–60).

16 See www.w3.org/Provider/Style/URI and W3C Interest Group (2008).

17 See http://purl.org/.

18 See www.handle.net/.

19 See www.doi.org/.

20 See https://confluence.ucop.edu/display/Curation/ARK.

21 See http://earth.google.co.uk/.

22 See http://maps.google.co.uk/.

23 See http://wellcomelibrary.org/.

24 See www2.lse.ac.uk/library/collections/digital/projects/PhoneBooth.aspx.

25 See http://booth.lse.ac.uk/.

26 See http://edina.ac.uk/.

27 See the project blog at http://jiscphonebooth.wordpress.com/.

10

Future trends

10.1 Introduction

Attempts to predict trends in technology beyond the very short term are fraught with difficulty, and frequently offer little more than unintentional entertainment for future readers. Having said that, in as rapidly changing a field as digital preservation, there is some value in considering the areas of progress that are most apparent, and how they may manifest. This chapter looks at emerging technologies and trends within the digital preservation community and beyond, where they are likely to have an impact on that community.

10.2 Preservation tools and services

To date, the majority of research into, and implementation of, digital preservation services has taken place within the public sector, led by the national memory institutions. As a result, the market for commercial solutions has remained relatively small, but there are indications that the private sector is now beginning to grapple with these issues in earnest. The potential demand from sectors such as banking, pharmaceuticals and aerospace is colossal (see 'The current market' in Chapter 4). These organizations typically look for commercial, 'off-the-shelf' solutions. If this trend continues, it could substantially change the shape of the market, encouraging a wide range of vendors to offer digital preservation solutions. Such a development can only be positive, creating a healthy degree of competition.

Current commercial services have typically emerged from the incubators of flagship public sector projects: for example, Ex Libris' Rosetta from the National Library of New Zealand's National Digital Heritage Archive, and Tessella's SDB from the UK National Archives' digital archive. These vendors have tended to market their products to the large cultural memory institutions, focusing on consolidating their positions in these sectors. However, this is a small market and easily saturated, and they are increasingly looking to diversify, targeting smaller organizations, with correspondingly more modest budgets. One manifestation of this is likely to be a growth in utility preservation services in the Cloud, such as Tessella's Preservica (see Chapter 4, 'Models for implementing a digital preservation service' and later in this chapter). Another might be 'lite' versions of products, offering lower implementation and support costs at the price of less flexibility.

Existing suppliers of other types of information management product, such as collections management systems and EDRMSs, may also increasingly look to acquire, develop or offer integration with digital preservation tools in order to maintain a one-stop-shop solution within their domains. Meanwhile, the established open-source repository platforms look set to continue developing very actively. It is likely that the consolidation of this latter sector into a few mature systems will benefit smaller organizations, as this should lead to improvements in usability and support, as well as functionality.

Almost all repository solutions rely extensively on specialized third-party tools for a wide range of tasks, from virus and integrity checking, to characterization and format migration. This requires the development of some form of 'wrapper' for each tool, code that allows each repository to control and use it. The range of tools supported is undoubtedly a key differentiator between systems, and suppliers therefore need to invest a significant proportion of their effort in growing that range, ensuring that it remains comprehensive and up to date. This in turn may lead tool developers to develop more standardized interfaces, making it as simple as possible for repository suppliers to use them. The range of specialized tools is itself likely to continue growing at a substantial rate. New tools are appearing regularly, as a result of research projects, commercial development, hackathons and individual initiative.

As well as tools to be installed and run locally, many digital preservation functions can be operated as remote services, offered by a third party. We are already starting to see examples of organizations offering specific services as a general good, such as the UK National Archives' PRONOM technical registry, and this may well become increasingly widespread. From this could emerge a new information economy comprising distributed preservation micro-service providers: a repository might be able to use provider A for format identification, provider B for validation and metadata transformation, and provider C for preservation planning. Indeed, it could be much more granular, with provider D (an audiovisual archive) offering preservation planning for sound and moving image objects, while provider E, a national library, does the same for e-book formats.

Such an environment would also raise potential challenges in areas such as information security and legal compliance. These challenges will tend to apply mostly to services that require the actual digital objects to be processed by a third-party service provider, such as format migration, rather than those that depend only on the processing of metadata, or local processing using third-party tools, such as DROID. For example, organizations holding sensitive personal data are likely to be restricted in the extent to which they can send that data to third parties, or outside a particular geographical area. Therefore any such network of brokered services might focus, in the first instance, primarily on metadata-centric services, rather than data-centric ones. It may also be that such an environment will be more immediately attractive to, and more tailored towards the needs of, libraries and other institutions holding a greater proportion of non-unique, published information.

The ever-growing range of tools and services in turn brings the challenge of how to keep track of them, and identify the right tool for the right job. For this we need registries or 'service brokers' – systems to help repositories identify and select between the tools and services they need. PRONOM was perhaps the prototypical example of such a registry, but other examples are now emerging, such as the Library of Congress' Tools Showcase.[1] The SPRUCE project maintains a meta-list of such tool registries.[2]

It is most likely that in future a mixed economy of tool, service and platform providers will emerge, offering organizations a sophisticated range of options from which to assemble their digital repositories.

10.3 Preservation-as-a-Service

The emergence of Preservation-as-a-Service (PraaS) looks likely to develop into a significant trend, and is sufficiently different to standard commercial models to merit considering separately. The few existing examples, such as DuraCloud and Preservica, have been described in Chapter 4, 'Models for implementing a digital preservation service', but it is probable that further examples will appear in the near future, with existing digital repository software providers positioning themselves to provide services alongside their more traditional software offerings.

So what might PraaS look like? For the institution, it will require no more physical infrastructure than an internet connection, a desktop workstation with a web browser, and possibly some form of temporary local storage area for collating content before ingest. Staff will interact with the repository entirely through the browser, whether launching new ingests, managing data, executing preservation plans or searching for content. The service provider will be completely responsible for the repository infrastructure, and the services it provides. Indeed, they may offer a wider range of services than conventional repositories. For example, they might well provide a complete preservation planning service, in which the customer is simply notified of content at risk, offered a proposed mitigation (or range of mitigations, perhaps at different prices), and asked to approve its execution. PraaS providers may also be able to leverage a wide customer base to help shape and refine their services; one might, for example, foresee a preservation plan recommendation service, which takes account of other customers' choices when weighting particular options.

PraaS has a number of attractions for the smaller organization, not least a pay-per-use pricing model – you only pay for the volume of data you actually need to preserve at a given time, and for the level of preservation you require, with no up-front capital investment. Flexibility is another benefit – if you suddenly need to ingest a large and unexpected volume of data, then you can do so, subject to costs; equally, if demand should drop, you can scale back immediately to suit, rather than pay for unused capacity. These potential benefits can also bring attendant risks and disadvantages, as discussed with reference to the Cloud in general in Chapter 8, 'Preserving digital objects'.

PraaS could require a compromise between flexibility and control on the one hand, and ease of use on the other. For smaller organizations, that may well be considered a compromise worth accepting, in return for the opportunity to actually engage with digital preservation on a practical level. However, PraaS providers will need to price their services keenly if they are to realize their full potential, and especially if they are to tap into the vast market represented by small organizations, and the developing world (see later in this chapter).

10.4 Representation information registries

Representation information registries are widely recognized as one of the key elements of an international digital preservation infrastructure. Whichever current or future preservation strategies may be practised, it seems inevitable that they will depend on reliable information about the technologies required to provide access to digital objects. The ultimate goal must be for an open, universally accessible portal to comprehensive, authoritative representation information, whether it derives from a single source or a distributed system, and whatever the underpinning technologies and governance structures. Although major progress has already been made in this area, as described later in this section, we are still some distance from achieving this ambition.

For any registry, content is very much king; however sophisticated the technology or governance model, it ultimately stands and falls by the quality and quantity of its information, and the ease with which it can be accessed. The most frequently heard criticism of PRONOM, the longest-standing and most widely used registry, is that it doesn't contain details of a particular format or software tool; in some cases this is a genuine gap, in others it is due to the user being unable to find content which is actually present, perhaps because of the complexity of the interface.

The effort and time required to maintain such a registry cannot be underestimated; at the same time, it is by no means an insurmountable problem. If we limit ourselves to file formats, for example, it is possible to estimate the number that a registry might need to record. On 29 November 2012, Wikipedia listed 3607 format extensions.[3] A minority of these extensions (perhaps 10%) applied to multiple versions of a format; allowing for this, and the inevitable incompleteness of the list, it is unlikely that the true number of formats in existence exceeds 8000. However, if one were to draw a graph representing the number of files ever created in each of these formats, it would reveal an exponential distribution; in other words, a small number of formats account for the majority of actual digital objects. This is because the majority of these formats are either very obscure, and therefore unlikely to be encountered in real-world preservation scenarios, or system files which would only be relevant in very specific emulation scenarios. A representation information registry can therefore prioritize a relatively small number of formats (certainly less than 1000) and still expect to cover the vast majority of objects requiring long-term preservation. The content of PRONOM has been primarily developed by a handful of staff in one organization (although latterly with significant contributions from a number of other institutions) and, on the same date that Wikipedia was consulted above, included information on 934 formats. Admittedly, perhaps half of these are only outline records, and lack the full detail ultimately required. Nonetheless, this illustrates that some concentrated effort by a small number of institutions could easily develop and maintain a comprehensive and authoritative registry – the biggest obstacle is developing the organizational will and co-ordination to make it happen.

The development of such a registry is undoubtedly a strong candidate for a collaborative approach, not only as a means of spreading the workload, but also because it enables the registry to draw on the expertise of a wide range of organizations and individuals; for example, a sound archive could contribute information on audio formats, while an archaeological data archive might be well placed to supply information on geospatial data standards. Increasingly, the focus is on community action, such as 'hackdays', or the 'Solve the file format problem month' action proposed by Jason Scott of the Archive Team,[4] which involved a dedicated month (November 2012) of concerted action by online volunteers, to collect as much file format documentation as possible and collate it into a wiki.[5] Taking a slightly different approach, in 2012 the SPRUCE project (see later in this chapter) launched the Crowd sourced Representation Information for Supporting Preservation (cRIsp) wiki, which aims to use crowd sourcing to identify online sources of representation information.[6] It is intended that these can then be harvested by web archives and fed into other representation registry initiatives.

These community initiatives are excellent for gathering information, and channelling the enormous pool of enthusiasm and expertise which exists across the web. They are likely to be less suited to structuring and maintaining the results as persistent, reliable information resources on which the digital preservation community will be willing to rely. The best answer may therefore be to draw on the respective strengths of each approach – use community action to gather the raw data, in genuine partnership with major memory institutions, which can develop and maintain that resource.

Perhaps the hardest problem to solve will be how to foster continued community input, to ensure that the registry remains current. The idea of collaborative maintenance first found limited expression in PRONOM's facility for submitting new information, and was subsequently more fully developed in the Global Digital Format Registry (GDFR) model,[7] although the latter never materialized as an operational service. A number of current initiatives are developing these ideas further, as described below.

Unified Digital Format Registry

The Unified Digital Format Registry (UDFR) initiative aims to develop a single, shared format registry, based on the previous work of a number of institutions, and most notably PRONOM and GDFR.[8] In particular, it arises from the desire of many of the major international cultural memory institutions to combine the well developed content and mature technology base of the former with the innovative model for shared governance, co-operative data contribution, and distributed data hosting developed by the latter.

To this end, an *ad hoc* governing body was established in 2009, chaired by Libraries and Archives Canada, the other institutions represented being The National Archive of the UK, Harvard University Library, the British Library, the University of Illinois at Urbana-Champaign, Georgia Institute of Technology, the National Archives and Records Administration in the USA (NARA), the Koninklijke Bibliotheek, the Library of Congress, the California Digital Library, the German National Library and the National Library of New Zealand.

Work to develop the UDFR is being led by the California Digital Library, with funding from the Library of Congress' National Digital Information Infrastructure and Preservation Program (NDIIPP). In its present form, it comprises a central format registry, hosted by the California Digital Library and populated with the entire contents of PRONOM and the IANA MIME-type registry, with a mechanism to allow shared contribution of new content by multiple organizations, and quality vetting for contributed data.

The UDFR went live in July 2012, but has received a mixed reception from the community; while some have welcomed it as a 'great day for practical approaches to electronic records',[9] others have been critical of its usability and sustainability.[10] A permanent operational home and governance structure are still to be agreed, and the final ambition to create a distributed registry network, with a mechanism to automatically replicate content between multiple instances hosted by various institutions, remains unfulfilled and unfunded at present. Whether UDFR can become a vital piece of global digital preservation infrastructure, or will wither away, remains to be seen.

The Open Planets Foundation registry ecosystem

The Open Planets Foundation (OPF) has now taken the distributed registry idea further, allying it to the possibilities of linked data, in its proposal for a 'registry ecosystem', which it outlined in 2011.[11] This concept is based on a set of disparate, but linked, information sources rather than a single, centralized registry. These might include memory institutions, technology suppliers and standards bodies, or even be derived from crowd sourcing, and could have varying levels of trustworthiness. For example, one might take information on Microsoft Word 2010 from Microsoft, and on XHTML from the W3C, both of which could be considered authoritative; at the same time, one might choose to accept crowd sourced information of more doubtful provenance about an obsolete format, and choose to research an obscure format of purely local interest for oneself.

At the heart of this, OPF proposes a 'dashboard client', a piece of software through which an organization can control what information it derives from which source, using linked data as the underlying technology. This client then effectively becomes your local registry instance, configured to contain the content you need, taken from the sources you choose to trust.

This approach requires two things for success: first, that existing registries expose their content as linked data, and second, the development and widespread uptake of a suitable dashboard client. As will be seen in the following sections, the first of these is already starting to happen, and OPF has stated its intention to support the second by:

- establishing a core data model and exchange format for registry information
- developing a prototype dashboard client
- creating guidelines to help existing or planned registries achieve interoperability with the ecosystem
- developing a standard corpus of registry information.

Provided the client is stable and easy to use by a wide variety of organizations, this approach offers many attractions, and should enable smaller organizations to benefit from access to representation information tailored to their specific requirements.

The OPF also proposes the separation of factual representation information from the policy decisions that an organization may take, based on that information. It suggests that the latter should be maintained in local 'preservation policy registries', which will be the subject of separate OPF proposals.[12]

The P2 registry

An example of the kind of distributed registry environment envisioned by the OPF is provided by the P2 registry,[13] which was developed under the auspices of two JISC-funded projects in the UK – initially Preserv[14] and subsequently KeepIt.[15] Led by Southampton University, the P2 registry seeks to provide a semantically enhanced registry to support digital preservation. It combines data from two sources, PRONOM and DBpedia,[16] a linked data version of Wikipedia. In addition to making format information from PRONOM available in a much more flexible form, this enables new relationships to be built between these two sources. The substantial background information held by DBpedia on specific file formats can be linked to the detailed data on format versions and migration pathways in PRONOM. New connections can then be made – for example, the number of tools identified as being able to read one particular format (PDF 1.4) jumped from 19 in PRONOM to 70 in the P2 registry.[17]

Linked data PRONOM

Meanwhile, the UK National Archives is working to develop a linked data version of PRONOM, and published a proposed RDF vocabulary to underpin this in 2011.[18] This should make future initiatives such as the P2 registry much simpler – whereas P2 had to develop a tool specifically to harvest PRONOM data and translate it into RDF, the new version of PRONOM will provide its content in this form natively.

KEEP

The EU-funded KEEP project (discussed more generally later in this chapter) is researching the representation information required specifically to support emulation-based preservation strategies. These require the re-creation of entire technology environments, including software, operating system and hardware layers, and consequently depend on detailed representation information to describe such environments. KEEP is therefore developing an information model for describing the technology platforms required to support emulation of both simple and complex digital objects. Such research is essential if emulation is to become a mainstream preservation strategy, and should underpin the development of more mature emulators, suitable for use by smaller organizations.

10.5 Storage

We are creating digital information at an ever greater rate; one need only consider how our commonplace metrics for talking about data volumes have changed in magnitude over a few decades, from kilobytes and megabytes, to petabytes and exabytes. In 2000, the terabyte (1000 gigabytes) was a unit of measurement reserved for very large data archives; by 2010, it had become the norm for consumer hard drives. We regularly encounter new initiatives that require us to redefine our notions of what 'big' means in the digital world. For example, the Large Hadron Collider at CERN, which went into full operation in 2010, produces about 15 petabytes (15,000 terabytes) of data each year.[19] Even this will be dwarfed by the Square Kilometre Array, a radio telescope currently under construction in Australia and South Africa. When this goes into full operation in 2024, it is expected to generate over one exabyte (1000 petabytes) of raw data every day, approximately twice the current volume of daily global internet traffic. Even after processing, up to 1.5 exabytes of data will need to be stored each year.[20]

Storage technology vendors are engaged in a relentless cycle of innovation to meet this insatiable demand, which has tended to drive unit costs down. For example, storage capacities for magnetic disk have tended to increase at a predictable, exponential rate known as Kryder's Law, doubling every 12 months, while storage costs have halved at the same rate. We have therefore always been able to budget on the basis that the cost of storing a gigabyte next year will be significantly cheaper than today. This in turn has helped organizations to manage data growth without escalating budgets.

Conventional spinning magnetic disk (HDD) technology continues to evolve, with vendors experimenting with new techniques such as heat-assisted magnetic recording (HAMR) and bit-patterned media (BPM) recording to increase the density with which data can be recorded on a disk, and hence its storage capacity. Although HDDs remain the norm, other storage technologies continue to develop. Solid state drives (SSDs), usually based on flash memory, are becoming increasingly widespread as alternative secondary storage devices. They offer much faster access times than HDDs and – lacking any moving parts – are also more physically robust, making them especially suited to use in mobile devices, such as laptops. Storage capacities are currently lower, and unit costs higher, than spinning disk, although this may change in future.

Holographic disks have often been touted as representing the future for data storage, but recent initiatives appear to have fallen into abeyance, partly due to difficulties with the technology, but also because the continued development of HDD and SSD technologies has reduced the commercial impetus. In the meantime, experimental storage technologies based on concepts such as molecular memory, nanotechnology and quantum holography continue to be explored; some of these may ultimately yield the next storage revolution.

The Cloud is also likely to feature increasingly in the calculations of any organization considering data storage needs. Cloud storage, also commonly referred to as Infrastructure-as-a-Service (IaaS), offers both opportunities and threats for digital preservation, which have already been considered in some detail in Chapter 8, 'Preserving digital objects'. In the context of future trends in storage, the most obvious advantage is that it insulates organizations from the need to worry about storage technologies – they are simply buying a specified storage space without having to think about the technology used to provide it. It is also likely that offerings tailored to the specific requirements of archival storage will emerge as cloud services mature. For example, these may offer rigorous control over which legal jurisdictions data is stored in, and increased durability levels.

Few repositories are so far using the Cloud, but this may change if it can offer a compelling economic argument. Cloud suppliers may be able to offer services that appear very keenly priced in relation to conventional technologies. For example, in 2012 Amazon launched a new storage service, Glacier, priced at $0.01 per GB per month.[21] However, assessing the economics of preservation is not simple, and requires careful modelling of the total cost of ownership of each alternative, over a defined period.

Some commentators are predicting a fast-approaching crisis in digital storage, occasioned by demand outstripping the ability of vendors to meet it at affordable prices. The standard assumption that unit storage costs will continue to fall at current rates may cease to be valid, as vendors struggle to overcome the physical limitations that current technologies place on storage densities. For example, David Rosenthal, Chief Scientist for the LOCKSS programme, notes on his blog[22] that, while demand for storage is increasing by 60% per annum, some analysts predict that unit costs may only drop by 20% each year. Elsewhere, he has cast doubt on the idea that cloud storage providers will be able to reduce their prices at the same rate as the underlying storage technologies.[23] This would mean that, while cloud storage might initially appear very competitive compared to in-house storage, the longer-term prognosis might be very different.

For business archives and others, which may depend on corporate IT support, the economics of storage may change in ways that are not immediately obvious. For example, corporate IT strategies may dictate an increasing move of services to the Cloud. This may have the effect of increasing the cost of any remaining in-house infrastructure, and hence alter the economic balance of arguments for an in-house versus outsourced digital repository. Smaller organizations certainly need to consider the economics of their storage solution very carefully, to ensure that it is sustainable and offers best value for money.

10.6 Training and professional bodies

Any organization seeking to build digital preservation capabilities needs to be able to recruit or develop staff with appropriate skills. This in turn requires the provision of high-quality training, as part of existing graduate and postgraduate courses in the information management and information technology domains, and as free-standing vocational training. The current provision of such training has been discussed in Chapter 4, 'Models for implementing a digital preservation service'.

It is likely that digital preservation skills will continue to form an increasingly large element of postgraduate information management courses, especially in archival and library sciences, while further courses wholly dedicated to digital curation may continue to emerge. It is to be hoped that this will be coupled by the availability of a much wider range of shorter training courses suitable for in-service staff training and continuing professional development.

Existing professional bodies, not only for curators but also IT, such as the BCS, the Chartered Institute for IT in the UK,[24] have a role to play here too, while it is possible that entirely new bodies for the digital curator may emerge. Such bodies could provide a means to establish benchmarks for professional skills and competencies, support continuing professional development, and contribute significantly to the increasing recognition and professionalization of the discipline.

Advocacy and knowledge sharing bodies, such as the UK's Digital Preservation Coalition[25] and the Netherlands Coalition for Digital Preservation[26] will continue to play a vital role in supporting professional development. Likewise, organizations such as the OPF may have much to offer. The OPF is a membership organization 'established to provide practical solutions and expertise in digital preservation, building on the research and development outputs of the Planets project'.[27] While at present its membership rates are likely to be too high to attract many smaller organizations, they can still benefit from the wealth of information it publishes online, as well as events such as hackathons, which it regularly organizes.

10.7 Certification schemes

The various standards for certifying trusted digital repositories may be expected to mature and rationalize within the next few years. It is to be hoped that a small, practical and complementary set of standards will emerge, offering genuine benefits and a compelling case for adoption by repositories of all sizes. At present, the development of the European Framework for Audit and Certification of Digital Repositories (see Chapter 4, 'Models for implementing a digital preservation service') seems to offer the best hope for rationalization and, although Europe-centric, should be equally applicable worldwide. Whether or not it proves capable of scaling down to the smallest organizations, as well as upwards, will need to be demonstrated through practical application.

10.8 New paradigms

Digital preservation will need to evolve to reflect the new ways in which we create, manage and consume information. For example, vast amounts of personal data now exist on social networks, and the impact that the unintended or malicious reuse of that information can have features regularly in news stories. From embarrassment to more serious consequences, such as losing one's job, we continue to discover that, while the digital information we want to preserve can prove terribly fragile, what we would prefer to destroy or hide may turn out to be all too persistent. This is driving legislative changes, such as the European Commission's planned introduction of a 'right to be forgotten', due to form part of an overhaul of EU privacy laws. Such changes may prove inimical for memory institutions, not only because they may affect what content they are allowed to collect, and for how long, but also because the content may be destroyed long before it ever reaches them. Libraries and archives will need to lobby hard to ensure that their requirements are not ignored.

The development of the Semantic Web also poses challenges to traditional views of curation: what do you seek to preserve in an environment composed of vast numbers of interlinked units of information, and how do you describe the provenance of that information? But there are opportunities here, too, enabling institutions not only to offer new modes of access to their digital information holdings, but also to diminish some of the boundaries between physical and digital information holdings.

Many libraries and archives are experimenting with linked open data (LOD) to expose the content of their traditional collections management systems, and to provide consistent, integrated information about their physical and digital collections, linked to the actual content wherever possible, including digital surrogates. For example, the JISC-funded 'Step Change' project has developed LOD functionality in CALM, one of the leading commercial collections management systems for archives, libraries and museums.[28] LOD also offers the potential to extend traditional approaches to arranging and managing information, without requiring those approaches to be abandoned or altered. For example, archival description based on ISAD (G) remains as relevant as ever for physical collections, and can be applied equally well to digital records. However, it may not allow the full potential of those digital records to be realized. A linked data approach can allow new facts about, and relationships between, digital objects to be defined, at any level of granularity. These new forms of descriptive information don't negate or supersede the traditional ones; they enhance and complement them.

The role of social media and community engagement in tackling digital preservation challenges is also starting to be recognized. A great example of this is the JISC-funded project SPRUCE in the UK.[29] Hosted by the OPF, in partnership with the University of Leeds, British Library, Digital Preservation Coalition and London School of Economics, SPRUCE is pioneering a range of online and face-to-face community events, which bring together digital preservation practitioners and developers to solve practical problems. Funding is available to help participants continue developing the activities started during these events, and eventually embed them into business as usual, and the aim is to foster a self-sustaining community. The SPRUCE website maintains a list of such community initiatives.[30]

10.9 Current and future research

There is no sign that research activity in digital preservation is abating; if anything, an ever greater range of projects is being undertaken, by a growing pool of organizations. In Europe, the European Commission remains the major funder, through its Seventh Framework Programme (FP7),[31] as evidenced by the range of projects being funded as of 2012, which include:

- **APARSEN**: a network of excellence supporting digital preservation practitioners and researchers[32]
- **ARCOMEM**: using the social web to support content appraisal, selection and preservation, including the development of next-generation web archiving tools[33]
- **BlogForever**: creating tools to preserve, manage and provide long-term access to weblogs[34]
- **ENSURE**: extending the state of the art in digital preservation to data held by commercial organizations, in domains such as aerospace, health care, finance and clinical trials[35]
- **KEEP**: building portable emulators for static and dynamic digital objects[36]
- **PrestoPRIME**: developing tools and services to provide long-term preservation of, and access to, digital audiovisual content[37]
- **SCAPE**: developing a scalable infrastructure and tools to undertake preservation actions, a framework for running automated, quality-assured preservation workflows, and a policy-based preservation planning system[38]
- **TIMBUS**: integrating digital preservation with business continuity management, to address the challenges of ensuring continued access to services and software[39]
- **Wf4Ever**: developing methods and tools to preserve scientific workflows.[40]

In the USA an equally diverse range of projects continues to be funded from a number of sources. The NDIIPP, led by the Library of Congress, has funded an enormous variety of research since 2000, and that work is today being extended through the National Digital Stewardship Alliance,[41] which is focusing on content, standards and practices, infrastructure, innovation and outreach. Other regular sources of research funding include the Andrew W. Mellon Foundation,[42] the National Historical Publications and Records Commission[43] and the National Science Foundation.[44]

Outside the USA and Europe, research tends to be more focused at an institutional level, or as part of global groups such as the International Internet Preservation Consortium, but this does not limit its scope to deliver results of worldwide value, from the National Library of New Zealand's funding of Rosetta, to the National Archives of Australia's Xena tool. Although research activity beyond the west is currently much more limited, it is to be hoped that this will change in future.

While keeping abreast of this wealth of research may sometimes seem intimidating, if not overwhelming, it promises to yield many advances for the future, from which practitioners everywhere will benefit. There are a number of excellent sources which summarize current digital preservation activity, including the bi-monthly *D-Lib Magazine*,[45] the Library of Congress' monthly *Digital Preservation Newsletter*[46] and the plethora of relevant blogs, Twitter feeds and other social media. Chapter 8, 'Preserving digital objects', lists further sources (see 'Preservation planning in practice' in Chapter 8).

10.10 Digital preservation in the developing world

Digital preservation has hitherto been considered a 'luxury' activity, exclusive to a developed world which generates and depends on vast and ever-increasing volumes of digital information, and has the resources and capacity to address the concomitant preservation challenges. By contrast, the developing world has lacked the ubiquitous digital infrastructure, information landscape and financial wherewithal to address an issue that, by most measures, pales into insignificance in the face of civil war, famine, disease and poverty.

However, there are already signs that this is beginning to change, and it seems inevitable that, over the next decade, countries in the developing world will increasingly implement digital preservation solutions too. Partly, this is simply an emergent response to the development of national digital infrastructures, but the primary impetus is transparency and accountability.

It has for many years been recognized that good records management is fundamental to achieving transparency and accountability within public administrations, and organizations such as the International Records Management Trust[47] have long led the way in this, working with governments, aid agencies and others to establish a tradition of rigorous recordkeeping in developing countries. Of necessity, this has previously focused on paper-based systems, but electronic records management is now an increasing feature of their work. This, in turn, is driving a growing recognition of the need to underpin current information systems with the solid foundations of digital preservation. To begin with, the emphasis was on providing guidance, such as the IRMT's Training in Electronic Records Management programme;[48] however, in countries like Tanzania the development of practical digital preservation capability is being pioneered through institutions such as the Eastern and Southern African Management Institute's Centre of Excellence for the Management of Electronic Records.[49] The emergence of PraaS is likely to stimulate and accelerate this trend, by providing access to affordable preservation services with minimal infrastructure or expertise overheads.

10.11 Moving to the mainstream

Perhaps the greatest challenge for digital preservation, and the truest yardstick for its success, will be to embed itself fully into the mainstream of information management and IT processes, becoming a routine background activity – in effect, to disappear. For memory institutions, this requires the availability of tools and services every bit as robust and mature as those on which they depend for managing traditional collections. But, as the rise of the 'digital native' continues, so we expect our personal digital information assets – our photographs, videos, music collections and blogs – to enjoy the same longevity as institutional archives.

Digital preservation must therefore also establish itself at a personal level, becoming a basic function of our personal computing devices – intrinsic to the operation of every software application – on a par with, say, the ability to create folders and move files between them, or to open and save files.

What might this mean in practice? We could imagine an operating system that automatically detects when any file under its control ceases to be accessible using available software. It might do this proactively, or at the point the user tries to access it. It could then automatically undertake the necessary preservation actions to allow access to continue, which might include downloading new or updated software, migrating the file to another format, or launching it in an appropriate emulation environment. The operating system could perform these actions automatically or with user permission.

Operating systems may also develop more sophisticated support for bitstream preservation. With its Time Machine back-up tool, Apple has already demonstrated a seamless, user-friendly approach to back-up, and there are a growing range of products that provide automatic data replication to the Cloud, for improved resilience. Automated integrity checking could easily become a basic desktop function.

Embedding digital preservation functions will provide the guarantee that any file a user saves will remain intact and accessible, as standard operating system feature.

The operating system may well also take on a wider range of information management functions, including:

- true version control
- rich metadata support, extrinsic to files
- the ability to move beyond simply managing files, to managing information; this might include support for aggregations of data, or for alternative manifestations of the same information object
- disposal scheduling
- semi-automated classification of information
- support for flexible views of data, with multiple simultaneous hierarchies, rather than being restricted to a single folder structure.

An increasing proportion of functions that have traditionally been provided by locally installed software applications are also likely to be provided in future as online services, which users consume on demand from the Cloud. Major software vendors are already offering cloud-based versions of their traditional desktop products, such as Microsoft Office 365,[50] while native cloud alternatives, such as Google Drive,[51] Zoho[52] and ThinkFree[53] continue to emerge. Users will increasingly store and share their data via the Web, whether through these cloud-based productivity suites, dedicated hosting sites for particular types of data (e.g. Flickr for images[54]) or generic file hosting tools such as DropBox.[55] With their data and software online, the traditional notion of an operating system may even cease to be relevant to users; Google, for one, has long pioneered the concept of a browser-based desktop operating system. In this ecosystem, digital preservation functions may simply become one more standard online service, consumed by all with no more thought or fuss than receiving updated antivirus definitions.

10.12 Conclusion

While reiterating the caveats about futurology from the beginning of this chapter, it is unlikely to be controversial to predict that digital preservation will become an increasingly mainstream activity over the next few years, with ever more mature and sophisticated services available to a wider range of audiences, at a decreasing cost; this can only accelerate its move from the preserve of the major cultural memory institutions to a function simply and easily adopted by organizations of all sizes.

10.13 Notes

1   See www.digitalpreservation.gov/tools/.
2   See http://wiki.opf-labs.org/display/SPR/Digital+Preservation+Tools.
3   Information extracted from
    http://en.wikipedia.org/wiki/List_of_file_formats_(alphabetical).
4   See http://ascii.textfiles.com/archives/3645.
5   See http://fileformats.archiveteam.org/wiki/Main_Page.
6   See http://wiki.opf-labs.org/display/SPR/Crowd+sourced+Representation+
    Information+for+Supporting+Preservation+%28CRISP%29.
7   See http://gdfr.info/.
8   See www.udfr.org/.
9   See http://e-records.chrisprom.com/happy-day-udfr-released/.
10 See, for example, http://fileformats.wordpress.com/2012/08/25/registries-2/.
11 Roberts (2011).
12 Roberts (2011, 4–5).
13 See http://p2-registry.ecs.soton.ac.uk/.
14 See http://preserv.eprints.org/.
15 See http://preservation.eprints.org/keepit/.
16 See http://dbpedia.org/About.
17 Tarrant, Hitchcock and Carr (2009, 190).
18 The National Archives (2011).
19 See http://user.web.cern.ch/public/en/LHC/Computing-en.html.
20 See www-03.ibm.com/press/us/en/pressrelease/37361.wss.
21 See http://aws.amazon.com/glacier/.
22 See http://blog.dshr.org/2012/07/three-numbers-presage-crisis.html.

23 See, for example, http://blog.dshr.org/2012/08/amazons-announcement-of-glacier.html#more, http://blog.dshr.org/2012/02/cloud-storage-pricing-history.html, and http://blog.dshr.org/2012/06/cloud-vs-local-storage-costs.html.

24 See www.bcs.org/.

25 See www.dpconline.org/.

26 See www.ncdd.nl/.

27 See www.openplanetsfoundation.org/about.

28 See http://openmetadatapathway.blogspot.co.uk/.

29 See www.dpconline.org/advocacy/spruce and http://wiki.opf-labs.org/display/SPR/Home.

30 See http://wiki.opf-labs.org/display/SPR/Collaborate+with+the+digital+preservation+community.

31 See http://cordis.europa.eu/fp7/.

32 See www.alliancepermanentaccess.org/.

33 See www.arcomem.eu/.

34 See http://blogforever.eu/.

35 See http://ensure-fp7.eu/.

36 See www.keep-project.eu/.

37 See www.prestoprime.org/.

38 See www.scape-project.eu/.

39 See http://timbusproject.net/.

40 See www.wf4ever-project.org/.

41 See www.digitalpreservation.gov/ndsa/.

42 See www.mellon.org/.

43 See www.archives.gov/nhprc/.

44 See www.nsf.gov/.

45 See www.dlib.org/.

46 See www.digitalpreservation.gov/news/.

47 See http://irmt.org/.

48 Millar (2009).

49 See www.esami-africa.org/.

50 See http://office.microsoft.com/en-gb/.

51 See https://drive.google.com/.

52 See www.zoho.com/.

53 See www.thinkfree.com/.

54 See www.flickr.com/.

55 See https://www.dropbox.com/.

Appendices

Appendix 1 Creating a digital asset register

This appendix provides a template and explanatory notes for creating a digital asset register, as described in Chapter 2, 'Making the case for digital preservation' (Table A1.1).

Key:

Reference: A unique reference number for each asset.

Asset name: A brief name for the asset.

Owner: The person or group responsible for creating or maintaining the asset.

Type: The category of asset, e.g. digitized images, office documents, application.

Volume:

  Current: The current size of the asset, expressed in standard units such as GBs.

  Accrual rate: The annual rate of growth, if applicable, expressed in standard units such as GBs.

Estimated value: The estimated financial value of the asset, e.g. the cost to re-create or investment value. Example formulae for calculating this are provided later in this appendix.

Potential benefits: The projected long-term benefits of continued access to the asset, including the potential for reuse.

Vulnerability types: The type(s) of threat to the continued accessibility of the resource. An example categorization is provided in Table A1.2.

Risk type: The category of risk faced if the asset were to be lost, e.g. financial, operational, reputational.

Risk assessment: A quantification of the risk associated with losing the asset, expressed as a combination of the probability of the asset being

Table A1.1 Template for a digital asset register

Ref.	Asset name	Owner	Type	Volume		Estimated value	Potential benefits	Vulnerability	Risk type	Risk assessment			Risk score
				Current	Accrual rate					Probability	Impact	Proximity	

lost, the impact if it were to be lost, and the proximity of the threat, all expressed as numerical scores. An example scoring system is provided in Table A1.3.

Risk score: A numerical score, calculated by multiplying the probability, impact and proximity scores.

Table A1.2	Vulnerability types
Type	Description
1	Content at risk of immediate corruption or loss, due to storage on vulnerable removable media, or lack of adequate back-up arrangements.
2	Content that is currently inaccessible because of technology obsolescence.
3	Content for which no permanent, controlled storage environment is available.
4	Content for which there is no current provision for public access.
5	Where other systems have specific milestones to be able to export content to a repository for permanent preservation.
6	Content created externally, where the repository has no control over creation standards.
7	Content at risk due to management and system configuration issues.

Table A1.3	Example risk scoring system		
Score	Probability	Impact	Proximity
	The proportion of the asset which is predicted to be lost	The reputational, operational, or commercial impact of any loss	The timeframe within which loss is predicted
5	100% loss	Severe damage to the organization	Loss currently occurring
4	80% loss	Serious damage to the organization	Loss expected within 3 years
3	60% loss	Moderate damage to the organization	Loss expected within 5 years
2	40% loss	Minor damage to the organization	Loss expected within 10 years
1	20% loss or less	Minimal damage to the organization	Loss expected after 10 years

Example formulae for estimating value

Some simple formulae for calculating values are provided below. Much more sophisticated analyses of economic impact are also possible (see, for example, Charles Beagrie Ltd and Centre for Strategic Economic Studies (2012)).

Contractor costs

If an external contractor was paid to create the asset, for example on a digitization project, either the value of the contract or a unit creation cost quoted by the contractor may be used.

Staff time

This may be helpful for valuing internally created assets, such as documents held in a corporate EDRMS. It can be calculated using the following formula:

$$S \times C \times N \times A$$

where:

S = estimated proportion of staff time spent creating the assets (e.g. 5%)
C = average staff cost (this should be available from human resources information)
N = estimated number of staff who create assets (typically the organization's headcount)
A = estimated proportion of assets having archival value (e.g. 5–10% for corporate records, or 100% of digitized images).

Re-acquisition costs

If the asset originates outside the organization, it may be possible to quantify the cost of obtaining a replacement copy, for example the cost of staff time, as follows:

$$T \times S \times N$$

where:

T = estimated time to replace one item
S = time cost for staff undertaking work
N = Number of items to replace

Profiling opportunity costs

You can use the register as the basis for calculating the savings that will accrue from implementing a digital repository, and the costs of doing nothing. For example, it can be used to calculate a profile of the opportunity costs for re-creating or rescuing the identified assets over the life of the project. For each asset, a proportion of the re-creation cost can be included, based on the probability of loss; the year(s) in which these costs are assigned can then be based on the proximity of the threat. Thus, for example, an asset that scored 4 for probability would have 80% of the re-creation costs included in the profile; if it also scored 4 for proximity, those costs would then be assigned from Year 3 of the project onwards.

Appendix 2 Digital preservation maturity model

This appendix expands on the maturity model introduced in Chapter 4, 'Models for implementing a digital preservation service', and provides example definitions for all three capability levels (Levels 3–5) within each process perspective.

Table A2.1 Digital preservation maturity model for capability levels 3–5

A Organizational viability	
1 Awareness	Not applicable
2 Roadmap	Not applicable
3 Basic process	• Staff have assigned responsibilities, and the time to undertake them. • A suitable budget has been allocated. • Staff development requirements have been identified and funded.
4 Managed process	• Budgets, staff roles and development needs are regularly assessed in response to changing circumstances.
5 Optimized process	• Budgets, staff roles and development needs are proactively assessed in anticipation of future changes. • The efficacy of staff development is regularly monitored.
B Stakeholder engagement	
1 Awareness	Not applicable
2 Roadmap	Not applicable
3 Basic process	• Key stakeholders have been identified. • Objectives and methods of communication have been identified.
4 Managed process	• Stakeholders are communicated with on a regular basis.
5 Optimized process	• Stakeholders proactively engage with the repository, seeking and offering information.

Continued on next page

C Legal basis	
1 Awareness	Not applicable
2 Roadmap	Not applicable
3 Basic process	• Key legal rights and responsibilities, together with their owners, have been identified.
4 Managed process	• Legal issues are regularly reviewed. • A process for managing new issues which arise exists.
5 Optimized process	• Legal issues are proactively monitored and mitigated.
D Policy framework	
1 Awareness	Not applicable
2 Roadmap	Not applicable
3 Basic process	• A written, approved digital preservation policy exists.
4 Managed process	• The policy fully articulates with other organizational policies and is regularly reviewed.
5 Optimized process	• The policy is proactively monitored and updated to reflect internal changes, changes in other policies, or other external factors.
E Acquisition and ingest	
1 Awareness	Not applicable
2 Roadmap	Not applicable
3 Basic process	• An acquisition policy exists which defines the types of digital content which may be acquired. • A documented accession and ingest procedure exists, including basic guidance for depositors. • Some individual tools are used to support accession and ingest.
4 Managed process	• The acquisition policy is regularly reviewed and updated. • Detailed guidance is provided for depositors. • Parts of the accession and ingest process are automated.
5 Optimized process	• The repository co-ordinates with potential depositors to support best practice lifecycle management. • The accession and ingest workflow is managed as a single, automated process.

Continued on next page

F Bitstream preservation	
1 Awareness	Not applicable
2 Roadmap	Not applicable
3 Basic process	• Dedicated storage space on a network drive, workstation, or removable media. • At least three copies maintained of each object, with back-up to removable media. • Basic integrity checking performed. • Virus checking performed. • Existing access controls and security processes applied.
4 Managed process	• Managed storage environment with automated replication and back-up. • Specialized repository platform used to manage content. • Automated integrity checking. • Automated virus checking. • Repository-specific security measures applied as required. • Reactive storage management, which identifies and manages threats to bitstream preservation as they arise.
5 Optimized process	• Hierarchical storage management or storage appliances, with dedicated storage management software. • Security and access controls proactively monitored and reviewed. • Proactive storage management to predict and mitigate threats to bitstream preservation before they occur, including automated repair of integrity failures.
G Logical preservation	
1 Awareness	Not applicable
2 Roadmap	Not applicable
3 Basic process	• Basic characterization capability exists, allowing at least format identification. • *Ad hoc* preservation planning takes place. • *Ad hoc* preservation actions can be performed if required. • Ability to manage multiple manifestations of digital objects.
4 Managed process	• Advanced characterization capability exists, including automated metadata extraction. • Reactive logical preservation: The institution can identify and react to threats to the usability of stored objects, mitigating them in a timely fashion.
5 Optimized process	• Proactive logical preservation: The institution can identify and predict threats to the usability of stored objects before they arise, proactively identifying, testing and implementing appropriate mitigations before the threat materializes.

Continued on next page

H Metadata management	
1 Awareness	Not applicable
2 Roadmap	Not applicable
3 Basic process	• Documented minimum metadata requirement exists. • Consistent approach to organization of data and metadata implemented. • Metadata stored in a variety of forms using spreadsheets, text files or simple databases. • Capability exists to maintain persistent links between data and metadata. • Persistent unique identifiers are assigned and maintained for all digital objects.
4 Managed process	• Metadata managed in a consistent form using spreadsheets, text files or simple databases.
5 Optimized process	• Metadata managed in complex, reusable forms, such as XML, LOD, or sophisticated databases.
I Dissemination	
1 Awareness	Not applicable
2 Roadmap	Not applicable
3 Basic process	• Basic finding aids exist for all digital content. • Users can view or download data and metadata, either online or on-site.
4 Managed process	• A range of access options are provided. • Access systems are updated to reflect feedback from the user community.
5 Optimized process	• Advanced resource discovery tools are provided. • The user community is proactively consulted to establish needs and expectations.
J Infrastructure	
1 Awareness	Not applicable
2 Roadmap	Not applicable
3 Basic process	• Sufficient storage capacity is available, and plans exist to meet future storage needs. • IT systems are documented, supported and fit for purpose
4 Managed process	• Future storage needs are regularly predicted and updated. Storage capacity is monitored and revised accordingly. • IT systems are regularly patched and updated. • New tools and systems are deployed when required.
5 Optimized process	• A detailed roadmap exists for future development of IT systems. • Potential new tools and systems are proactively identified and tested.

Appendix 3 Systems, tools and services

This appendix provides examples of software systems, tools and services that may be useful in providing a variety of digital preservation functions. These range from simple utilities to full-blown digital repository systems, and from free software to commercial products. No such list can ever hope to be comprehensive, and new tools are emerging all the time. However, it seeks to be representative, and to include the most widely used tools, with a particular focus on those likely to be most useful to smaller organizations.

The inclusion of any product here does not constitute an endorsement or recommendation.

A3.1 Repository platforms

This section lists examples of general repository management platforms.

Commercial

Table A3.1 gives examples of the most common commercial digital repository systems.

Table A3.1 Commercial digital repository systems	
System	**Notes/Website**
DIAS	The Digital Information Archiving System (DIAS) was originally developed by IBM for the Dutch Royal Library, and is now available as a commercial product. **www-935.ibm.com/services/ch/gts/pdf/ br-storage-lza-en-01-04-08.pdf**
Rosetta	The Rosetta system was developed by Ex Libris for the National Library of New Zealand, and is now available commercially. **www.exlibrisgroup.com/category/RosettaOverview**

Continued on next page

Table A3.1 Commercial digital repository platforms (*continued*)

System	Notes/Website
scopeArchiv	Developed by Scope Solutions AG, scopeArchiv is a commercial archives management system designed for both analogue and digital collections, the latter capability being provided principally through the scopeOAIS module. **www.scope.ch/en/scopeArchiv/SystemArchitecture.aspx**
SDB	The UK National Archives developed a digital archive to store the electronic records of government and subsequently licensed its developer, Tessella, to resell the software as SDB. The system has subsequently been further developed commercially and through the EU-funded Planets Project. **www.digital-preservation.com/solution/safety-deposit-box/**

Open source

A number of open-source digital repository management systems have been developed, primarily by the academic community. Although varying in the level of preservation functionality that they offer directly, they may all be used to provide the basis for such a facility. The most widely used systems are shown in Table A3.2.

Table A3.2 Open-source digital repository management systems

System	Notes/Website
Archivematica	A repository platform with bitstream and logical preservation services, developed by Artefactual Systems in collaboration with a range of institutions. Archivematica also incorporates a range of other open-source preservation tools. In 2012 it had only been released in beta form. **http://archivematica.org/wiki/index.php?title=Main_Page**
DAITSS	DAITSS was developed by the Florida Center for Library Automation, and used by the Florida Digital Archive, DAITSS provides bitstream and logical preservation functions. **http://daitss.fcla.edu/**
DSpace	Originally developed jointly by MIT and HP Labs, DSpace is now maintained by DuraSpace, a not-for-profit organization. **www.dspace.org/**
EPrints	This is developed and maintained by the University of Southampton. **www.eprints.org/**
Fedora Commons	While not offering the out-of-the-box functionality of systems like DSpace or EPrints, Fedora provides a very flexible and powerful underlying architecture for building digital repositories. Originally developed by Cornell University and the University of Virginia Library, it is now maintained by DuraSpace. **http://fedora-commons.org/**

Continued on next page

Table A3.2 Open-source digital repository management systems (*continued*)

System	Notes/Website
Hydra	Created and maintained jointly by a range of organizations, primarily US and UK universities, Hydra is a repository platform built using a combination of open-source components, including Fedora Commons. Its name derives from an architecture based on the concept of a single digital repository supporting multiple 'heads' – digital asset management applications and tailored workflows for specific users and types of content. **http://hydraproject.org/**
iRods	A rule-driven repository system developed by the University of North Carolina and the University of California San Diego. **https://www.irods.org/**
LOCKSS	Created by Stanford University, LOCKSS stands for 'Lots of Copies Keeps Stuff Safe'. A LOCKSS system uses a distributed peer-to-peer network of servers, usually hosted by a number of co-operating institutions. Each institution's content is replicated among the various nodes of the network, and regular integrity checks ensure that all copies are identical; if a discrepancy is found, the system comes to a quorum on which copies are correct, and replaces the changed files from a known 'good' copy. Public or private LOCKSS networks can be created. **www.lockss.org/**
RODA	The Repository of Authentic Digital Objects (RODA) system was developed by the Portuguese National Archives, and is supported by a commercial company, Keep Solutions. Using Fedora as its underlying repository platform, it builds a range of bitstream and logical preservation services on top. **http://redmine.keep.pt/projects/roda-public**

Service providers

There is a growing number of providers offering managed repository services. This is a rapidly evolving market, but examples of current commercial services are shown in Table A3.3.

Table A3.3 Providers offering managed repository services

Service	Notes/Website
Chronopolis	Chronopolis is a digital repository service provided under the management of the San Diego Supercomputer Center. **http://chronopolis.sdsc.edu/**
DuraCloud	This is a cloud-based repository service provided by DuraSpace. **www.duracloud.org/**
OCLC Digital Archive	An online digital repository service provided by OCLC, this is primarily designed to preserve the outputs from library digitization projects. **www.oclc.org/digitalarchive/default.htm**

Continued on next page

Table A3.3 Providers offering managed repository services (*continued*)

Service	Notes/Website
Portico	Portico is an international digital preservation service for the academic community, which is used by participating libraries and publishers to preserve electronic books and journals, and digitized historical collections. It is a membership organization provided by ITHAKA, a US-based non-profit organization, and funded principally through annual subscriptions. **www.portico.org/digital-preservation/**
Preservica	Preservica is a cloud-based repository solution provided by Tessella, and based on SDB. **www.digital-preservation.com/solution/preservica/**
ULCC	The University of London Computer Centre (ULCC) provides a number of specific digital preservation services for individual customers, repository platforms and consultancy services. **www.ulcc.ac.uk/services/research-technology**

In addition to the commercial service providers, there is a wide range of data services that support the academic sector. Some are discussed in Chapter 4.

A3.2 Tools

This section lists examples of individual tools and toolkits for performing specific repository functions.

Ingest

Ingest tools (Table A3.4) are designed to support the accession and ingest process, either with individual tasks or by providing workflow systems that may incorporate a number of third-party utilities.

Table A3.4 Ingest tools

Tool	Notes/Website
Bagger	One of a number of tools developed by the Library of Congress for validating and transferring data that conforms to the BagIt specification. **http://sourceforge.net/projects/loc-xferutils/files/loc-bagger**
BagIt Library	One of a number of tools developed by the Library of Congress for validating and transferring data that conforms to the BagIt specification. **http://sourceforge.net/projects/loc-xferutils/**
BagIt Transfer Utilities	One of a number of tools developed by the Library of Congress for validating and transferring data that conforms to the BagIt specification. **http://sourceforge.net/projects/loc-xferutils/**

Continued on next page

Table A3.4 Ingest tools (*continued*)

Tool	Notes/Website
CINCH	The CINCH (Capture, INgest, & CHecksum) tool automates the transfer of online content to a repository, including the assignment of unique identifiers, virus checking, metadata extraction, integrity checking and creation of audit trails. CINCH was developed by the State Library of North Carolina. **http://cinch.nclive.org/Cinch/**
Curator's Workbench	The Curator's Workbench is a collection preparation and workflow tool for digital materials, based on METS and MODS, and developed by the University of North Carolina, Chapel Hill. **https://github.com/UNC-Libraries/Curators-Workbench**
DPSP	The Digital Preservation Software Platform (DPSP) is a collection of software applications, which support the goal of digital preservation, developed by the National Archives of Australia. It includes Xena (see Table A3.11), a workflow management tool, Checksum Checker (see Table A3.9) and a manifest generator. **http://dpsp.sourceforge.net/**
Duke Data Accessioner	A tool for ingesting digital content from removable media, developed by Duke University Libraries. **http://library.duke.edu/uarchives/about/tools/data-accessioner.html**
Fedora SIP Creator	A tool for creating SIPs for ingest into a Fedora repository. **www.fedora.info/download/2.2/services/sipcreator/doc/index.html** **www.fedora.info/download/2.2/services/diringest/doc/index.html**
Karen's Directory Printer	A utility for generating basic information about the contents of a directory structure. **www.karenware.com/powertools/ptdirprn.asp**
Prometheus	A workflow tool to support the transfer of data from removable media to a digital repository, developed by the National Library of Australia. Prometheus incorporates a range of primarily open-source tools, for processes such as media imaging, file identification and metadata extraction. **http://prometheus-digi.sourceforge.net/index.html**
SCAT	A suite of tools for creating and managing SIPs and AIPs, developed by Gloucestershire Archives. It incorporates a range of existing open-source utilities. **www.gloucestershire.gov.uk/archives/article/103644/ Digital-curation**

Forensic toolkits

Table A3.5 lists forensic tools that may be useful, especially for ingest.

Table A3.5 Forensic tools

Tool	Notes/Website
AFF Open Source Computer Forensics Software	A forensic toolkit based around the Advanced Forensics Format (AFF), developed by Simson L. Garfinkel and Basis Technology Corp. **http://afflib.org/**
BitCurator	A digital forensics framework designed specifically for memory institutions, developed by the University of North Carolina, Chapel Hill and the Maryland Institute for Technology in the Humanities. It incorporates a range of free and open-source digital forensics tools and associated software libraries, modified and packaged for increased accessibility and functionality for memory institutions. **www.bitcurator.net/**
FTK	A commercial digital forensic platform developed by AccessData. A Lite version of the imaging tool (FTK Imager) is also available. **http://accessdata.com/products/computer-forensics/ftk**
Gumshoe	A prototype tool for searching metadata extracted from forensic disk images. **https://github.com/anarchivist/gumshoe**

Metadata and arrangement

Table A3.6 lists tools that support description and arrangement of digital collections.

Table A3.6 Metadata and arrangement tools

Tool	Notes/Website
ArchiveSpace	An archives management application for describing analogue and born-digital archival materials, developed by the New York University Libraries, UC San Diego Libraries and the University of Illinois Urbana-Champaign Libraries. **www.archivesspace.org/**
Archivists' Toolkit	An archival data management system developed by the UC San Diego Libraries, the New York University Libraries and the Five College Libraries. **http://archiviststoolkit.org/**
ICA-AtoM	A web-based archival description tool based on International Council on Archives (ICA) standards, and developed by Artefactual Systems in collaboration with the ICA Program Commission (PCOM) and a growing network of international partners. **https://www.ica-atom.org/**
PREMIS in METS Toolbox	A set of open-source tools to support the implementation of PREMIS in the METS container format, developed by Florida Center for Library Automation for the Library of Congress. **http://pim.fcla.edu/** **http://sourceforge.net/projects/pimtoolbox/**

Web archiving

Table A3.7 lists tools for web archiving.

Table A3.7 Web archiving tools	
Tool	**Notes/Website**
Archive-It	A subscription-based web archiving service provided by the Internet Archive. **www.archive-it.org/**
Heritrix	An archival web crawler developed and maintained by the Internet Archive. **http://crawler.archive.org**
NetarchiveSuite	A complete web archiving software package originally developed by the two national deposit libraries in Denmark, the Royal Library and the State and University Library, with more recent support from the French and Austrian National Libraries. **https://sbforge.org/display/NAS/NetarchiveSuite**
Web Curator Tool	A web archiving workflow management tool developed jointly by the British Library and the National Library of New Zealand. **http://webcurator.sourceforge.net/**

Characterization

Table A3.8 lists tools that perform a variety of characterization tasks, including format identification, validation and metadata extraction.

Table A3.8 Characterization tools	
Tool	**Notes/Website**
DIFFER	Utility developed by the National Library of the Czech Republic to characterize selected still image file formats, which includes a tool to compare the properties of an image in different formats. **http://differ.nkp.cz/**
DROID	Format identification tool developed and maintained by the UK National Archives, which uses regularly updated signatures files automatically downloaded from PRONOM. DROID (Digital Record Object Identification) is probably the format identification tool in widest production use for digital preservation purposes internationally. **www.nationalarchives.gov.uk/information-management/our-** **services/dc-file-profiling-tool.htm** **https://groups.google.com/forum/?fromgroups#!forum/droid-list** **http://digital-preservation.github.com/droid/**
ExifTool	Tool for reading, writing and editing metadata in a wide variety of image file formats. **http://owl.phy.queensu.ca/~phil/exiftool/**
FIDO	FIDO (Format Identification for Digital Objects) is a format identification tool developed by the OPF. It is unclear if further development is envisaged. **www.openplanetsfoundation.org/software/fido**

Continued on next page

Table A3.8 Characterization tools (*continued*)

Tool	Notes/Website
File	Originally developed for Unix, but now also available for other platforms, File is perhaps the most venerable format identification utility. **http://unixhelp.ed.ac.uk/CGI/man-cgi?file** **http://gnuwin32.sourceforge.net/packages/file.htm**
FITS	FITS (File Information Tool Set) provides a framework for executing a number of existing characterization tools, including DROID, ExifTool, the NLNZ Metadata Extractor, JHOVE, FFIdent and File, as well as two original tools. **http://code.google.com/p/fits/**
JHOVE	JHOVE is a widely used format identification, validation and metadata extraction tool developed by Harvard University Library. **http://jhove.sourceforge.net/**
JHOVE2	JHOVE2 is a successor to JHOVE developed by the California Digital Library, Portico and Stanford University. It provides advanced characterization, including identification, validation, feature extraction and policy-based assessment, and is designed for simple and complex digital objects. **https://bitbucket.org/jhove2/main/wiki/Home**
Jpylyzer	A validator and metadata extractor for JPEG 2000 (JP2) images, developed by the OPF. **www.openplanetsfoundation.org/software/jpylyzer**
Metadata Extraction Tool	Metadata extraction utility developed by the National Library of New Zealand. **http://meta-extractor.sourceforge.net/**
NARA File Analyzer and Metadata Harvester	Utility for performing automated actions on files, such as filename validation, file size statistical analysis, checksum calculation and file type extraction. **https://github.com/usnationalarchives/File-Analyzer**
PREMIS Creation Tool	Uses JHOVE, DROID and the National Library of New Zealand's Metadata Extractor to generate PREMIS files. **http://pigpen.lib.uchicago.edu:8888/pigpen/40**
Tika	Developed by the Apache Software Foundation, the Tika toolkit detects and extracts metadata and structured text content from various file formats. **http://tika.apache.org/**
TrID	Format identification utility. **http://mark0.net/soft-trid-e.html**
XCDL Comparator	Tool for extracting and comparing the properties of digital objects, developed primarily by Cologne University as part of the Planets project. **http://planetarium.hki.uni-koeln.de/planets_cms/about-xcl**

Checksums

Table A3.9 lists tools for generating and comparing checksums for the purposes of integrity management.

Table A3.9 Checksum tools

Tool	Website
ACE (Audit Control Environment)	https://wiki.umiacs.umd.edu/adapt/index.php/Ace
Checksum Checker	http://checksumchecker.sourceforge.net/
Checksums for Windows	http://sourceforge.net/projects/checksumwindows/
ExactFile	www.exactfile.com/
FastSum	www.fastsum.com/
Fsum Frontend	http://fsumfe.sourceforge.net/index.php?page=home
HashMyFiles	www.nirsoft.net/utils/hash_my_files.html
Jacksum	http://sourceforge.net/projects/jacksum/ www.jonelo.de/java/jacksum/
md5deep and hashdeep	http://md5deep.sourceforge.net/
MD5Summer	www.md5summer.org/

Preservation planning

Table A3.10 lists tools that support the preservation planning process.

Table A3.10 Preservation planning tools

Tool	Notes/Website
PLATO	Online preservation planning service developed through the Planets project and maintained by the Technical University of Vienna. www.ifs.tuwien.ac.at/dp/plato/intro.html
PRONOM	Online technical registry developed and maintained by the UK National Archives. PRONOM is at present the longest-standing and most widely used format registry. www.nationalarchives.gov.uk/PRONOM/Default.aspx
UDFR	The Unified Digital Format Registry has been developed by the California Digital Library, with an international governing body. www.udfr.org/

Preservation action

Tables A3.11 and A3.12 list examples of tools that perform preservation actions.

Migration

Table A3.11 Migration tools	
Tool	Notes/Website
HOPPLA	A back-up and fully automated migration tool for data collections in small office environments, developed by the Technical University of Vienna. **www.ifs.tuwien.ac.at/dp/hoppla/**
ImageMagick	Software suite for migrating between a wide variety of image formats. **www.imagemagick.org/**
Xena	Format migration toolkit developed by the National Archives of Australia, as part of its DPSP (see Table A3.4). **http://xena.sourceforge.net/**

Emulation

Table A3.12 Emulation tools	
Tool	Notes/Website
Dioscuri	A hardware emulator, which emulates an IBM PC platform. Dioscuri has been developed by the Koninklijke Bibliotheek (National Library of the Netherlands) and Nationaal Archief of the Netherlands, with support from Tessella. Recent development has taken place within the Planets and KEEP projects. **http://dioscuri.sourceforge.net/**
KEEP emulation framework	A modular emulation framework developed as part of the KEEP project, which supports seven emulators including Dioscuri, Qemu, VICE, UAE, BeebEm, JavaCPC and Thomson. **http://emuframework.sourceforge.net/**

Other sources

There are several excellent online sources of information about digital preservation tools and services, including:

- **Cairo**:
  http://cairo.paradigm.ac.uk/projectdocs/cairo_tools_listing_pv1.pdf
- **Digital Curation Centre**: www.dcc.ac.uk/resources/external/tools-services
- **Library of Congress Digital Preservation Tools Showcase**:
  www.digitalpreservation.gov/tools/
- **OPF Digital Preservation Tool Registry**: http://wiki.opf-labs.org/display/TR/Home
- **SPRUCE Digital Preservation Tools list**: http://wiki.opf-labs.org/display/SPR/Digital+Preservation+Tools.

Bibliography

Standards

ANSI/NISO Z39.87 – 2006 *Data Dictionary – Technical Metadata for Digital Still Images.*

DIN 31644: 2012 *Information and Documentation – Criteria for Trustworthy Digital Archives.*

ISO 2709: 2008 *Information and Documentation – Format for Information Exchange*

ISO 14721: 2003 *Space Data and Information Transfer Systems – Open Archival Information System – Reference Model* [equivalent to CCSDS (2012)].

ISO 15489-1: 2001 *Information and Documentation – Records Management – Part 1: General.*

ISO 15489-2: 2001 *Information and Documentation – Records Management – Part 2: Guidelines.*

ISO 15836: 2009 *Information and Documentation – The Dublin Core Metadata Element Set.*

ISO 16175-1: 2010 *Information and Documentation – Principles and Functional Requirements for Records in Electronic Office Environments – Part 1: Overview and Statement of Principles.*

ISO 16175-2: 2011 *Information and Documentation – Principles and Functional Requirements for Records in Electronic Office Environments – Part 2: Guidelines and Functional Requirements for Digital Records Management Systems.*

ISO 16175-3: 2010 *Information and Documentation – Principles and Functional Requirements for Records in Electronic Office Environments – Part 3: Guidelines and Functional Requirements for Records in Business Systems.*

ISO 16363: 2012 *Space Data and Information Transfer Systems – Audit and Certification of Trustworthy Digital Repositories.*

ISO/DIS 16919 *Space Data and Information Transfer Systems – Requirements for Bodies Providing Audit and Certification of Candidate Trustworthy Digital Repositories [draft standard].*

ISO/IEC 21000 Parts 1–19. *Information Technology – Multimedia Framework (MPEG-21).*

ISO 21127: 2006 *Information and Documentation – A Reference Ontology for the*

Interchange of Cultural Heritage Information.

ISO 23081-1: 2006 *Information and Documentation – Records Management Processes – Metadata for Records – Part 1: Principles.*

ISO 23081-2: 2009 *Information and Documentation – Managing Metadata for Records – Part 2: Conceptual and Implementation Issues.*

ISO/TR 23081-3: 2011 *Information and Documentation – Managing Metadata for Records – Part 3: Self-assessment Method.*

ISO/IEC 27001: 2005 *Information technology – Security techniques – Information Security Management Systems – Requirements.*

ISO 28500: 2009 *Information and Documentation – WARC File Format.*

Legislation

Basel III Accord,
   www.bis.org/bcbs/basel3.htm.

Copyright, Designs and Patents Act 1988,
   www.legislation.gov.uk/ukpga/1988/48/contents.

Copyright (Librarians and Archivists) (Copying of Copyright Material) Regulations 1989,
   www.legislation.gov.uk/uksi/1989/1212/contents/made.

Legal Deposit Libraries Act 2003,
   www.legislation.gov.uk/ukpga/2003/28/contents.

Sarbanes-Oxley Act 2002,
   www.gpo.gov/fdsys/pkg/PLAW-107publ204/pdf/PLAW-107publ204.pdf.

Other works

AIMS Work Group (2012) *AIMS Born-Digital Collections: an inter-institutional model for stewardship,*
   www2.lib.virginia.edu/aims/whitepaper/AIMS_final_A4.pdf.

Aitken, B., McCann, P., McHugh, A. and Miller, K. (2012) *Digital Curation and the Cloud: final report,* produced by the Digital Curation Centre for JISC's Curation in the Cloud Workshop, Hallam Conference Centre, 7–8 March 2012, Digital Curation Centre,
   www.jisc.ac.uk/media/7/C/1/%7B7C1A1FD7-44B4-4951-85A8-FC2C4CEB1564%7DCuration-in-the-Cloud_master_final.pdf.

APARSEN Project (2012) *Report on Peer Review of Digital Repositories,* Alliance for Permanent Access,

www.alliancepermanentaccess.org/wp-content/uploads/downloads/2012/04/
APARSEN-REP-D33_1B-01-1_0.pdf.

Au, Y., Kandalaft, R., Kuang, M. and Nair, S. (2010) *Digital Preservation and Long Term Access Functionality*, Judge Business School,
www.scribd.com/doc/45412331/Cambridge-Judge-Business-School-Market-
Research-Digital-Preservation.

Beagrie, N., Semple, N., Williams, P. and Wright, R. (2008) *Digital Preservation Policies Study*, Joint Information Systems Committee,
www.jisc.ac.uk/media/documents/programmes/preservation/
jiscpolicy_p1finalreport.pdf.

Becker, C., Antunes, G., Barateiro, J. and Vieira, R. (2011) A Capability Model for Digital Preservation: analyzing concerns, drivers, constraints, capabilities and maturities, in Borbinha, J., Jatowt, A., Foo, S., Sugimoto, S., Khoo, C. and Buddharaju, R. (eds), *Proceedings of the 8th International Conference on Preservation of Digital Objects (iPRES 2011), 1–4 November 2011, Singapore*, National Library of Singapore and Nanyang Technological University, 1–10,
http://ipres2011.sg/conference-procedings.

Bolton, K. (2008) *Web Archiving in Greater Manchester*, PowerPoint presentation,
www.dpconline.org/docs/reports/dpconsultBolton.pdf.

Boyko, A., Kunze, J., Littman, J., Madden, L. and Vargas, B. (2012) *The BagIt File Packaging Format (V0.97)*, IETF Internet-Draft,
http://tools.ietf.org/html/draft-kunze-bagit-07.

Boyle, F., Eveleigh, A. and Needham, H. (2009) Preserving Local Archival Heritage for Ongoing Accessibility, *Ariadne*, **58**,
www.ariadne.ac.uk/issue58/boyle-et-al.

Bradner, S. (1997) *RFC 2119: key words for use in RFCs to indicate requirement levels*, Internet Engineering Task Force,
www.ietf.org/rfc/rfc2119.txt.

Brown, A. (2000) Documenting Digital Archives: a case study. In Richards, J. and Robinson, D. (eds) *Digital Archives from Excavation and Fieldwork: a guide to good practice*, Oxbow, 48–56,
http://ads.ahds.ac.uk/project/goodguides/excavation/.

Brown, A. (2002a) *Centre for Archaeology Digital Archiving Strategy*, 2nd edn, English Heritage,
http://citeseerx.ist.psu.edu/viewdoc/
download?doi=10.1.1.184.3003&rep=rep1&type=pdf.

Brown, A. (2002b) *Digital Archiving Programme: preservation management procedures manual*, English Heritage,

www.english-heritage.org.uk/publications/digital-archiving-
programme/dapmanualpreservation.pdf/.

Brown, A. (2003) From Theory to Practice: the Centre for Archaeology Digital
Archiving Programme. In Doerr, M. and Sarris, A. (eds), *The Digital Heritage of
Archaeology: computer applications and quantitative methods in archaeology: proceedings
of the 30th conference, Heraklion, Crete, April 2002*, 313–18.

Brown, A. (2006) *Archiving Websites: a practical guide for information management
professionals*, Facet Publishing.

Brown, A. (2008a) *Digital Preservation Guidance Note 2: selecting storage media for long-
term preservation*, The National Archives,
www.nationalarchives.gov.uk/documents/information-management/
selecting-storage-media.pdf.

Brown, A. (2008b) *Digital Preservation Guidance Note 3: care, handling and storage of
removable media*, The National Archives,
www.nationalarchives.gov.uk/documents/information-management/
removable-media-care.pdf.

Brown, A. (2008c) *White Paper: representation information registries*, Planets Project,
www.planets-project.eu/docs/reports/
Planets_PC3-D7_RepInformationRegistries.pdf.

Brown, A. (2011) *Best Practice and Minimum Standards in Digital Preservation*,
presentation given at Oracle Preservation and Archiving Special Interest Group
(PASIG) Meeting, 4–5 April 2011, British Library,
www.oracle.com/us/dm/h2fy11/
0900-adrian-brown-362563.pdf?evite=EMEAFM10041984MPP017.

Cabinet Office (2012) *Open Data White Paper: unleashing the potential*, Cm 8353,
HMSO,
www.cabinetoffice.gov.uk/resource-library/
open-data-white-paper-unleashing-potential.

Cedars Project (2002) *Cedars Guide to Digital Preservation Strategies*,
www.webarchive.org.uk/wayback/archive/20050410120000/http://www.leeds.
ac.uk/cedars/guideto/dpstrategies/dpstrategies.html.

Charles Beagrie Ltd and Centre for Strategic Economic Studies (2012) *Economic
Impact Evaluation of the Economic and Social Data Service*,
www.esrc.ac.uk/_images/ESDS_Economic_Impact_Evaluation_tcm8-22229.pdf.

Charlesworth, A. (2012) *Intellectual Property Rights for Digital Preservation*, DPC
Technology Watch Report 12-02, Digital Preservation Coalition,
www.dpconline.org/component/docman/doc_download/796-dpctw12-02.

Checkley-Scott, C. and Thompson, D. (2007) *Wellcome Library Preservation Policy for*

Materials Held in Collections, Wellcome Library,
http://wellcomelibrary.org/content/documents/policy-documents/
preservation-policy.

Cloud Sweden (2011) *Guidelines: areas and problems to consider within information security and digital preservation during procurement and use of cloud services*,
http://natverk.dfs.se/sites/natverk.dfs.se/files/
Cloud_Sweden_Security-DigitalPreservation_v1.1.1_English_final.pdf.

Cochrane, E. (2012) *Rendering Matters: report on the results of research into digital object rendering*, Archives New Zealand,
http://archives.govt.nz/resources/information-management-research/
rendering-matters-report-results-research-digital-object-r.

Collections Trust (2009) *SPECTRUM: the UK Museum Documentation Standard, version 3.2*,
www.collectionslink.org.uk/programmes/spectrum.

Columbia University Libraries (2006) *Policy for Preservation of Digital Resources*,
http://library.columbia.edu/services/preservation/dlpolicy.html.

Consultative Committee on Space Data Systems (2012) *Reference Model for an Open Archival Information System (OAIS): recommended practice CCSDS 650.0 M 2, Magenta Book, Issue 2*, [equivalent to ISO 14721: 2003],
http://public.ccsds.org/publications/archive/650x0m2.pdf.

Cothey, V. (2010) Digital Curation at Gloucestershire Archives: from ingest to production by way of trusted storage, *Journal of the Society of Archivists*, **31** (2), 207–28.

Dappert, A. and Farquhar, A. (2009) Significance is in the Eye of the Stakeholder. In Agosti, M. et al. (eds) *Research and Advanced Technology for Digital Libraries: 13th European Conference, ECDL 2009, Corfu, Greece, September 27 – October 2, 2009: proceedings*, Lecture Notes in Computer Science 5714, Springer-Verlag, 297–308,
www.planets-project.eu/docs/papers/
Dappert_SignificantCharacteristics_ECDL2009.pdf.

Data Seal of Approval Board (2010) *Quality Guidelines for Digital Research Data*,
http://assessment.datasealofapproval.org/sitemedia/files/DSA_booklets/
DSA-booklet_1_June2010.pdf.

DDI Alliance (2009) *Data Documentation Initiative (DDI) Technical Specification, version 3.1*,
www.ddialliance.org/specification.

Digital Curation Centre and DigitalPreservationEurope (2007) *Digital Repository Audit Method Based on Risk Assessment (DRAMBORA), version 1.0*,
http://repositoryaudit.eu/download.

DigitalPreservationEurope (2008) *Repository Planning Checklist and Guidance*,
www.digitalpreservationeurope.eu/platter/.

DLM Forum Foundation (2011) *MoReq2010: modular requirements for records systems — core services and plug-in modules, version 1.1*,
http://moreq2010.eu/pdf/moreq2010_vol1_v1_1_en.pdf.

Donaldson, D. R. (2011) Users' Trust in Trusted Digital Repository Content. In Borbinha, J., Jatowt, A., Foo, S., Sugimoto, S., Khoo, C. and Buddharaju, R. (eds), *Proceedings of the 8th International Conference on Preservation of Digital Objects (iPRES 2011), 1–4 November 2011, Singapore*, National Library of Singapore and Nanyang Technological University, 20–3,
http://ipres2011.sg/conference-procedings.

Dunedin Public Libraries (n.d.) *Collection Development Policy*,
www.dunedinlibraries.govt.nz/your-library/about-us/strategy-and-policy/collection-development-policy.

Eastlake, D. (2001) *RFC 3171:US Secure Hash Algorithm (SHA-1)*, Internet Engineering Task Force,
www.ietf.org/rfc/rfc3174.txt.

Educopia Institute (2012a) *MetaArchive Cooperative Charter: a charter describing the purposes and aims of the MetaArchive Cooperative, an association dedicated to the preservation of digital materials*,
www.metaarchive.org/public/resources/charter_member/2012_MetaArchive_Charter.pdf.

Educopia Institute (2012b) *The MetaArchive Cooperative: membership agreement*,
www.metaarchive.org/public/resources/charter_member/2012_Membership_Agreement.pdf.

Electronic Records Archives Program Management Office (2010) *Electronic Records Archives Requirements Document (RD v4.0)*, National Archives and Records Administration,
www.archives.gov/era/about/requirements.pdf.

ERPANET (2003) *Digital Preservation Policy Tool*,
www.erpanet.org/guidance/docs/ERPANETPolicyTool.pdf.

Erway, R. (2012) *You've Got to Walk Before You Can Run: first steps for managing born-digital content received on physical media*, OCLC, Inc.,
www.oclc.org/content/dam/research/publications/library/2012/2012-06.pdf.

European Commission (2008) *Model Requirements for the Management of Electronic Records: update and extension 2008*, INSAR Supplement VIII, Office for Official Publications of the European Communities: Luxembourg,
http://bookshop.europa.eu/is-bin/INTERSHOP.enfinity/

WFS/EU-Bookshop-Site/en_GB/-/EUR/
ViewPublication-Start?PublicationKey=KAAF08S08.

European Parliament and the Council of the European Union (2004) Directive
2004/18/EC of the European Parliament and the Council of 31 March 2004 on the
Coordination of Procedures for the Award of Public Works Contracts, Public
Supply Contracts and Public Service Contracts, *Official Journal of the European
Union*, L134/114,
http://eur-lex.europa.eu/LexUriServ/
LexUriServ.do?uri=OJ:L:2004:134:0114:0240:EN:PDF.

Eveleigh, A. (2010) *Digital Preservation Case Notes – Practical Preservation: the MLA
Yorkshire Archive at West Yorkshire Archive Service*, Digital Preservation Coalition,
www.dpconline.org/component/docman/
doc_download/511-casenotemlawyaspdf.

Fay, E. (2010) Repository Software Comparison: building digital library
infrastructure at LSE, *Ariadne*, **64**,
www.ariadne.ac.uk/issue64/fay.

Fay, E. (2011) *LSE Digital Library: how it was done*, presentation given to UCL
Department of Information Studies and UCL Centre for Digital Humanities
students on 29 November 2011,
www.slideshare.net/digitalfay/lse-digital-library-how-it-was-done.

Garrett, J. and Waters, D. (1996) *Preserving Digital Information: report of the Task Force
on Archiving of Digital Information*, Commission on Preservation and Access and
Research Libraries Group,
www.clir.org/pubs/reports/pub63watersgarrett.pdf.

Georgia Tech Library and Information Center (n.d.) *Georgia Tech Archives and Records
Management Collection Development Policy*, Georgia Institute of Technology,
www.library.gatech.edu/archives/forms/Collection_Policy.pdf.

Guildhall Library Manuscripts and London Metropolitan Archives (2008) *Interim
Digital Preservation Policy*,
www.history.ac.uk/gh/digprespol.pdf.

Hampshire Record Office (2010) *Digital Preservation Policy*,
www3.hants.gov.uk/archives/hro-policies/hro-digital-preservation-policy.htm.

Henshaw, C., Savage-Jones, M. and Thompson, D. (2010) A Digital Library
Feasibility Study, *Liber Quarterly*, **20** (1), 53–65,
http://liber.library.uu.nl/index.php/lq/article/view/7975.

Heslop, H., Davis, S. and Wilson, A. (2002) *An Approach to the Preservation of Digital
Records*, National Archives of Australia,
www.naa.gov.au/Images/An-approach-Green-Paper_tcm16-47161.pdf.

Human Interference Task Force (1984) *Reducing the Likelihood of Future Human Activities that Could Affect Geologic High-level Waste Repositories*, Office of Nuclear Waste Isolation, www.osti.gov/bridge/servlets/purl/6799619-fpYg48/6799619.pdf.

IFLA Study Group on the Functional Requirements for Bibliographic Records (2009) *Functional Requirements for Bibliographic Records: final report*, International Federation of Library Associations and Institutions, www.ifla.org/files/cataloguing/frbr/frbr_2008.pdf.

Iglesias, E. and Meesangnil, W. (2010) Using Amazon S3 in Digital Preservation in a Mid Sized Academic Library: a case study of CCSU ERIS digital archive system, *Code{4}Lib Journal*, **12**, http://journal.code4lib.org/articles/4468.

Innocenti, P., Aitken, B., Hasan, A., Ludwig, J., Maciuvite, E., Barateiro, J., Antunes, G., Mois, M., Jäschke, G., Pempe, W., Wilson, T., Hundsdoerfer, A., Krandstedt, A. and Ross, S. (2009) *SHAMAN Requirements Analysis Report (public version) and Specification of the SHAMAN Assessment Framework and Protocol*, SHAMAN Project, http://shaman-ip.eu/shaman/sites/default/files/ SHAMAN_D1_2Requirements%20Analysis%20ReportSHAMAN%20Assessment %20Framework.pdf.

International Council on Archives (2000) *ISAD(G): General International Standard Archival Description*, 2nd edn, www.icacds.org.uk/eng/ISAD%28G%29.pdf.

International Council on Archives (2004) *ISAAR (CPF): International Standard Archival Authority Record For Corporate Bodies, Persons and Families*, 2nd edn, www.icacds.org.uk/eng/ISAAR%28CPF%292ed.pdf.

Jackson, A. (2012) *Formats over Time: exploring UK web history*, paper presented at iPRES 2012, Toronto, 1–5 October 2012, http://arxiv.org/abs/1210.1714.

James, H. (2004) *Collections Preservation Policy*, Arts and Humanities Data Service, www.ahds.ac.uk/documents/colls-policy-preservation-v1.pdf.

Joint Steering Committee for Revision of AACR (2005) *Anglo-American Cataloguing Rules, 2nd Edition, 2002 Revision: 2005 Update*, American Library Association, Canadian Library Association and CILIP.

Jones, M. and Beagrie, N. (2001) *Preservation Management of Digital Materials: a handbook*, British Library. [The handbook is now maintained and updated in online form by the Digital Preservation Coalition at www.dpconline.org/advice/preservationhandbook.]

Lemieux, V. L. (2012) Envisioning a Sustainable Future for Archives: a role for visual analytics? In *Proceedings of the International Council on Archives Congress, Brisbane, Australia, 20–24 August 2012*, International Council on Archives, www.ica2012.com/files/data/Full%20papers%20upload/ica12Final00239.pdf.

Libraries and Archives Canada (2008) *Digital Preservation Policy.*

Lynch, C. A. (1999) Canonicalization: a fundamental tool to facilitate preservation and management of digital information, *D-Lib Magazine*, **5** (9), www.dlib.org/dlib/september99/09lynch.html.

Masanès, J. (ed) (2006) *Web Archiving*, Springer.

McGovern, N. (2007) *Digital Preservation Policy Framework*, Inter-University Consortium for Political and Social Research, www.icpsr.umich.edu/icpsrweb/content/datamanagement/preservation/policies/dpp-framework.html.

Millar, L. (ed.) (2009) *Training in Electronic Records Management*, International Records Management Trust, http://irmt.org/education-and-training/education-and-training-2.

MLA East of England (2008) *The State of Digital Record Keeping in a Selection of Typical Depositors to Local Archives Services: report of the East of England Digital Preservation Regional Pilot Project Phase 2*, www.museumsandschoolseast.org/filegrab/?ref=153&f=L.

MLA East of England and East of England Regional Archive Council (2006) *Report of the East of England Digital Preservation Regional Pilot Project*, www.data-archive.ac.uk/media/1680/DARP_finalreport.pdf.

Museum of London (2011) *Acquisition and Disposal Policy*, www.museumoflondon.org.uk/NR/rdonlyres/F0F8E5B1-0F59-421C-AE27-2CC68A62976A/0/AcquisitionandDisposalPolicy.pdf.

The National Archives (2011) *PRONOM Vocabulary Specification: Draft*, http://labs.nationalarchives.gov.uk/wordpress/wp-content/uploads/2011/06/draft-pronom-vocabulary-specification.pdf.

National Library of Australia (1999) *Preservation Metadata for Digital Collections: exposure draft*, http://pandora.nla.gov.au/tep/25498.

National Library of Australia (2013) *Digital Preservation Policy*, 4th edn, www.nla.gov.au/policy-and-planning/digital-preservation-policy.

National Library of Medicine Digital Repository Working Group (2007) *National Library of Medicine Digital Repository: policies and functional requirements specification*, National Library of Medicine, www.nlm.nih.gov/digitalrepository/NLM-DigRep-Requirements-rev032007.pdf.

National Museum of Australia (2012) *Digital Preservation and Digitisation Policy*,

POL-C-028, version 2.2, www.nma.gov.au/about_us/ips/policies/
digital_preservation_and_digitisation_policy.

nestor Working Group on Trusted Repositories Certification (2006) *Catalogue of
Criteria for Trusted Digital Repositories, version 1*, nestor project,
http://nbn-resolving.de/urn:nbn:de:0008-2006060703.

OCLC (2006) *Digital Archive Preservation Policy and Supporting Documentation*, Online
Computer Library Center,
http://web.archive.org/web/20120731072305/http://www.oclc.org/support/
documentation/digitalarchive/preservationpolicy.pdf.

OCLC and Center for Research Libraries (2007) *Trustworthy Repositories Audit and
Certification: criteria and checklist*, Online Computer Library Center and Center for
Research Libraries, www.crl.edu/sites/default/files/attachments/pages/trac_0.pdf.

Padfield, T. (2010) *Copyright for Archivists and Records Managers*, 4th edn, Facet.

Parliamentary Archives (2009) *A Digital Preservation Policy for Parliament*,
www.parliament.uk/documents/upload/digitalpreservationpolicy1.0.pdf.

Parliamentary Archives (2012) *Collection and Acquisition Policy, version 4*,
www.parliament.uk/documents/parliamentary-archives/
Collection%20Acquisition%20Policy%20v4%202012.pdf.

Pinsent, E. and Good, K. (2012) *Future Proofing: enabling practical preservation of born-
digital records: final report*, University of London and JISC,
http://11kitbid.jiscinvolve.org/wp/files/
2012/03/ULCC_FutureProofing_final_report_2012_V2.pdf.

Posner, R. (ed.) (1984) And into Eternity... Communication over 10000s of Years: how
will we tell our children's children where the nuclear waste is?, *Zeitschrift für
Semiotik*, **6** (3),
http://ling.kgw.tu-berlin.de/semiotik/english/ZFS/Zfs84_3_e.htm.

Potter, M. (2002) Researching Long Term Digital Preservation Approaches in the
Dutch Digital Preservation Testbed (Testbed Digitale Bewaring), *RLG DigiNews*,
6 (3),
http://worldcat.org/arcviewer/1/OCC/2007/07/10/0000068882/viewer/
file1.html#feature2.

PREMIS Editorial Committee (2012) *PREMIS Data Dictionary for Preservation Metadata
version 2.2*, Library of Congress,
www.loc.gov/standards/premis/v2/premis-2-2.pdf.

Reich, V. and Rosenthal, D. (2009) Distributed Digital Preservation: lots of copies
keep stuff safe. In *Proceedings of the Indo-US Workshop on International Trends in
Digital Preservation, National Digital Preservation Program, Pune, India, March 2009*,
http://lockss.org/locksswiki/files/ReichIndiaFinal.pdf.

Repositories Support Project (2008) *Specifying Repository Requirements: briefing paper*,
www.rsp.ac.uk/documents/briefing-papers/repoadmin-requirements.pdf.

Rivest, R. (1992) *RFC 1321: The MD5 Message-Digest Algorithm*, Internet Engineering
Task Force,
www.ietf.org/rfc/rfc1321.txt.

RLG and OCLC (2002) *Trusted Digital Repositories: attributes and responsibilities*,
Research Libraries Group and Online Computer Library Center,
www.oclc.org/research/activities/past/rlg/trustedrep/repositories.pdf.

Roberts, B. (2011) *A New Registry for Digital Preservation: conceptual overview, version
1.1*, Open Planets Foundation,
www.openplanetsfoundation.org/
new-registry-digital-preservation-conceptual-overview.

Rosenthal, D. (2010) *Format Obsolescence: assessing the threat and the defenses*, Stanford
University Library,
http://lockss.org/locksswiki/files/LibraryHighTech2010.pdf.

Rosenthal, D., Robertson, T., Lipkis, T., Reich, V. and Morabito, S. (2005)
Requirements for Digital Preservation Systems: a bottom-up approach, *D-Lib
Magazine*, **11** (11),
www.dlib.org/dlib/november05/rosenthal/11rosenthal.html.

Russell, K., Sergeant, D., Stone, A., Weinberger, E. and Day, M. (2000) *Metadata for
Digital Preservation: the Cedars project outline specification*, Cedars Project,
www.webarchive.org.uk/wayback/archive/20050410120000/http://www.leeds.ac.
uk/cedars/colman/metadata/metadataspec.html.

Ruusalepp, R. (2003) *AHDS Archive Ingest Procedures Framework: AHDS preservation
procedures manual, final version*, Arts and Humanities Data Service,
www.ahds.ac.uk/preservation/ingest-procedures-review.pdf.

Schultz, M. (2010) *MetaArchive Cooperative: TRAC audit checklist*, Educopia Institute,
www.metaarchive.org/sites/metaarchive.org/files/
MetaArchive_TRAC_Checklist.pdf.

Simpson, D. (2005) *Digital Preservation in the Regions: sample survey of digital
preservation preparedness and needs of organisations at local and regional levels; an
assessment carried out from December 2004 to March 2005*, Museums, Libraries and
Archives Council,
http://webarchive.nationalarchives.gov.uk/20081209002411/http://www.mla.gov.
uk/programmes/digital_initiatives/digital_preservation/digital_preservation_in_
the_regions.

Sinclair, P. (2010) *The Digital Divide: assessing organisations' preparations for digital
preservation*, Planets Project,

www.planets-project.eu/docs/reports/planets-market-survey-white-paper.pdf.

Sinclair, P. and Bernstein, A. (2010) *An Emerging Market: establishing demand for digital preservation tools and services*, Planets Project, www.planets-project.eu/docs/reports/Planets-VENDOR-White-Paperv4.pdf.

Strodl, S., Petrov, P. and Rauber, A. (2011) *Research on Digital Preservation within projects co-funded by the European Union in the ICT programme*, report prepared for workshop 'The Future of the Past – shaping new visions for EU-research in digital preservation', 4–5 May 2011, Luxembourg, http://cordis.europa.eu/fp7/ict/telearn-digicult/report-research-digital-preservation_en.pdf.

Swiss Federal Archives (2009) *Digital Archiving Policy*, www.bar.admin.ch/themen/00876/index.html?lang=en&download=M3wBPgDB/8 ull6Du36WenojQ1NTTjaXZnqWfVp3Uhmfhnapmmc7Zi6rZnqCkkIN1gH5+bKbX rZ6lhuDZz8mMps2gpKfo.

Tarrant, D., Hitchcock, S. and Carr, L. (2009) Where the Semantic Web and Web 2.0 meet Format Risk Management: P2 registry. In *Proceedings of iPRES 2009: the Sixth International Conference on Preservation of Digital Objects*, California Digital Library, 187–93, http://escholarship.org/uc/item/8525r8cn.

Tarrant, D., O'Steen, B., Brody, T., Hitchcock, S., Jeffries, N. and Carr, L. (2009) Using OAI-ORE to Transform Digital Repositories into Interoperable Storage and Services Applications, *Code4Lib Journal*, **6**, http://journal.code4lib.org/articles/1062.

Tessella plc (2012) *Digital Archiving Maturity Model*, www.digital-preservation.com/wp-content/uploads/Maturity-Model-Web.pdf.

Thomas, S., Baker, F., Gittens, R. and Thompson, D. (2007) *Cairo Tools Survey: a survey of tools applicable to the preparation of digital archives for ingest into a preservation repository*, Cairo Project, http://cairo.paradigm.ac.uk/projectdocs/cairo_tools_listing_pv1.pdf.

Thomas, S., Gittens, R., Martin, J. and Baker, F. (2007) *Paradigm Workbook on Digital Private Papers*, Paradigm Project, www.paradigm.ac.uk/workbook/index.html.

UK Data Archive (2011) *Preservation Policy*, www.data-archive.ac.uk/media/54776/ukda062-dps-preservationpolicy.pdf.

US Department of Defence (2007) *Electronic Records Management Software Applications Design Criteria Standard*, DoD 5015.02-STD, http://jitc.fhu.disa.mil/cgi/rma/downloads/p50152stdapr07.pdf.

US Government Accountability Office (2010) *Report to Congressional Committees:*

Electronic Records Archive: status update on the National Archives and Records Administration's fiscal year 2010 expenditure plan, GAO-10-657, www.gao.gov/new.items/d10657.pdf.

US Government Printing Office (2005) *Code of Federal Regulations: Title 48 – Federal Acquisition Regulations System*, http://acquisition.gov/far/index.html.

Vermaaten, S., Lavoie, B. and Caplan, P. (2012) Identifying Threats to Successful Digital preservation: the SPOT model for risk assessment, *D-Lib Magazine*, **18** (9/10) , www.dlib.org/dlib/september12/vermaaten/09vermaaten.html.

W3C Interest Group (2008) *Cool URIs for the Semantic Web*, W3C, www.w3.org/TR/cooluris/.

Waller, M. and Sharpe, R. (2006) *Mind the Gap: assessing digital preservation needs in the UK*, Digital Preservation Coalition, www.dpconline.org/component/docman/doc_download/ 340-mind-the-gap-assessing-digital-preservation-needs-in-the-uk.

Wellcome Library (2008) *Specification of Requirements and ITT for the Wellcome Library Requirements for a Digital Object Repository*, www.webarchive.org.uk/wayback/archive/20120322230647/http://library. wellcome.ac.uk/assets/wtx055600.doc.

Wellcome Library (2010) *Specification of Requirements and ITT for a Wellcome Library Workflow Tracking System*, www.webarchive.org.uk/wayback/archive/20120322231050/http://library. wellcome.ac.uk/assets/WT_ITT_Package_Final.zip.

West Yorkshire Archive Service (2007) *Digital Archives Policy*, www.archives.wyjs.org.uk/documents/archives/ WYAS%20Digital%20Archives%20Policy.pdf.

Williams, G. (2010) *Prince2 Maturity Model (P2MM), version 2.1*, Office of Government Commerce, www.p3m3-officialsite.com/nmsruntime/saveasdialog.aspx?lID=462&sID=210.

Yale University Library (2007) *Policy for the Digital Preservation*, www.library.yale.edu/iac/DPC/revpolicy2-19-07.pdf.

Index